Reteaching and Practice Workbook

Grade 1

Scott Foresman·Addison Wesley

enVisionMATH®
Common Core

PEARSON

Glenview, Illinois • Boston Massachusetts • Chandler, Arizona • Upper Saddle River, New Jersey

ISBN-13: 978-0-328-69758-8

ISBN-10: 0-328-69758-3

3 4 5 6 7 8 9 10 V016 20 19 18 17 16 15 14 13 12

Contents

Name ______________________________

Reteaching
1-1

Spatial Patterns for Numbers to 10

You can use two-part patterns to show numbers.
Use each pattern to tell how many without counting.

This part shows 4.

This part shows 2.

The two parts together show 6 shoes in all.

Circle the number that tells how many in all.

1.

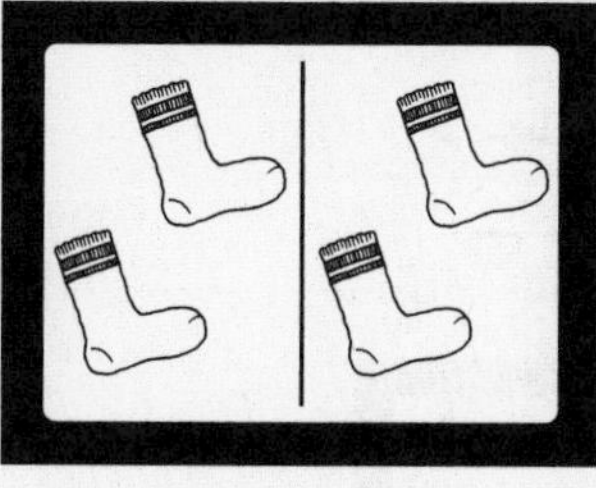

4 5 6

2.

6 7 8

3.

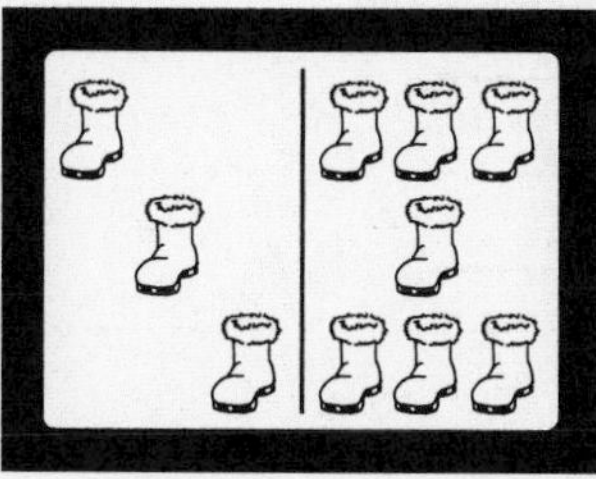

7 9 10

4.

8 10 12

Algebra

5. Draw the missing dot pattern for 9.

Name ____________________

Practice
1-1

Spatial Patterns for Numbers to 10

Write the number that tells how many.

1. 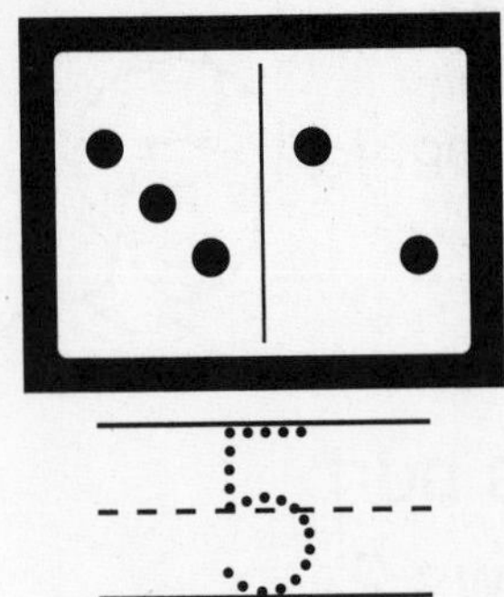

5

2. 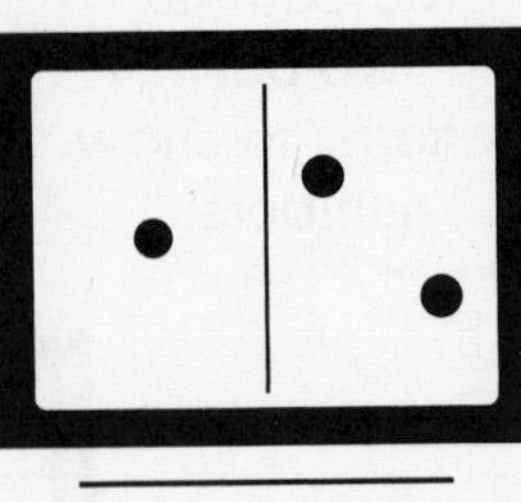

3. 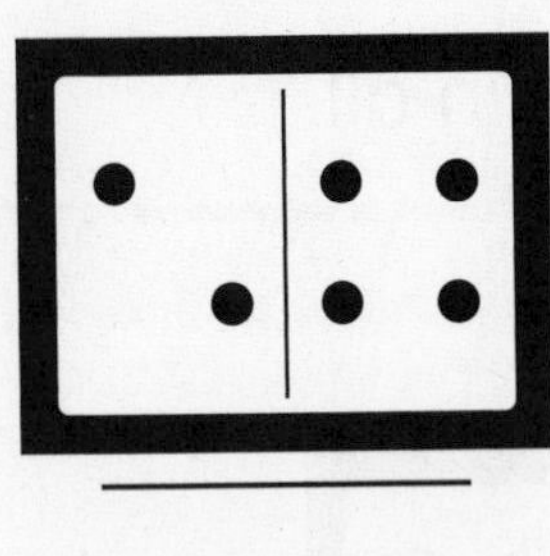

4. 

5. 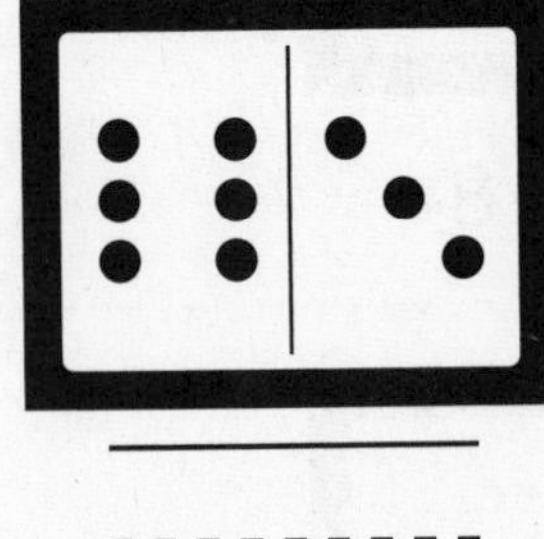

6. 

Number Sense

7. Tom has 7 dots.
Can he put the same number of dots on each flag?

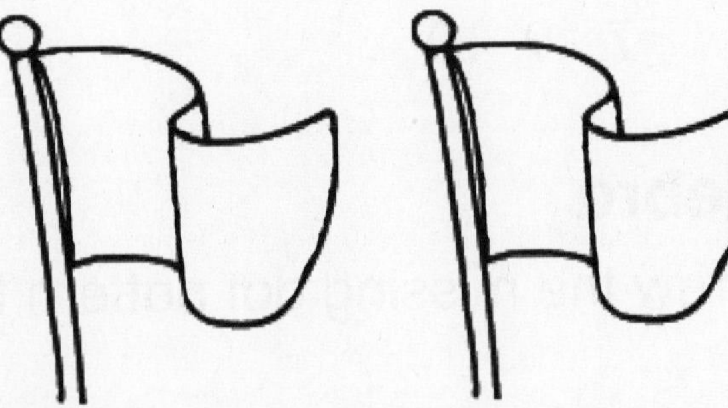

Yes **No**

Name ____________________

Reteaching
1-2

Making 6 and 7

You can use different ways to make 6.

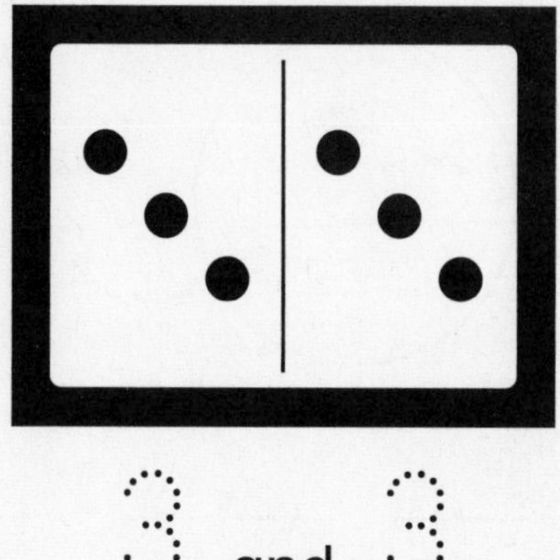

3 and 3

5 and 1

Write the numbers that show ways to make 6.

1.

2 and 4

2.

____ and ____

3.

____ and ____

4.

____ and ____

Name ______________________

Practice
1-2

Making 6 and 7

Write the number inside and outside.
Then write the number in all.

1.

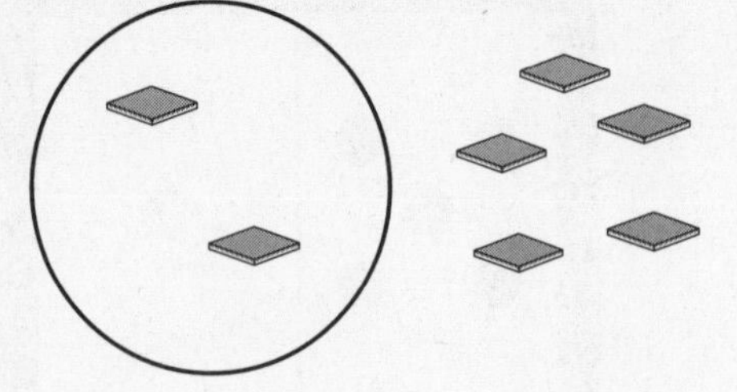

_____ inside _____ outside _____ in all

2.

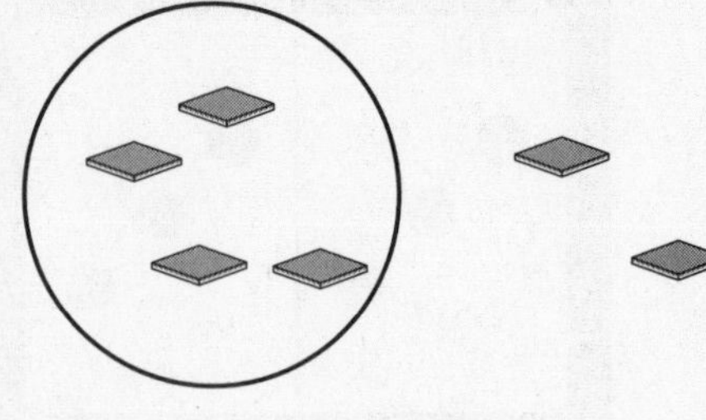

_____ inside _____ outside _____ in all

3.

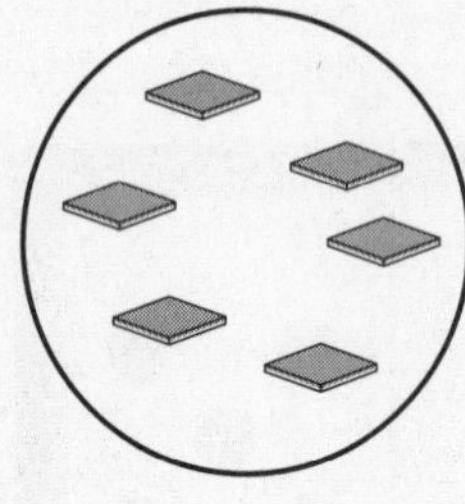

_____ inside _____ outside _____ in all

4.

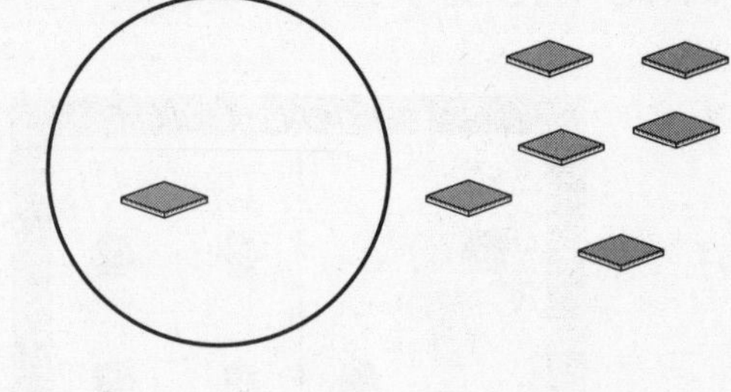

_____ inside _____ outside _____ in all

5. Draw 5 tiles inside the circle and 1 tile outside.
Then write how many in all.

_____

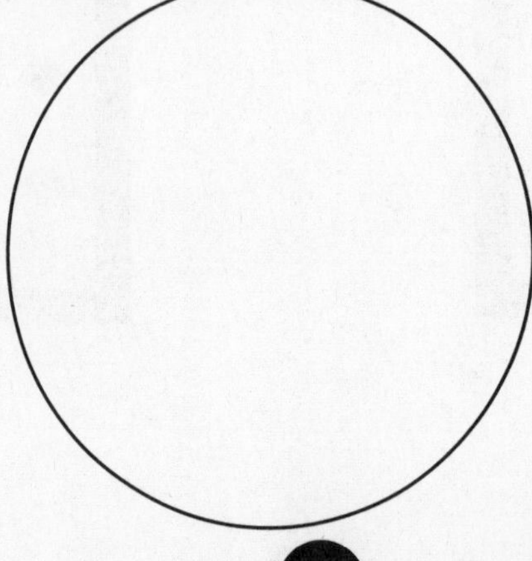

Name ______________________

Making 8

Reteaching
1-3

You can use different ways to make 8.

5 and 3

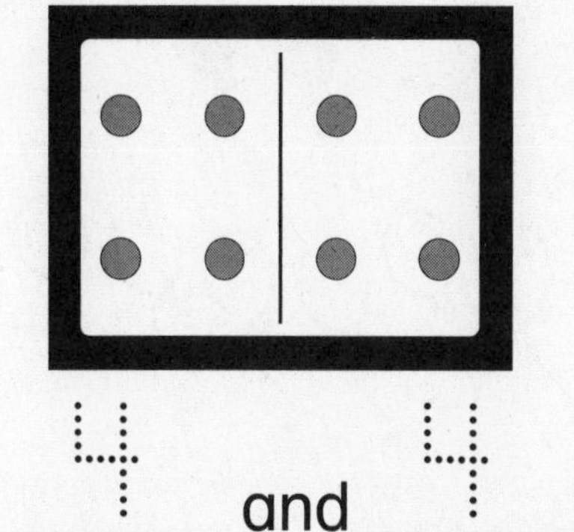

4 and 4

Write the numbers that show ways to make 8.

1.

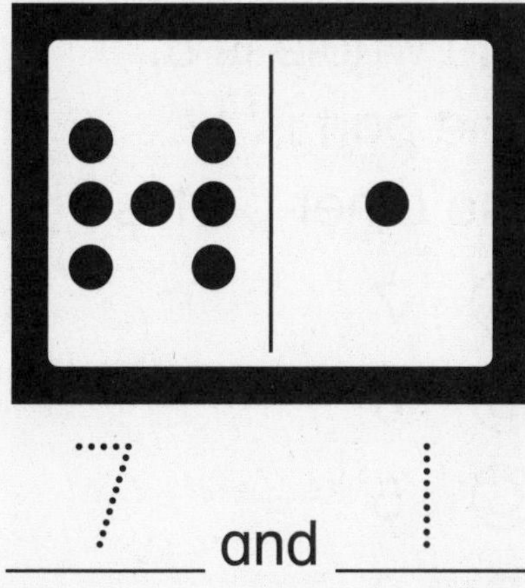

7 and 1

2.

______ and ______

3.

______ and ______

4.

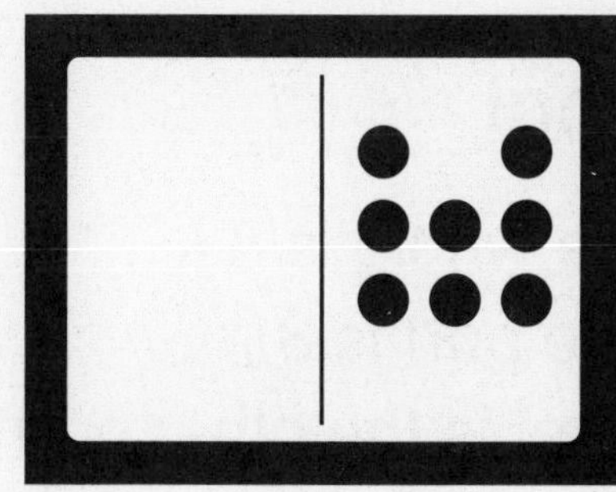

______ and ______

Name ______________________

Making 8

Write the numbers to show parts of 8.

1.

______ and ______

2.

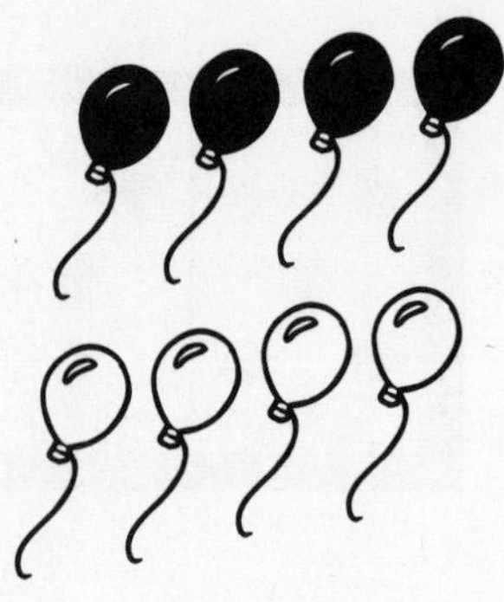

______ and ______

Algebra

3. The whole is 8.
One part is 3.
The other part is ______.

Ⓐ 3
Ⓑ 4
Ⓒ 5
Ⓓ 8

4. The whole is 8.
One part is 1.
The other part is ______.

Ⓐ 7
Ⓑ 6
Ⓒ 5
Ⓓ 2

Journal

5. The whole is 8.
One part is 8.
What is the other part? ______
Tell how you know.

____

____

Name ______________________

Reteaching 1-4

Making 9

You can make 9 in different ways.

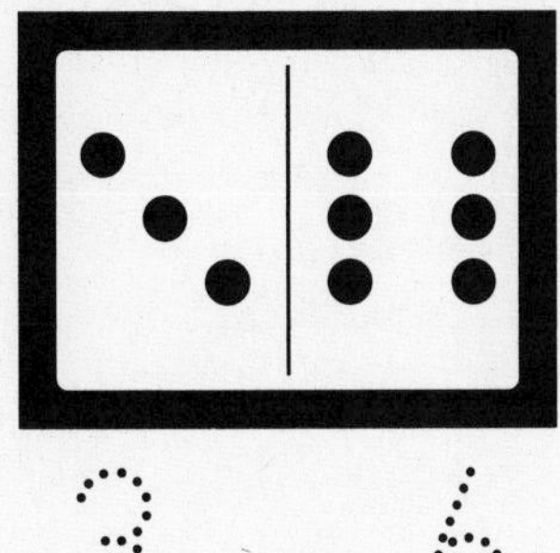

3 and 6

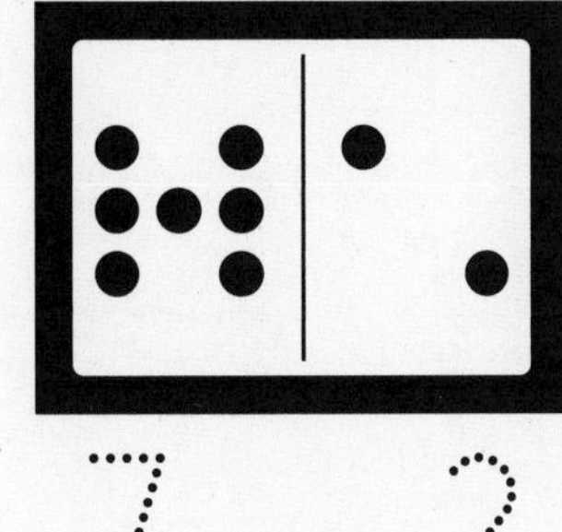

7 and 2

1 and 8

Write the numbers that show ways to make 8 and 9.

1.

3 and 5

____ and ____

____ and ____

2.

____ and ____

____ and ____

____ and ____

Name ____________________

Practice 1-4

Making 9

Write the numbers to show parts of 9.

1.

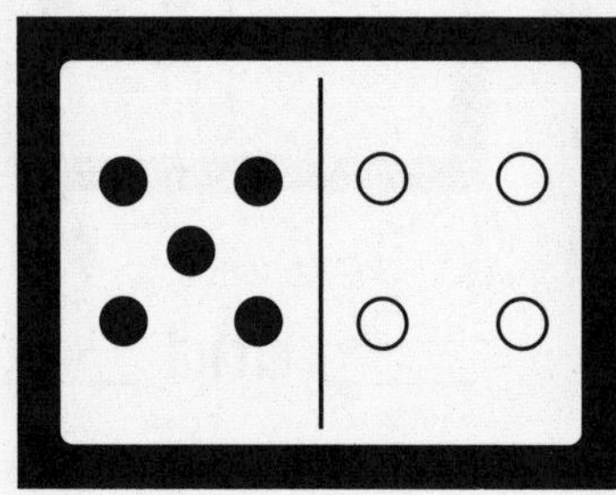

_____ ● and _____ ○

2.

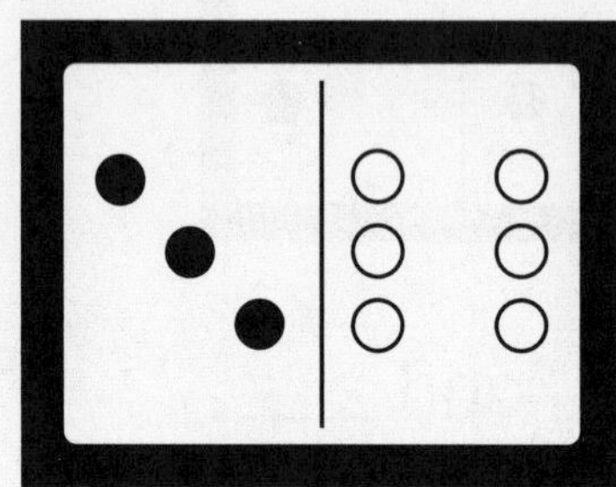

_____ ● and _____ ○

Visual Thinking

3. Which tells about the picture?

7 and 2	8 and 1	6 and 3	9 and 0
Ⓐ	Ⓑ	Ⓒ	Ⓓ

Name ______________________________

Introducing Addition Expressions and Number Sentences

Join the parts to make the whole.

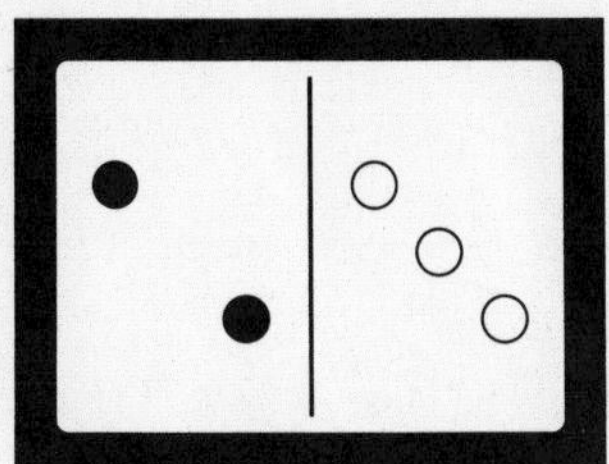

How many black counters? ______

How many white counters? ______

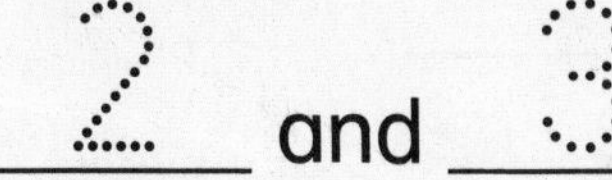

__2__ and __3__ is __5__ in all. 5 is the sum of 2 and 3.

Add to find the sum. Use counters if you like.

1.

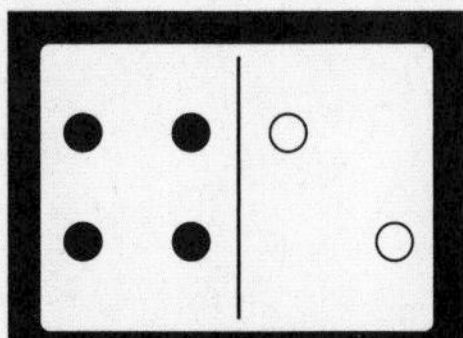

How many black counters? ______

How many white counters? ______

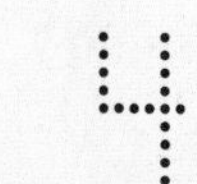

__4__ and __2__ is __6__ in all. 6 is the sum of 4 and 2.

2.

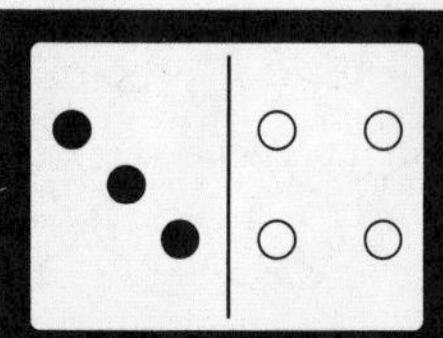

_____ and _____ is _____ in all.

3.

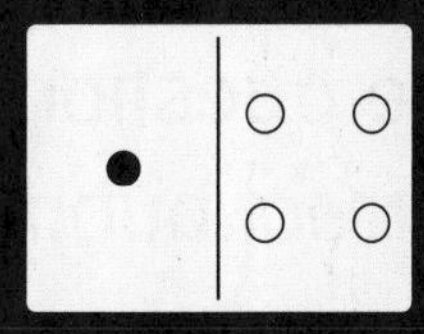

_____ and _____ is _____ in all.

4.

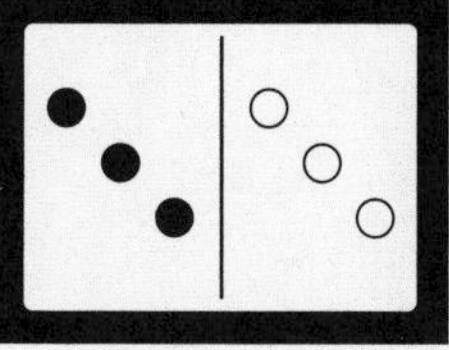

_____ and _____ is _____ in all.

5.

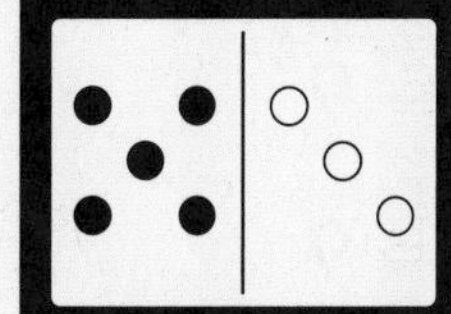

_____ and _____ is _____ in all.

Name ______________________

Practice 1-5

Introducing Addition Expressions and Number Sentences

Use the picture. Write the parts. Then write an addition sentence.

1.

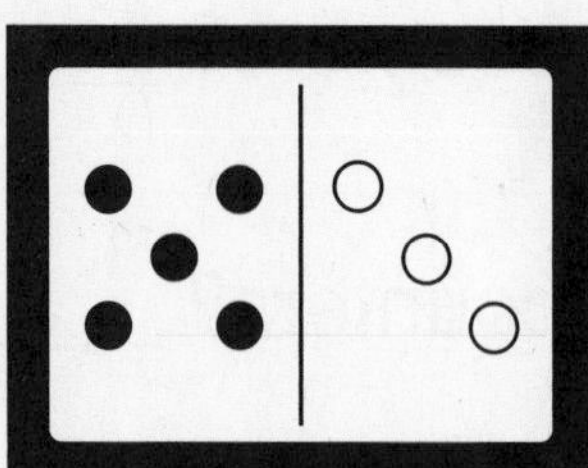

____ + ____

____ + ____ = ____

2.

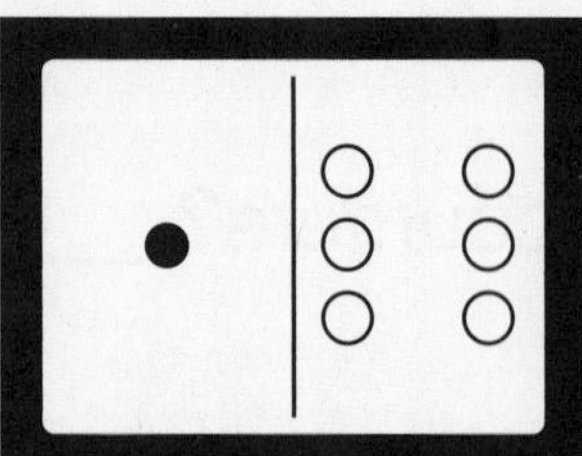

____ + ____

____ + ____ = ____

Visual Thinking

3. Which addition sentence goes with the question? Fill in the correct bubble.

There are 4 brown rabbits in the garden.
There are 5 white rabbits.
How many rabbits are there in all?

Ⓐ $4 + 5 = 9$

Ⓑ $2 + 7 = 9$

Ⓒ $4 + 4 = 8$

Ⓓ $4 + 1 = 5$

Name ________________________________

Reteaching **1-6**

Stories About Joining

Join the groups to find how many bugs in all.

Use a counter for each bug. Then count.

2 bugs are on the rock.

1 2

3 bugs are on the blanket.

3 4 5

How many bugs are there in all? _______ bugs

Tell a joining story for each picture.
Use counters to tell how many in all.

1. 2 birds are in a tree.

2 birds are in a nest.

How many birds are there in all? _______ birds

2. 3 fish are in a bowl.

2 fish are in another bowl.

How many fish are there in all? _______ fish

Name ______________________

Practice **1-6**

Stories About Joining

Solve. Write an addition sentence.

1. 5 children are reading books.
Then 3 more children join them.

How many children are reading books now?

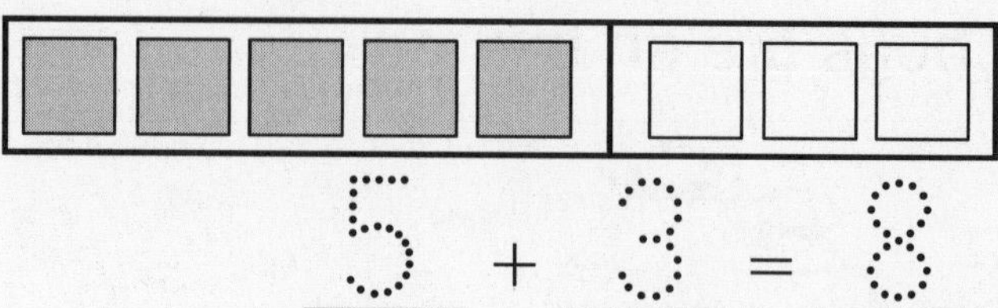

5 + 3 = 8

2. 7 children are running.
Then 2 more children join them.

How many children are running now?

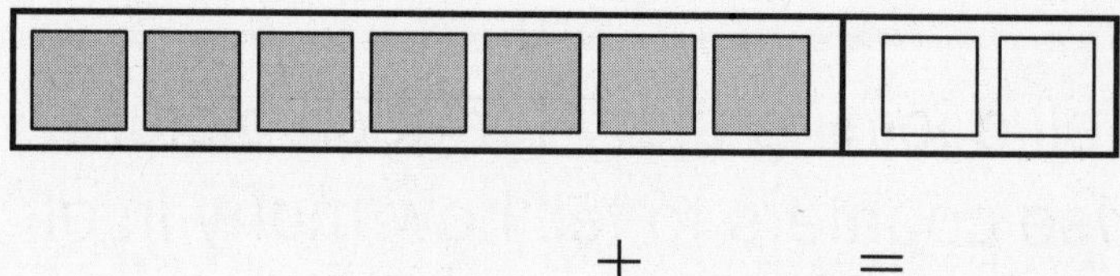

_____ + _____ = _____

3. 3 frogs are in the pond.
Then 3 more frogs join them.

How many frogs are in the pond now?

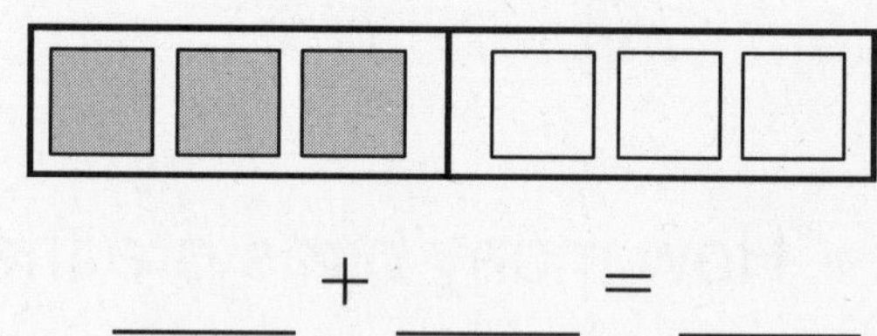

_____ + _____ = _____

Algebra

4. Which number makes the addition sentence true?

5 + _______ = 7

1	2	3	6
Ⓐ	Ⓑ	Ⓒ	Ⓓ

Name ____________________

Adding in Any Order

You can add in any order and get the same sum.

4 + 2 = 6

2 + 4 = 6

Add. Write an addition sentence with the addends in a different order.

1.  

5 + 2 = 7

2 + 5 = 7

2.  

4 + 1 = ____

____ + ____ = ____

3.

____ + ____ = ____

____ + ____ = ____

4.

$$\begin{array}{r} 5 \\ +4 \\ \hline \square \end{array}$$

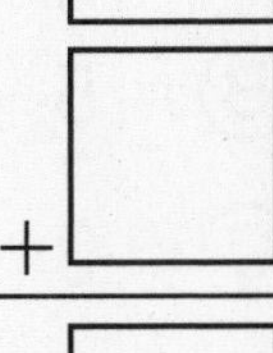

5. 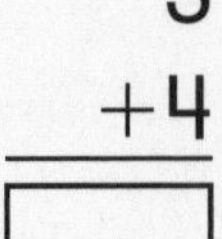

$$\begin{array}{r} 3 \\ +4 \\ \hline \square \end{array}$$

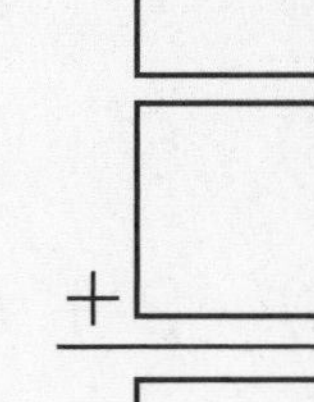

Name ______________________

Practice 1-7

Adding in Any Order

Write the sum.
Then change the order of the addends.
Write the new addition sentence.

1. 6 + 1 = ____

____ + ____ = ____

2. 5 + 4 = ____

____ + ____ = ____

3. 6 + 3 = ____

____ + ____ = ____

4.

  7
+ 1

  8

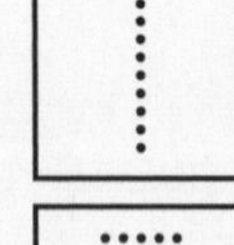

5.

  7
+ 2

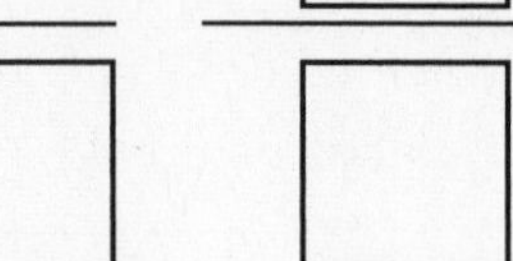

6.

  6
+ 0

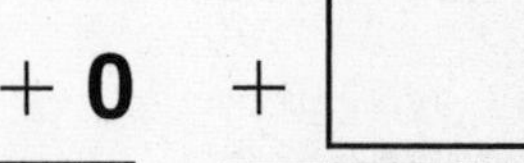

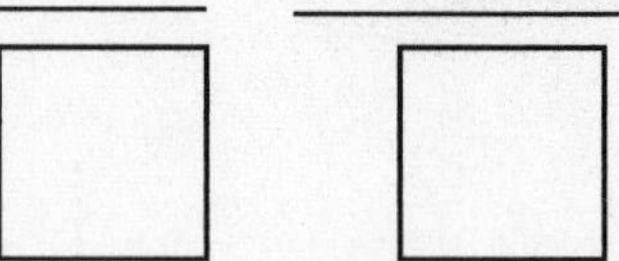

Algebra

7. Which is the same as 5 + 1?

Ⓐ 1 + 2
Ⓑ 5 + 3
Ⓒ 2 + 6
Ⓓ 1 + 5

8. Which is the same as 4 + 3?

Ⓐ 3 + 2
Ⓑ 5 + 4
Ⓒ 3 + 4
Ⓓ 7 + 2

Name ______________________________

Problem Solving: Use Objects

You can use objects to help you solve problems.

Bert has 3 pennies.
He put them in 2 pockets.
Use cubes to show the different ways Bert can do this.

Left **Right**

List the different ways.

Right Pocket	0	1	2	3
Left Pocket	3	2	1	0

Use cubes to help you list the different ways.

1. Marlene has 6 grapes.
   She puts them in 2 bowls.

Bowl 1	0	1	2	3	4	5	6
Bowl 2	6						0

2. Keith has 7 model airplanes.
   He wants to paint some white and some black.

Black	0							7
White	7							0

Name ______________________

Problem Solving: Use Objects

Use counters to solve.

1. Lisa puts 8 sweaters into two drawers.
   What are two different ways she can do this?

2. Jack puts 7 plates on two tables.
   What are two different ways he can do this?

Number Sense

3. Lynn is planting 9 flowers in two boxes.
   She plants 6 in the first box.
   Which shows how many she plants in the second box?

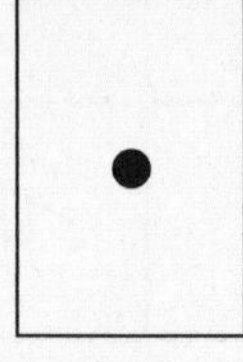
Ⓐ

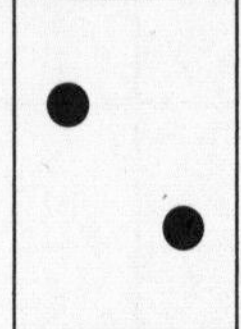
Ⓑ

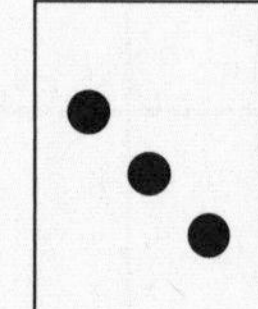
Ⓒ

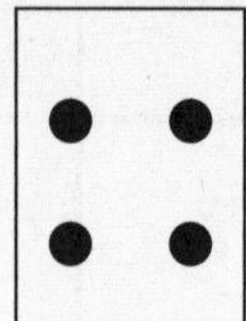
Ⓓ

Name ______________________

Finding Missing Parts of 6 and 7

You can draw a picture to help you find missing parts of 6 or 7.
Color the part you know.
Count the circles you did not color.
These circles are the missing part.
Write the number.

2 + ____ = 6

Whole

2 + __4__ = 6

Draw a picture to solve. Write the number.

1. Danielle has 6 toy trucks and cars.
I toy is a truck.
How many toys are cars?

I + __5__ = 6

2. There are 7 cats in all.
Some are black and some are white.
3 cats are black.
How many cats are white?

3 + ______ = 7

Reasoning

3. There are 6 ducks in the park.
Some ducks are in the water.
The same number are in the grass.
How many ducks are in the grass?

______ + ______ = 6

Name ______________________________

Practice **2-1**

Finding Missing Parts of 6 and 7

Find the missing part.
Write the numbers.

1. 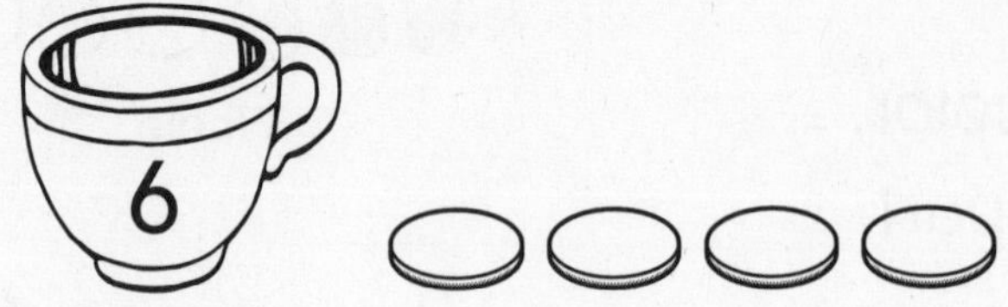

____ whole ____ part I know ____ missing part

2. 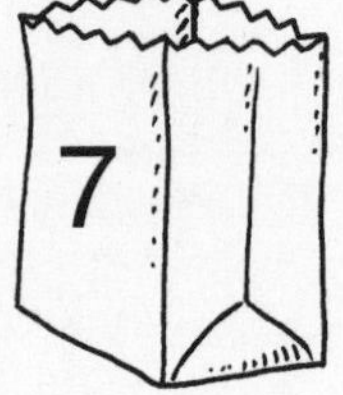

____ whole ____ part I know ____ missing part

Journal

3. Draw a picture to solve.
Write the number.
There are 7 crackers in all.
Melinda eats 2 crackers.
How many crackers are left on the plate?

____ crackers

Name ______________________

Reteaching
2-2

Finding Missing Parts of 8

You can draw a picture
to help you find missing parts of 8.
Color the part you know.
Count the circles you did not color.
These circles are the missing part.
Write the number.

7 + ____ = 8

Whole

7 + __1__ = 8

Draw a picture to solve.
Write the number.

1. There are 8 penguins.
2 penguins are small.
How many penguins are big?

2 + __6__ = 8

2. Andre has 8 puppies.
Some puppies are in the house.
4 puppies are playing in the yard.
How many puppies are in the house?

4 + ____ = 8

Reasoning

3. Use the picture to solve.
There are 8 marbles in all.

____ marbles are inside.

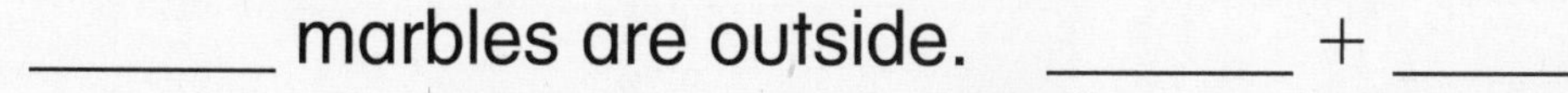

____ marbles are outside. ____ + ____ = 8

Name ______________________

Practice **2-2**

Finding Missing Parts of 8

1. Find the missing part.
Write the numbers.
There are 8 counters in all.

_______ part I know

_______ missing part

2. There are 8 counters in all.

_______ part I know

_______ missing part

Algebra

3. There are 8 books in all.
Which number sentence tells about the picture?

Ⓐ 8 − 1 = 7

Ⓑ 8 − 2 = 6

Ⓒ 8 − 3 = 5

Ⓓ 8 − 4 = 4

Name ______________________

Reteaching
2-3

Finding Missing Parts of 9

You can draw a picture
to help you find missing parts of 9.
Color the part you know.
Count the circles you did **not** color.
These circles are the missing part.
Write the number.

6 + ____ = 9

Whole

6 + 3 = 9

Draw a picture to solve. Write the number.

1. There are 9 horses in the field.
8 horses are big. The rest are small.
How many horses are small?

8 + 1 = 9

2. Alexis sees 9 frogs.
Some frogs are on a log.
2 frogs are in the grass.
How many frogs are on the log?

2 + ____ = 9

Reasoning

3. Sam has 9 balloons.
He has one more red balloon
than he has blue balloons.
Write the number sentence.

____ + ____ = 9

Name ______________________________

Finding Missing Parts of 9

1. Find the missing part.
Complete the model.
Then write the numbers.

_____ part I know _____ missing part

2. Maria sees 9 boats.
7 boats are in the water.
How many boats are **not** in the water?

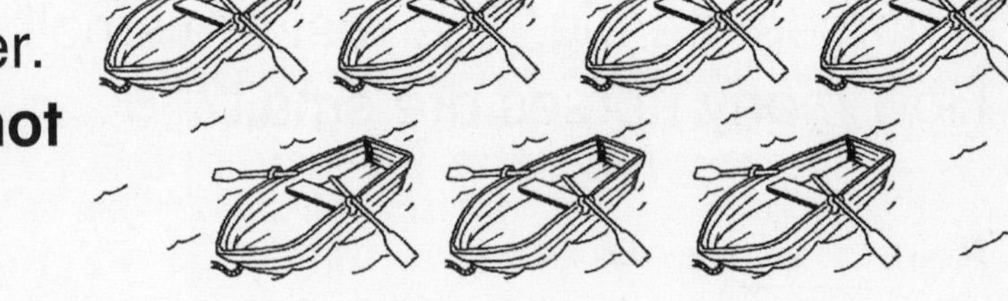

_____ boats

Journal

3. There are 9 apples in all.
Draw some on the tree.
Draw the rest of the apples on the ground.

Write the numbers.

_____ apples on the tree

_____ apples on the ground

Name ____________________

Reteaching
2-4

Introducing Subtraction Expressions and Number Sentences

Write the parts. Then you can write a subtraction sentence to find how many are left.

5 take away 2

These are the parts.

5 minus 2 equals 3.

5 − 2 = 3

This is a subtraction sentence.

Write the parts. Then write a subtraction sentence.

1.

____ − ____

4 minus 1 equals 3.

____ − ____ = ____

2.

____ − ____

7 minus 4 equals ____.

____ − ____ = ____

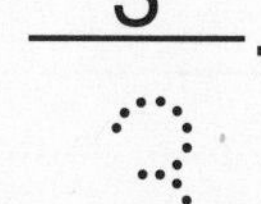

Journal

3. Draw a picture that shows subtraction.
Write a subtraction sentence that tells about your picture.

Name ______________________

Introducing Subtraction Expressions and Number Sentences

First write the parts. Then write a subtraction sentence.

1.

6 – 2

____ – ____ = ____

2.

____ – ____

____ – ____ = ____

3.

____ – ____

____ – ____ = ____

4.

____ – ____

____ – ____ = ____

Number Sense

5. Draw the missing dots.
Which subtraction sentence tells about the model?

Ⓐ 9 – 2 = 7
Ⓑ 9 – 5 = 4
Ⓒ 9 – 6 = 3
Ⓓ 5 – 4 = 1

Name ______________________

Stories About Taking Away

There are 6 birds on the branch.
4 birds fly away.
How many birds are left?

You need to find how many birds are left.
Write a subtraction sentence to find how many birds are left.

6 – 4 = 2

Check to see if your answer makes sense.

Write a subtraction sentence to answer each question.

1. There are 8 marbles in the bag.
3 marbles roll out.
How many marbles are left in the bag?

____ – ____ = ____

2. Mary has 10 pencils.
She gives 4 pencils to Jack.
How many pencils does Mary have left?

____ – ____ = ____

Name ______________________

Practice
2-5

Stories About Taking Away

Find the difference. Write a subtraction sentence.

1.

There are 5 children at the table.
2 children stop eating.
How many children are still eating?

2.

A man has 7 balloons.
2 balloons fly away.
How many balloons does the man have now?

Algebra

3. 8 girls are jumping rope.
6 girls leave to play hopscotch.
How many girls are still jumping rope?
Which subtraction sentence tells about the story?

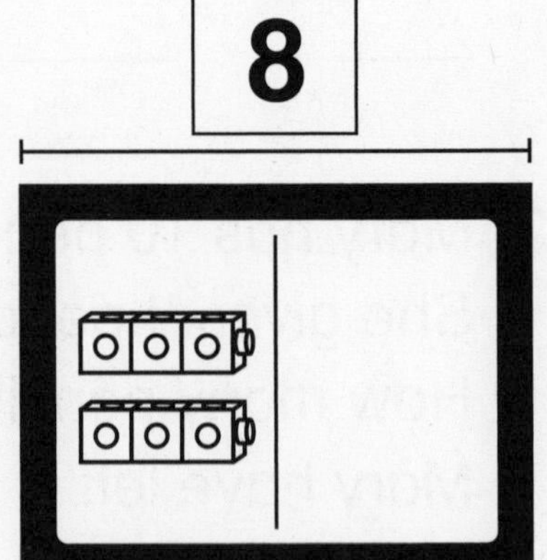

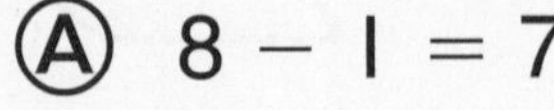
Ⓐ 8 − 1 = 7

Ⓑ 8 − 2 = 6

Ⓒ 8 − 5 = 3

Ⓓ 8 − 6 = 2

Name ______________________

Stories About Comparing

Match the white cubes with the gray cubes.
Then count how many more.

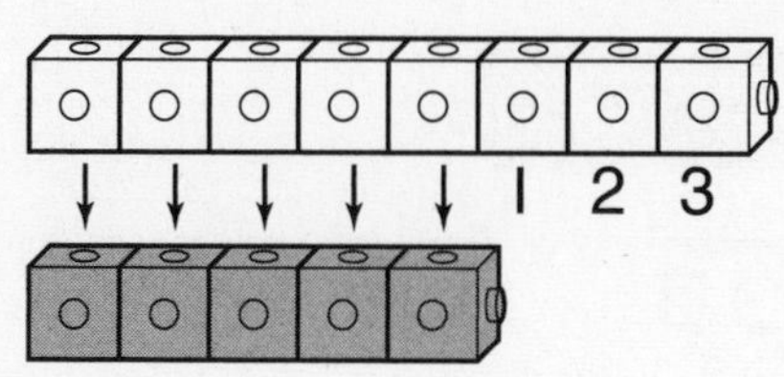

How many more white cubes? __3__ more white cubes

How many fewer gray cubes? __3__ fewer gray cubes

Write how many white cubes and how many gray cubes.
Then write how many more or how many fewer.

1. __4__ white cubes
__2__ gray cubes
__2__ more white cubes

2. ____ white cubes
____ gray cubes
____ more white cubes

3. ____ white cubes
____ gray cubes
____ fewer gray cubes

4. ____ white cubes
____ gray cubes
____ fewer gray cube

Name ______________________________

Stories About Comparing

Write a subtraction sentence.
Write how many more or fewer.

1. Sam sees 5 dogs.
Beth sees 3 dogs.
How many more dogs
does Sam see than Beth?

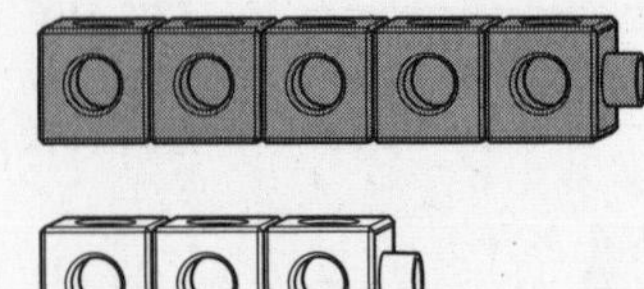

_____ − _____ = _____

_____ more dogs

2. Duane has 6 tickets.
Mimi has 2 tickets.
How many fewer tickets
does Mimi have than Duane?

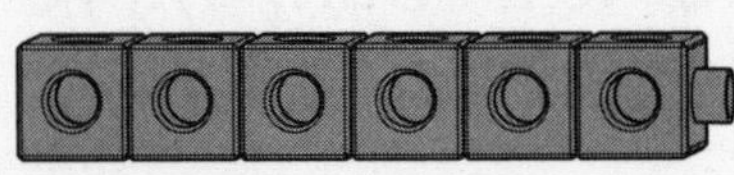

_____ − _____ = _____

_____ fewer tickets

Algebra

3. Use the picture.
Find the missing number.

7 − _____ = 1

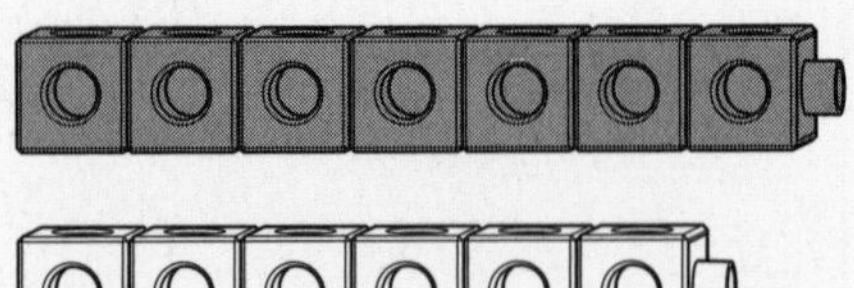

Ⓐ 5

Ⓑ 6

Ⓒ 7

Ⓓ 8

Name ______________________________

Stories About Missing Parts

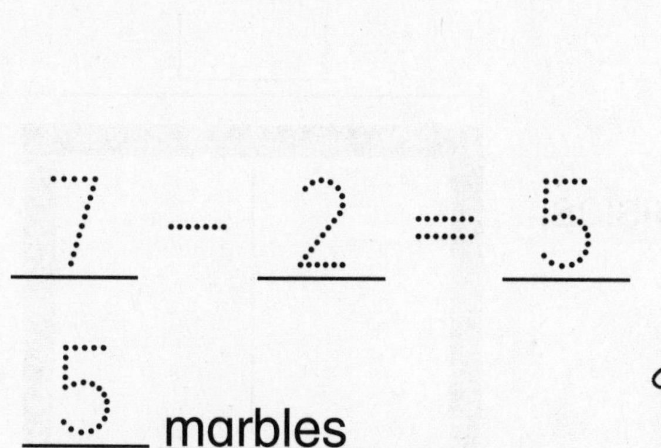

7 – 2 = 5

5 marbles

There are
7 marbles in all.
How many are in
my closed hand?

Find the missing number of marbles.

1. 9 marbles in all

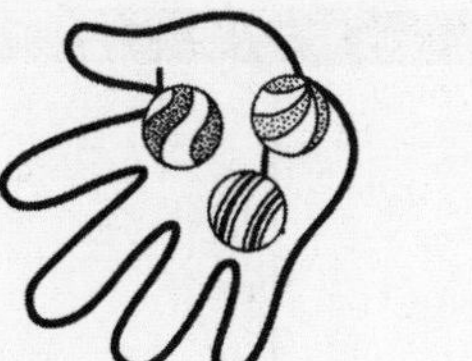

9 – 3 = 6

6 marbles

2. 8 marbles in all

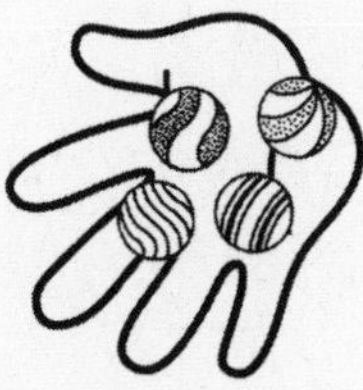

____ – ____ = ____

____ marbles

3. 6 marbles in all

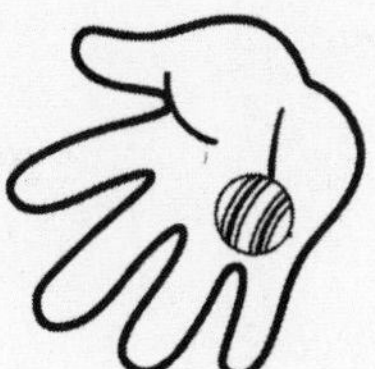

____ – ____ = ____

____ marbles

Name ______________________

Stories About Missing Parts

Draw the missing cubes.
Write a subtraction sentence.

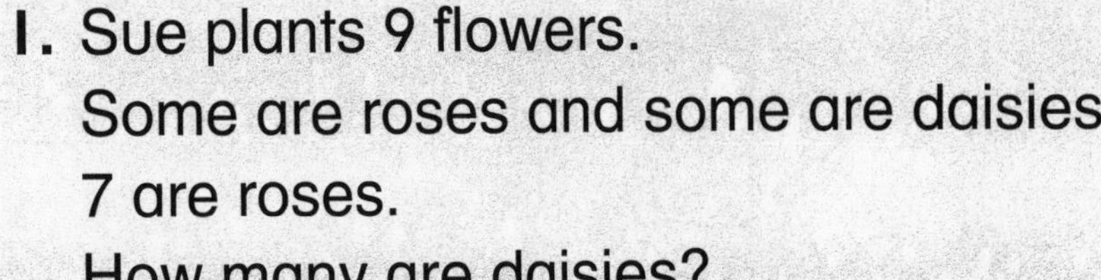

1. Sue plants 9 flowers.
Some are roses and some are daisies.
7 are roses.
How many are daisies?

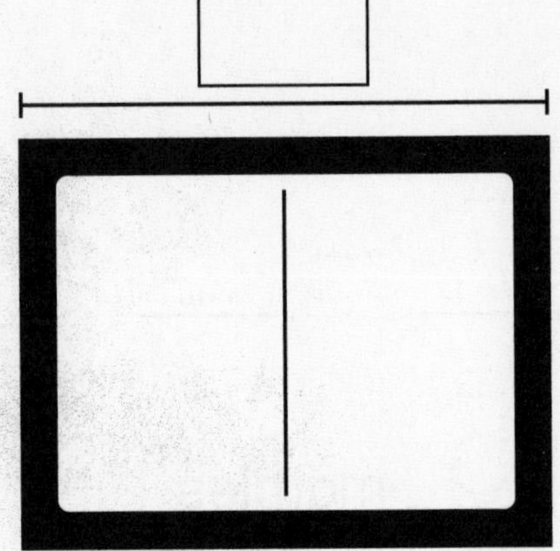

____ − ____ = ____

2. A friend gave Raul
1 baseball card.
Now Raul has 4 baseball cards.
How many baseball cards did he
have before?

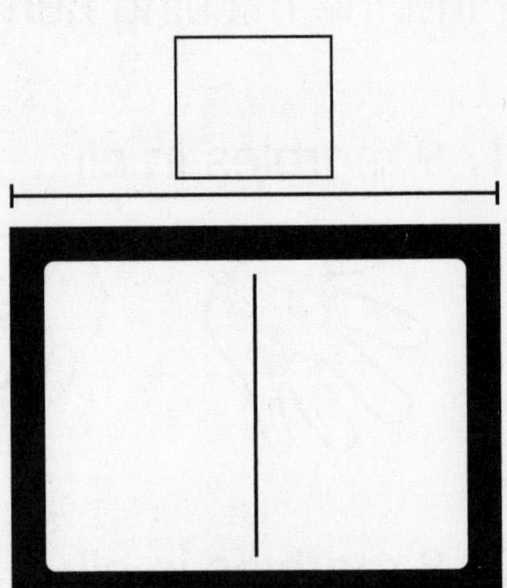

____ − ____ = ____

Reasoning

3. Amy has 9 shirts.
Some shirts are white and some shirts are red.
She has 2 white shirts.
How many red shirts does Amy have?

Ⓐ 6

Ⓑ 7

Ⓒ 8

Ⓓ 9

Name ______________________

All Kinds of Subtraction Stories

Talisa has 8 marbles.
Some are white and some are black.
If 5 are black, how many are white?

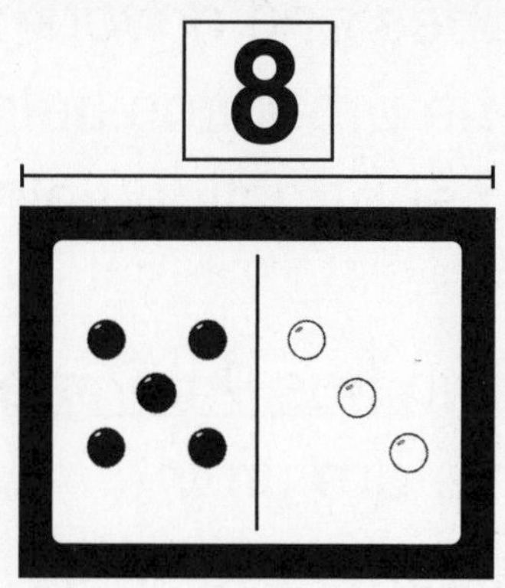

You can use cubes to show how many marbles are black.
Then write a subtraction sentence to help you find how many marbles are white.

8 – 5 = 3

3 white marbles

Use cubes to help you solve the problems below.
Then write a subtraction sentence.

1. Seth had 9 marbles.
He gave 3 marbles to a friend.
How many marbles does he have now?

_____ – _____ = _____

_____ marbles

2. Kristen has 7 pens.
Some are blue and some are red.
If 2 are red, how many are blue?

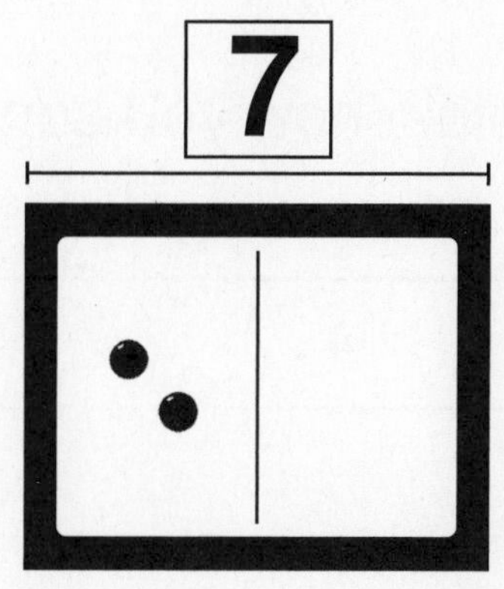

_____ – _____ = _____

_____ blue pens

Name ______________________

Practice
2-8

All Kinds of Subtraction Stories

Use cubes and a workmat to help solve the problems below. Write a subtraction sentence.

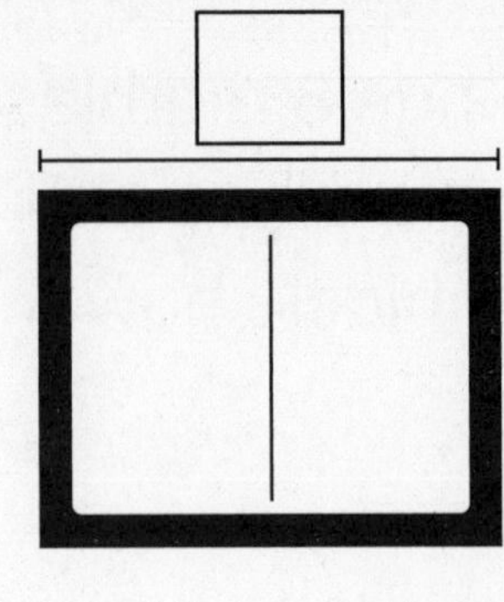

1. Shawn has 9 toy robots.
Some are gray
and some are white.
If 4 are gray, how many are white? ____ − ____ = ____

____ white robots

2. Libby has 8 postcards.
Chris has 2 postcards.
How many more postcards does
Libby have than Chris?

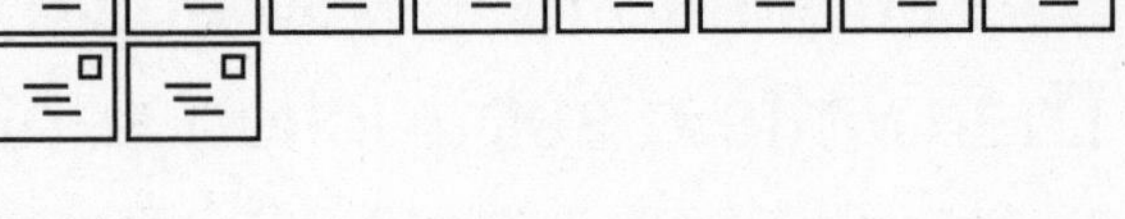

____ − ____ = ____

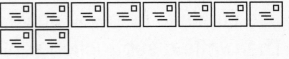

____ more postcards

Writing in Math

3. There were 7 birds on the roof.
Some flew away.
Now there is 1 bird left.
How many birds flew away?

Explain how you can solve this problem.

____

____

____

Name ______________________

Connecting Addition and Subtraction

4 + 3 = 7

7 − 3 = 4

The addition fact and the subtraction fact use the same numbers.

6 + 3 = 9

9 − 3 = 6

The sum of the addition sentence is the first number in the subtraction sentence.

Write a related addition and subtraction sentence for each picture.

1. 5 + 4 = 9
9 − 4 = 5

2. 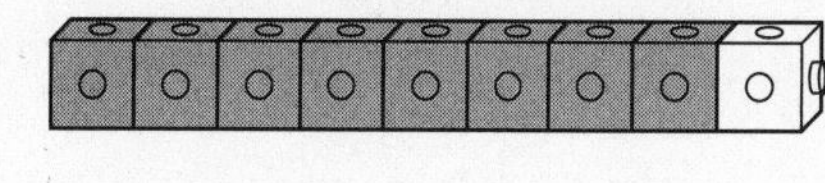
____ + ____ = ____
____ − ____ = ____

3. ____ + ____ = ____
____ − ____ = ____

4. 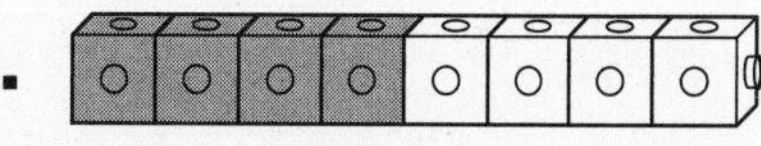
____ + ____ = ____
____ − ____ = ____

Name ______________________

Practice
2-9

Connecting Addition and Subtraction

Write an addition sentence and a subtraction sentence for each picture.

1. 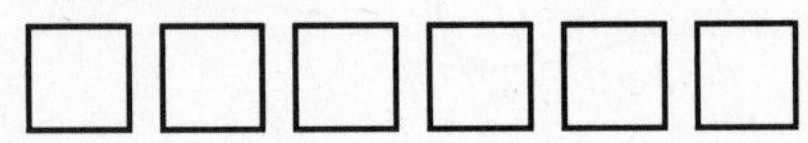

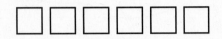

$2 + 6 = 8$

$8 - 2 = 6$

The first number in the subtraction sentence is the sum of the numbers in the addition sentence.

2. △△△△△△△
△

____ + ____ = ____

____ − ____ = ____

3. ☆☆
☆☆☆☆☆☆☆

____ + ____ = ____

____ − ____ = ____

Algebra

4. Which number is missing?

4 + ____ = 8

Ⓐ 2

Ⓑ 3

Ⓒ 4

Ⓓ 5

5. Which number is missing?

____ − 4 = 4

Ⓐ 8

Ⓑ 7

Ⓒ 6

Ⓓ 4

Name ______________________

Reteaching 2-10

Connecting Models and Symbols

9

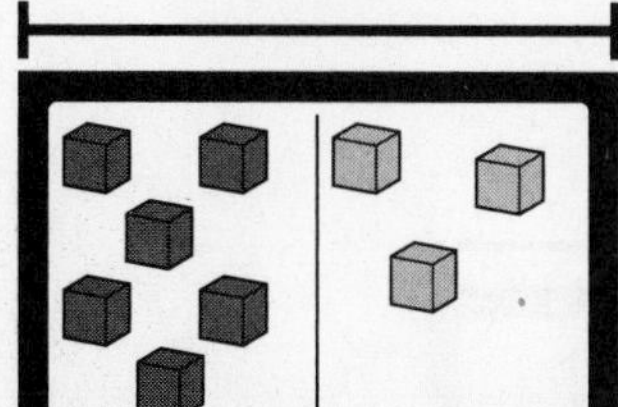

You can write a subtraction sentence this way.

9 − 6 = 3

You can also write a subtraction sentence like this.

3 = 9 − 6

The same amount is on each side of the equal sign.

Circle the number sentence that is true.
Draw a line through the number sentence that is false.
Then write another number sentence that is true about the model.

1.

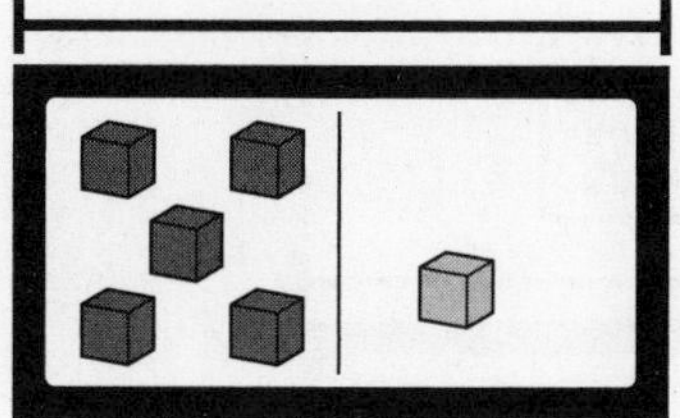

6 − 1 = 5

5 − 1 = 6

5 = 6 − 1

2.

6

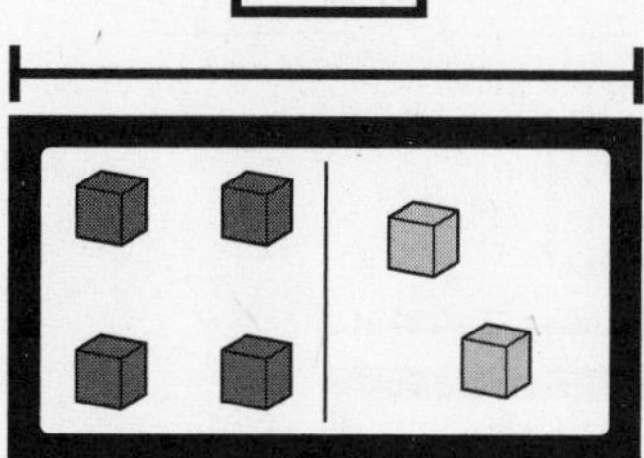

2 = 6 − 4

4 − 2 = 6

_____ − _____ = _____

3.

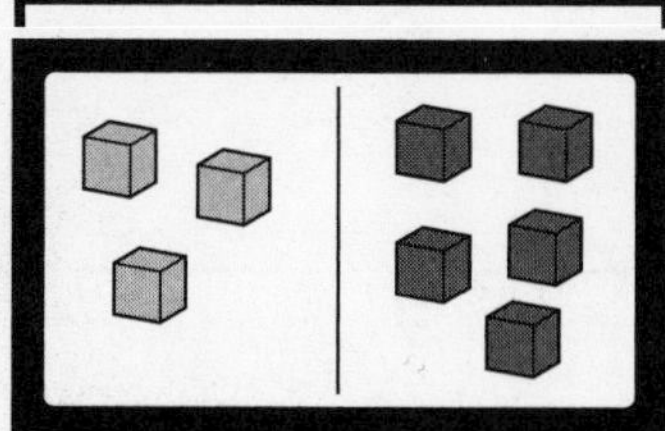

8 − 3 = 5

8 = 5 − 3

_____ − _____ = _____

4.

7

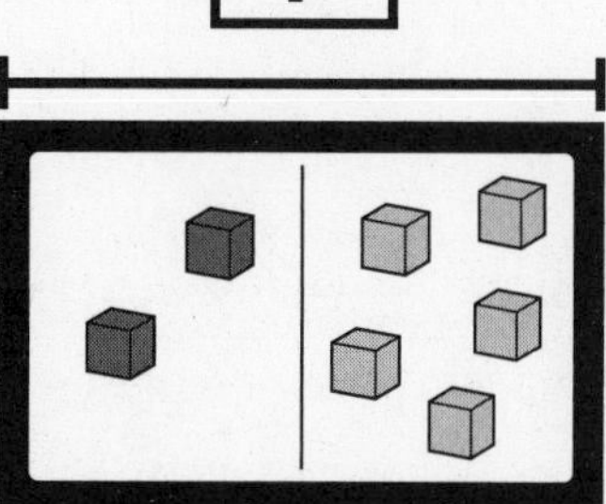

7 = 5 − 2

7 − 2 = 5

_____ = _____ − _____

Name ____________________

Practice
2-10

Circle the number sentence that is true.
Draw a line through the number sentence that is false.
Then write another number sentence that is true about the model.

1. 7

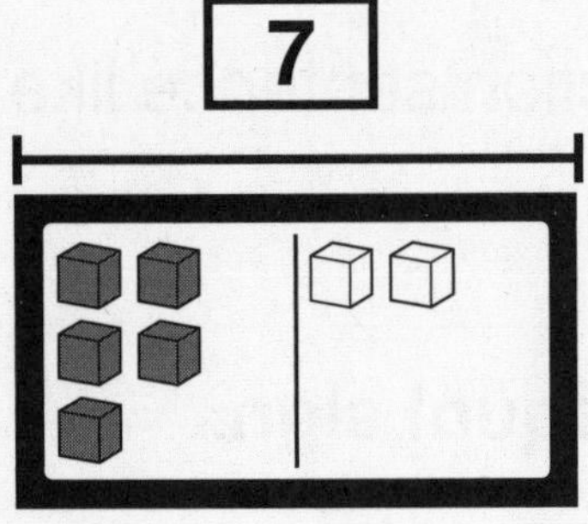

5 = 2 − 7

2 = 7 − 5

____ − ____ = ____

2. 10

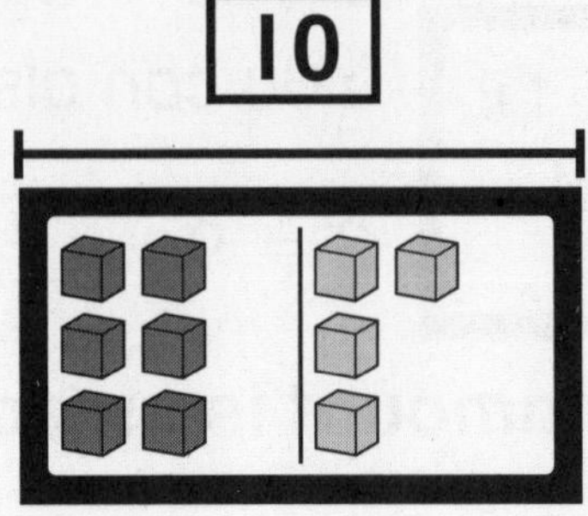

4 = 10 − 6

4 − 6 = 10

____ = ____ − ____

3. 11

11 = 4 − 7

7 = 11 − 4

____ − ____ = ____

4. 12

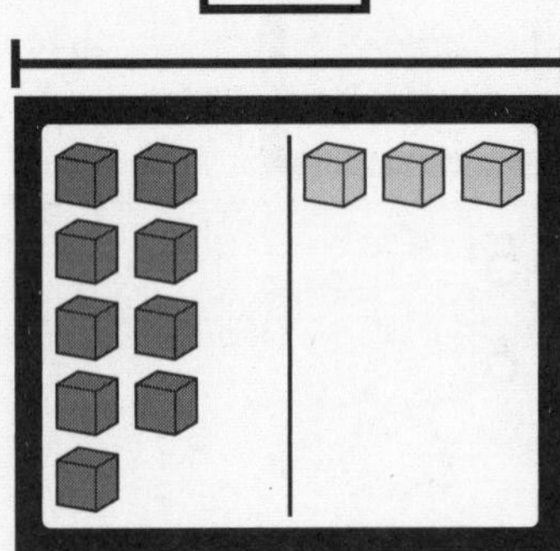

9 = 12 − 3

9 − 12 = 3

____ = ____ − ____

5. Number Sense Circle the number sentence that is correct.

4 − 3 = 5 − 1   8 − 4 = 9 − 5

Name ______________________

Problem Solving: Act It Out

You can use objects to show a story and write a number sentence.

There are 6 hats.
Ashley takes 2 hats.

How many hats are left? 4

Write the number sentence.

6 – 2 = 4

Cross out objects to show the story.
Write the number sentence.

1. There are 7 oranges.
Jeff takes 3 oranges.
How many oranges are left?

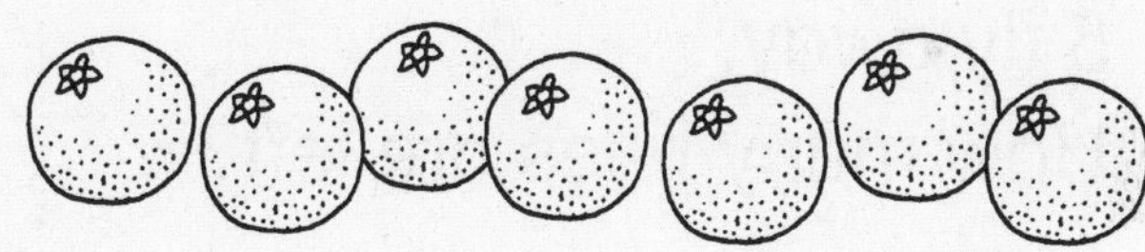

7 – ____ = ____

2. There are 5 airplanes.
4 airplanes take off.
How many airplanes are left?

____ – ____ = ____

Name ______________________

Practice
2-11

Problem Solving: Act It Out

Use counters to show the story.
Write the number sentence.

1. 9 boys are at the park.
5 go home.
How many boys are left?

_____ − _____ = _____

2. 6 ducks are in the pond.
3 fly away.
How many ducks are left?

_____ − _____ = _____

3. There are 8 books on the shelf.
Dana takes 2 books.
How many books are left?

_____ − _____ = _____

4. There are 4 pears.
Emily eats 1.
How many pears are left?

_____ − _____ = _____

5. 7 bees are in the garden.
5 fly away.
How many bees are left?

_____ − _____ = _____

6. There are 3 block towers.
2 get knocked over.
How many towers are left?

_____ − _____ = _____

Number Sense

7. You have 5 buttons.
Which is the greatest number of buttons you can give away?

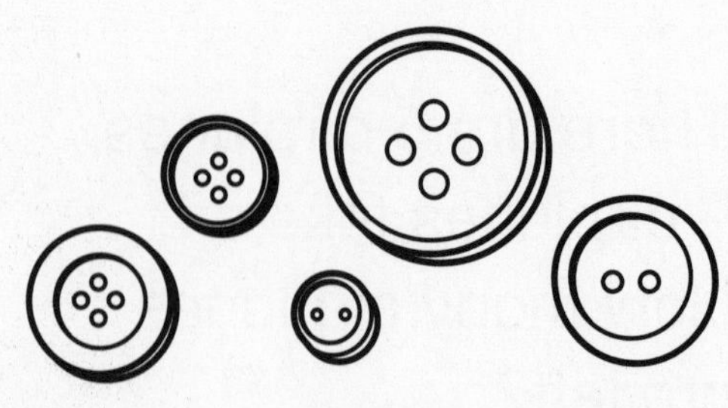

Ⓐ 6 Ⓑ 5 Ⓒ 3 Ⓓ 1

Name ____________________

Representing Numbers on a Ten-Frame

You can use a ten-frame to show numbers up to 10.

To show 3, start at the top left box. Count as you draw a counter for each number.

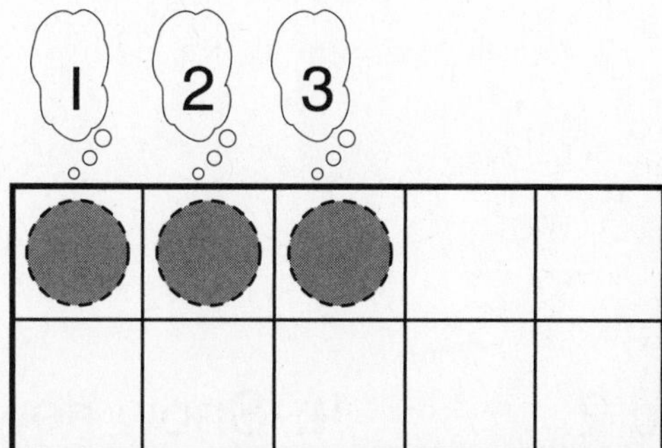

Draw counters in the ten-frame to show each number.

1. 6

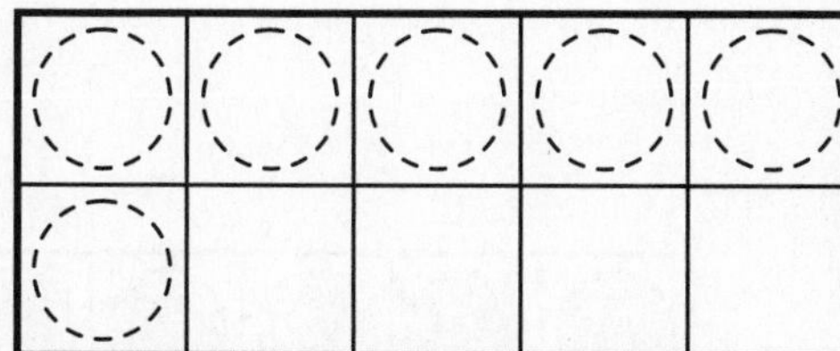

2. 8

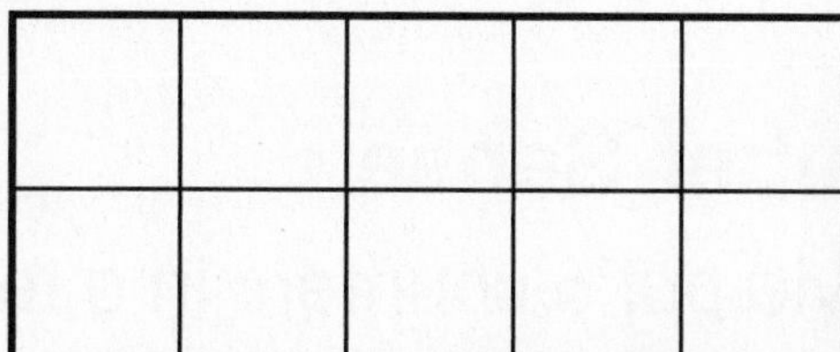

3. 7

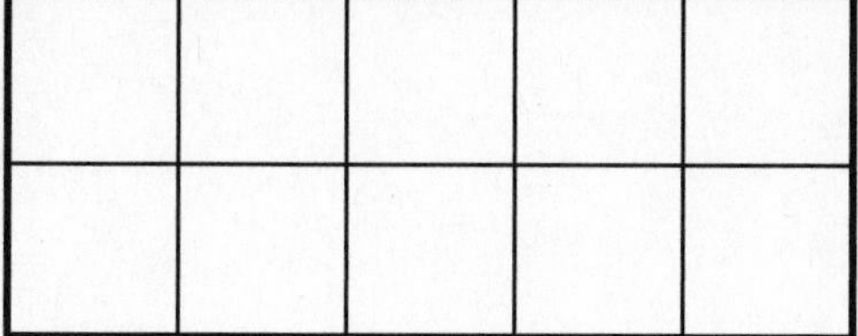

4. 9

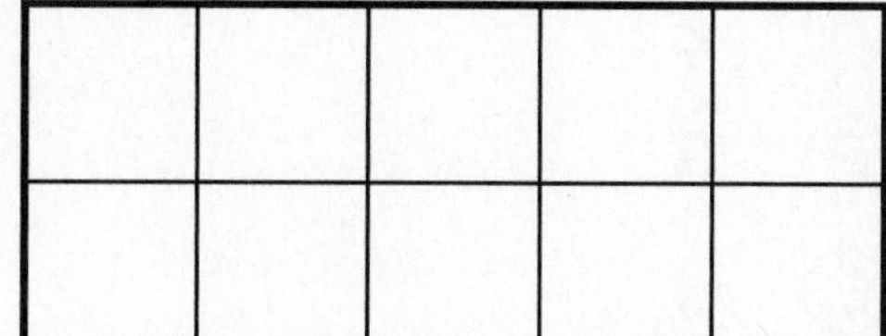

Name ______________________

Practice **3-1**

Representing Numbers on a Ten-Frame

Draw counters in the ten-frame to show each number.

1. 4

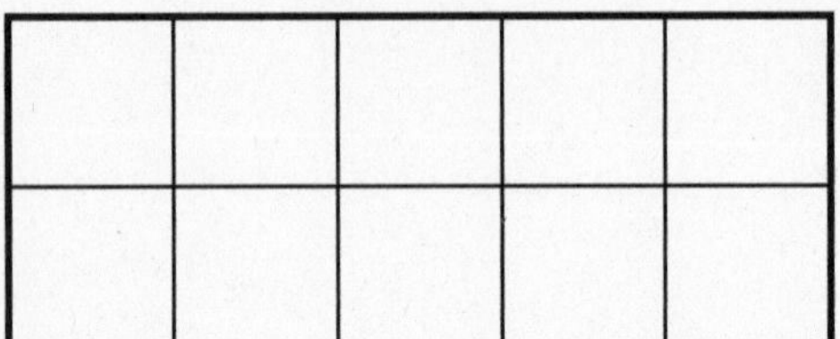

2. 6

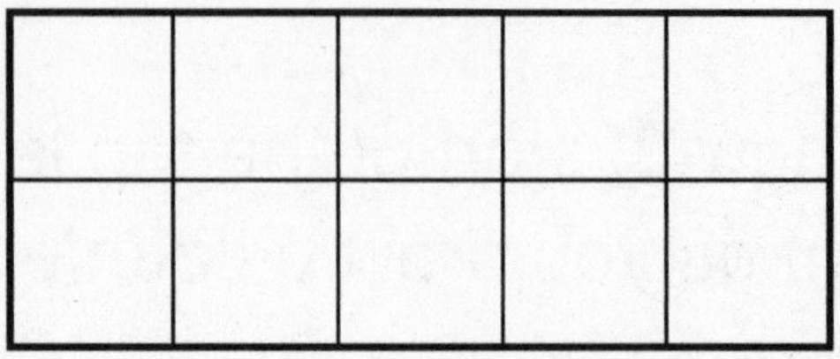

Algebra

Draw counters.

3. Show how 7 is 5 and 2.

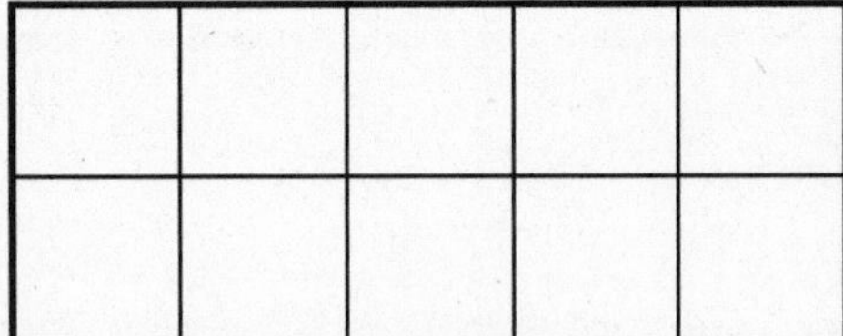

4. Show how 9 is 5 and 4.

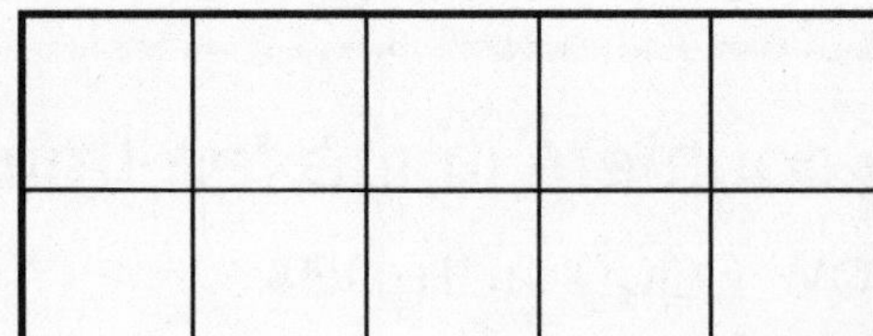

Number Sense

5. Kyle put 6 counters in a ten-frame. How many more counters should Kyle put in the frame to make 10?

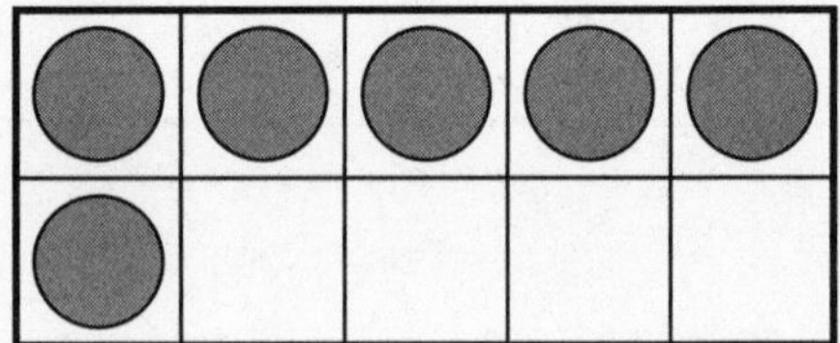

Ⓐ 2
Ⓑ 3
Ⓒ 4
Ⓓ 5

Name ______________________

Recognizing Numbers on a Ten-Frame

A ten-frame is made up of 2 five-frames. So, you can use what you learned about five-frames to help you read numbers on a ten-frame.
For example, the number 8 on a five-frame and a ten-frame looks very much alike.

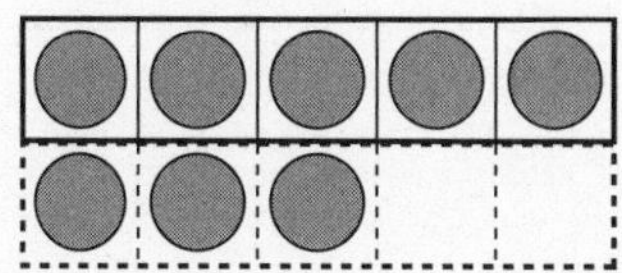

5 and 3 is 8.

Write the number shown on each ten-frame.

1. 7

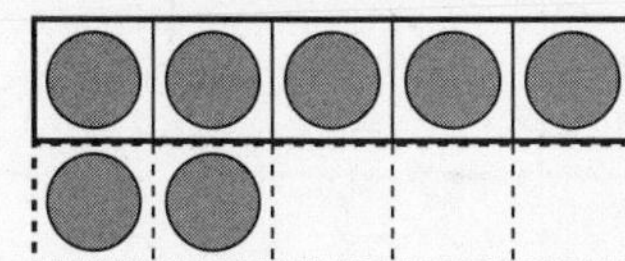

2. ______

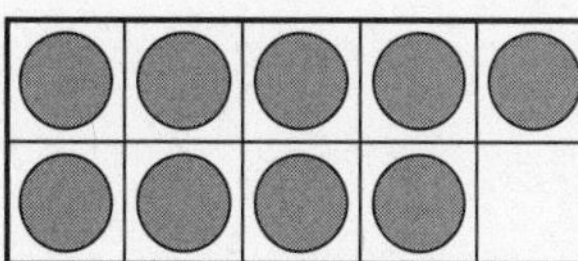

Spatial Thinking

Draw the counters.

3. Jim uses a ten-frame to show 5 and 5 more.

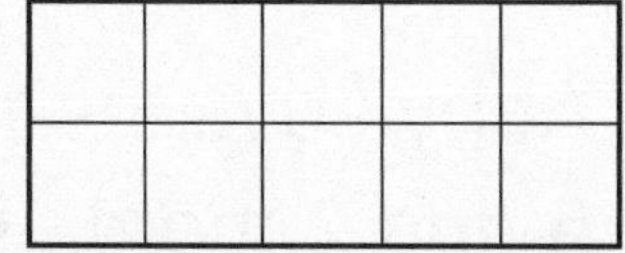

4. Bernice wrote about the ten-frame. Circle what Bernice wrote.

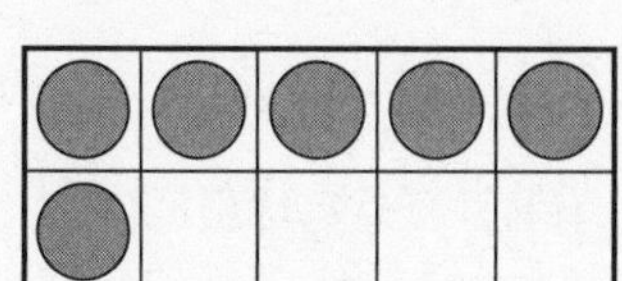

5 and 5 is 10. 4 away from 10 is 6. 5 and 2 is 7.

Name ________________________

Practice
3-2

Recognizing Numbers on a Ten-Frame

Write the number shown on each ten-frame.

1. 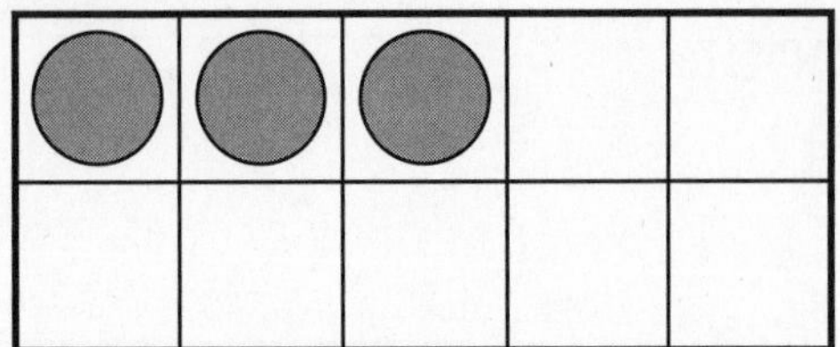

______

2. 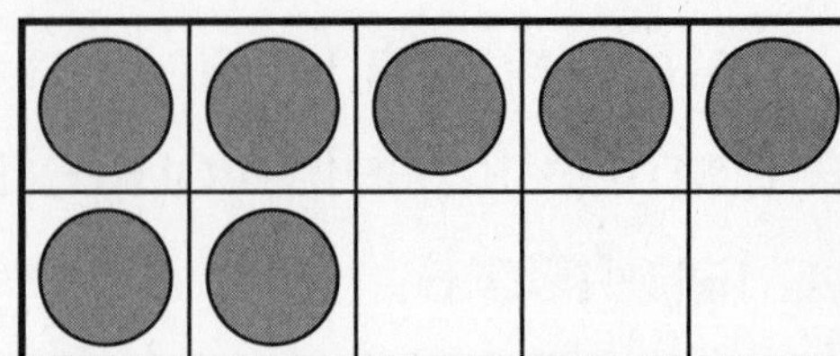

______

Spatial Thinking

Draw the counters. Then write the number.

3. Rob uses a ten-frame.
He shows 5 and 3 more.
What number does he show?

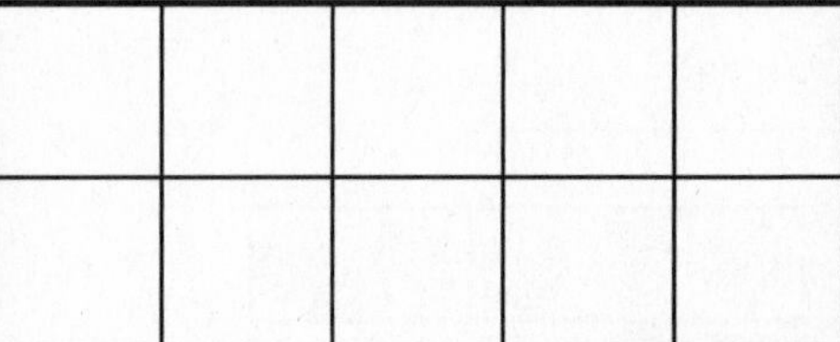

______

Number Sense

Draw the counters. Then solve the problem.

4. Abby says the ten-frame shows 5 and 2 more. Jake says it shows 3 away from 10.
What is the number in the ten-frame?

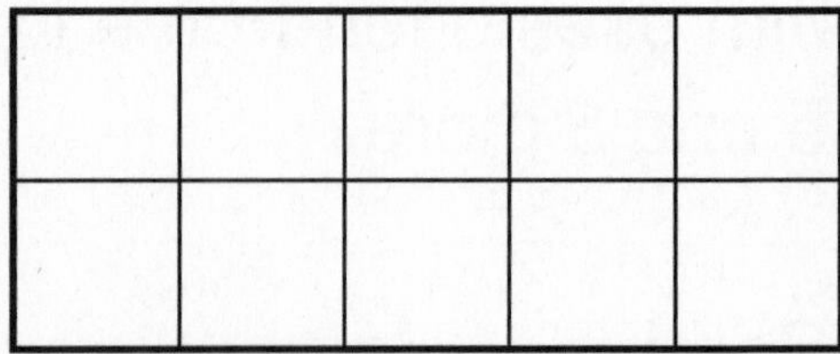

7	5	3	2
 Ⓐ	 Ⓑ	Ⓒ	Ⓓ

Name ___________________________

Reteaching 3-3

Parts of 10

Here are some different ways to make 10.

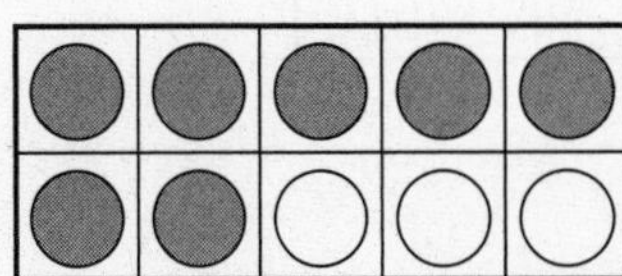

7 and 3

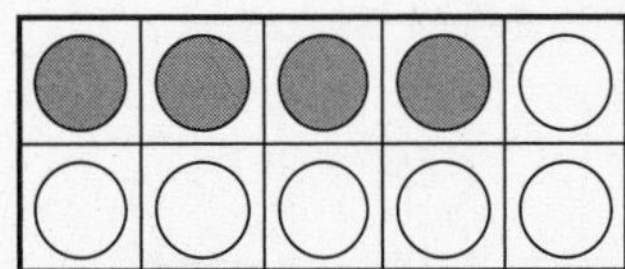

4 and 6

Write the numbers that show ways to make 10.

1. 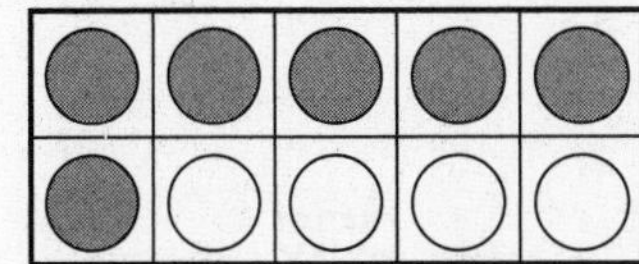

6 and 4

2. 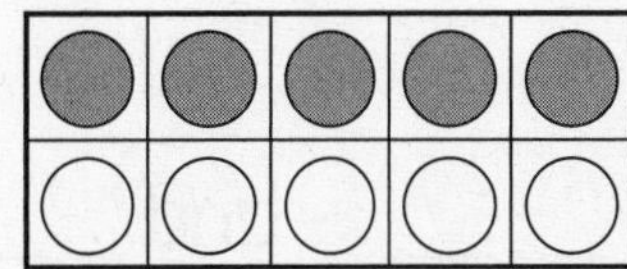

_______ and _______

3. 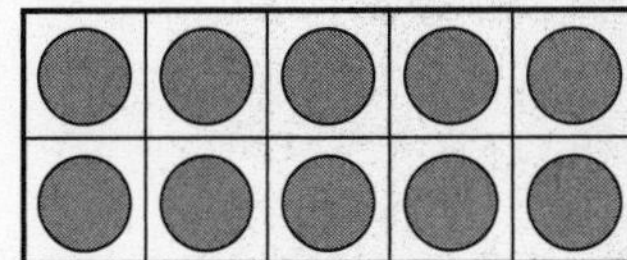

_______ and _______

4. 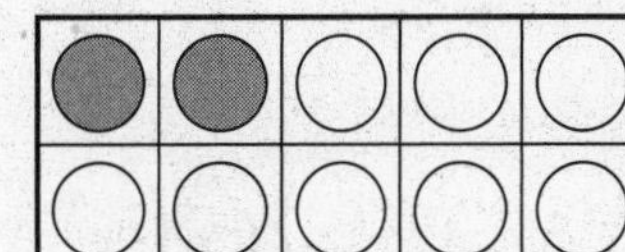

_______ and _______

5. 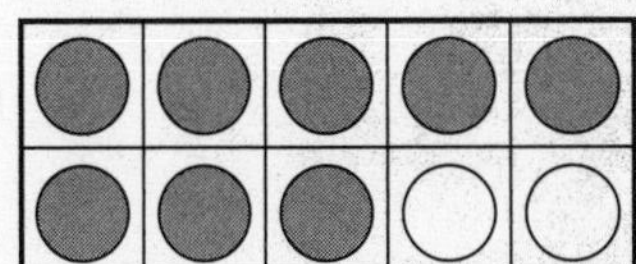

_______ and _______

6. 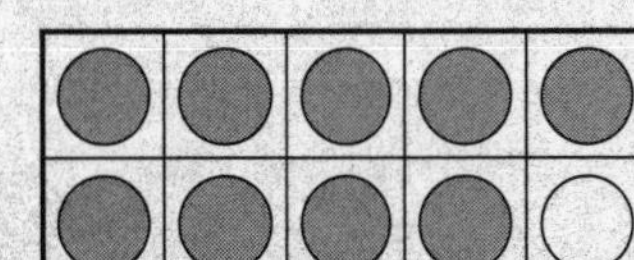

_______ and _______

Name ___________________________

Practice
3-3

Parts of 10

Write the numbers that show ways to make 10.

1. 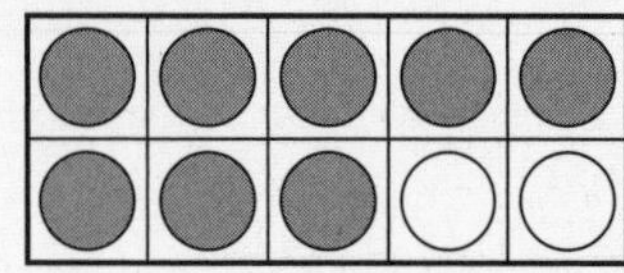

10 is __8__ and __2__.

2. 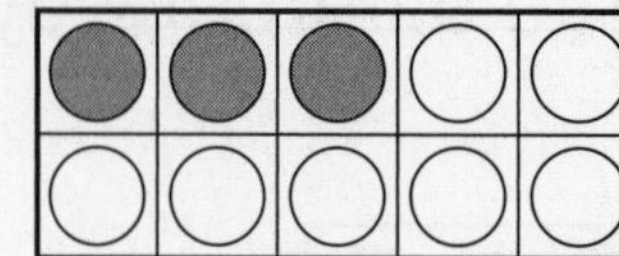

10 is ______ and ______.

3. 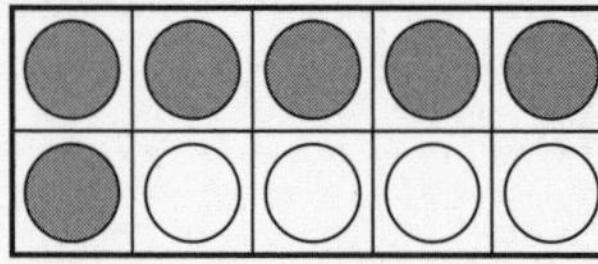

10 is ______ and ______.

4. 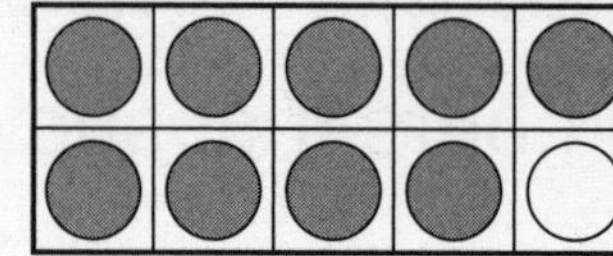

10 is ______ and ______.

5. 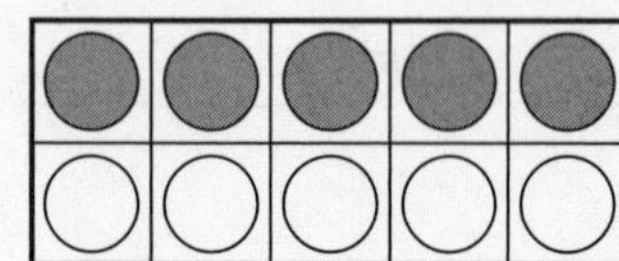

10 is ______ and ______.

6. 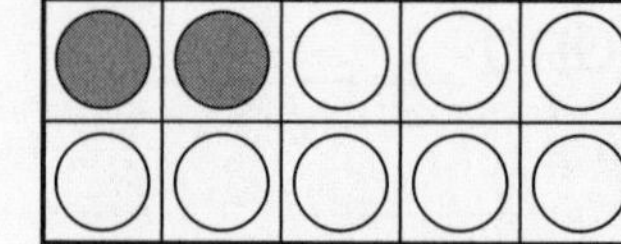

10 is ______ and ______.

Number Sense

7. Which numbers are parts of 10?

Ⓐ 1 and 8

Ⓑ 4 and 5

Ⓒ 7 and 3

Ⓓ 9 and 2

Name ____________________

Finding Missing Parts of 10

You can use a ten-frame to help you find missing parts of 10.

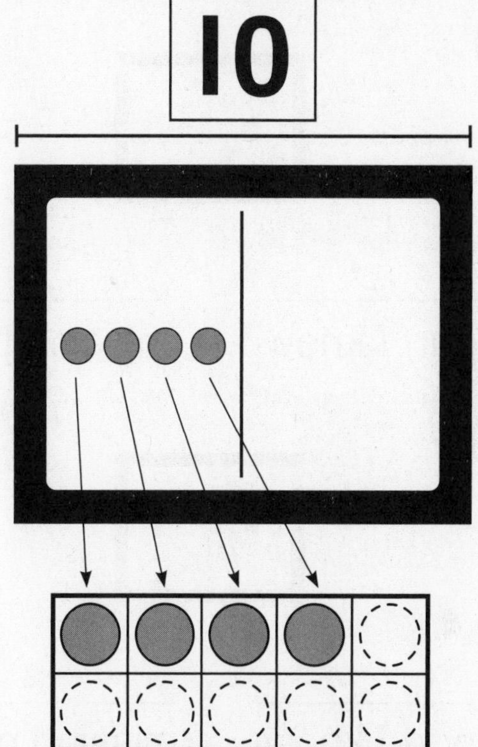

Draw the counters from the model in a ten-frame. This is the part you know.

To find the missing part, draw more counters to fill the frame.

Write the numbers.

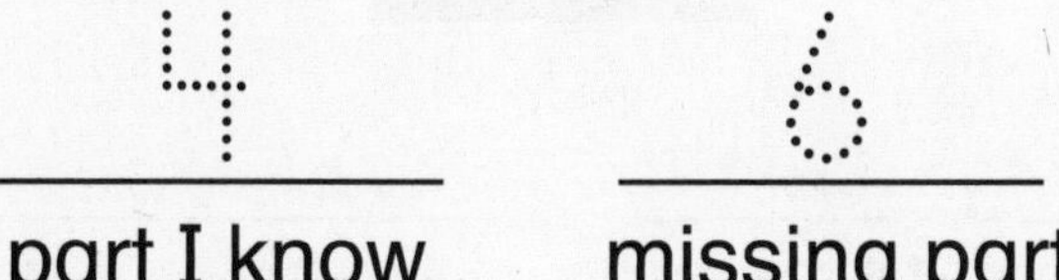

part I know   missing part

1. Look at the model.
Draw the missing part in the ten-frame.
Write the numbers.

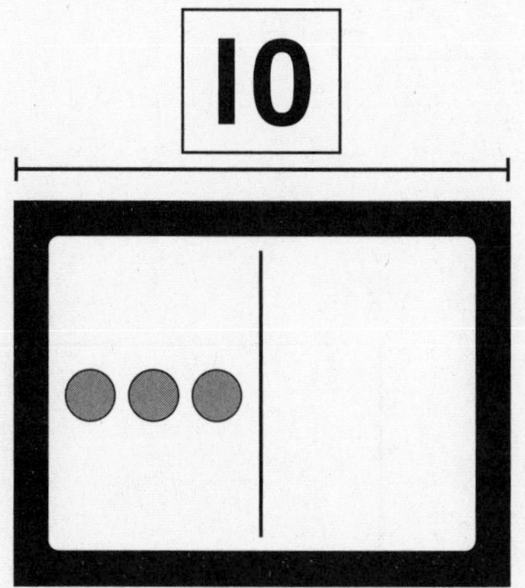

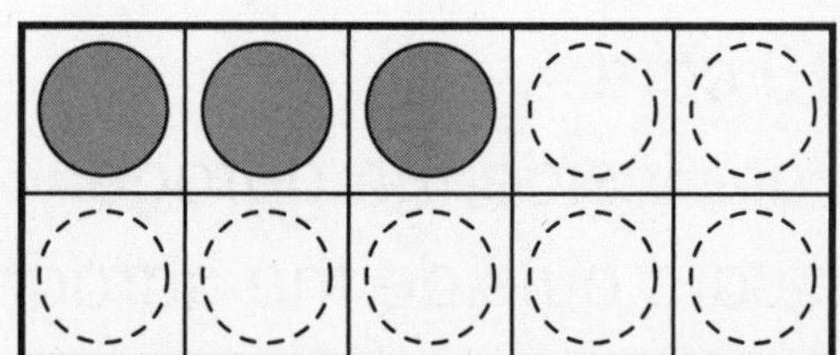

____________ ____________

part I know   missing part

Name ______________________

Practice
3-4

Finding Missing Parts of 10

Draw the missing part. Write the numbers.

1.

5 ______ 5 ______

part I know missing part

2.

______ ______

part I know missing part

3.

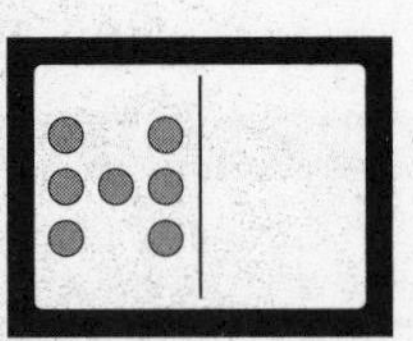

______ ______

part I know missing part

4.

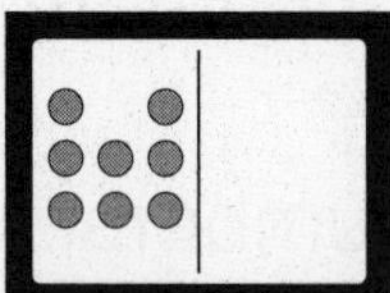

______ ______

part I know missing part

Algebra

Write the missing part.

5. 4 + ______ = 10

6. 1 + ______ = 10

Journal

Draw a picture to solve the problem.

7. There are 10 cars.
Some cars are inside the garage.
Draw some cars outside the garage.
Write the parts.

______ ______

part I know missing part

Name ______________________

Problem Solving: Make a Table

Katrina has purple marbles and yellow marbles. She can only fit 5 marbles in her pocket. How many different ways can Katrina put 5 marbles in her pocket?

To solve the problem, you need to find how many different ways Katrina can put the marbles in her pocket.

You can make a table and then count how many ways you made.

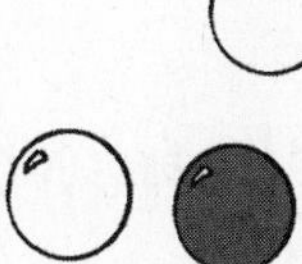

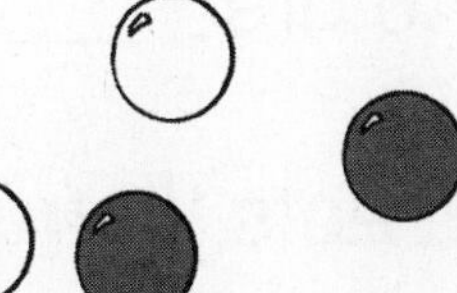

1. Complete the table.

2. There are ______ different ways.

3. What is the sum of each row in your table?

______

Purple Marbles	Yellow Marbles
5	0
4	1
3	2

Name ______________________

Problem Solving: Make a Table

Make a table to solve the problem.

1. Ed eats 6 pieces of fruit.
He can eat strawberries or grapes.
Show the ways Ed could pick which fruit to eat.

Strawberries	Grapes
0	
	3
6	

2. Complete the sentence.

There are ______ ways.

3. If Ed eats 4 strawberries, how many grapes does he eat?

______

Reasoning

4. Kathy has red balloons and blue balloons.
She gives away 5 balloons.

If she gives away 3 red balloons, how many blue balloons does she give away?

Ⓐ 3
Ⓑ 2
Ⓒ 1
Ⓓ 0

Red	Blue

Name ___

Adding with 0, 1, 2

You can count on to add with 0, 1, and 2.

(3) + 2 = ___

Circle the greater number.

Start with the greater number.

Then count on to add.

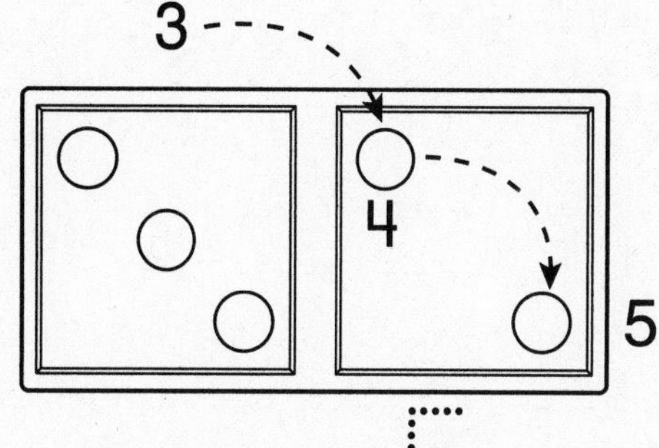

3 + 2 = 5

Circle the greater number. Count on to find each sum.

1.

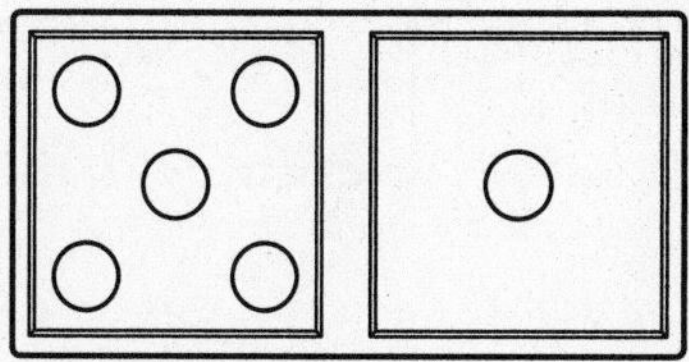

(5) + 1 = 6

2.

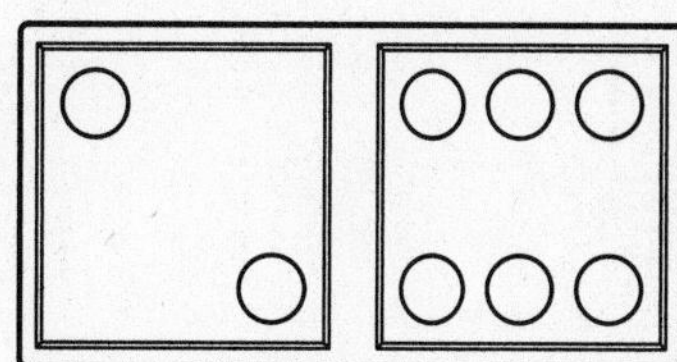

2 + (6) = ___

3.

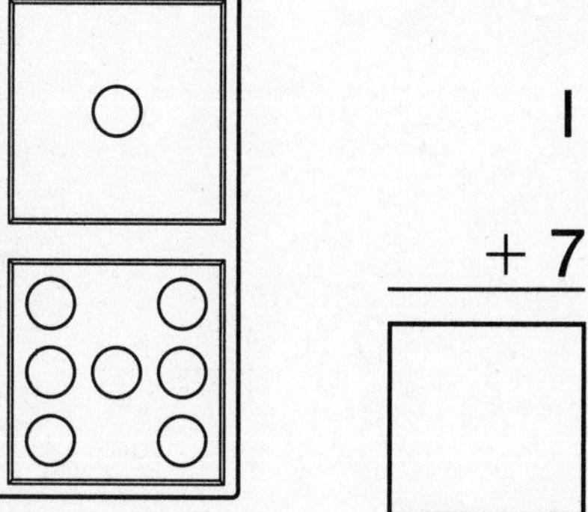

$$\begin{array}{r} 1 \\ +\ 7 \\ \hline \end{array}$$

4.

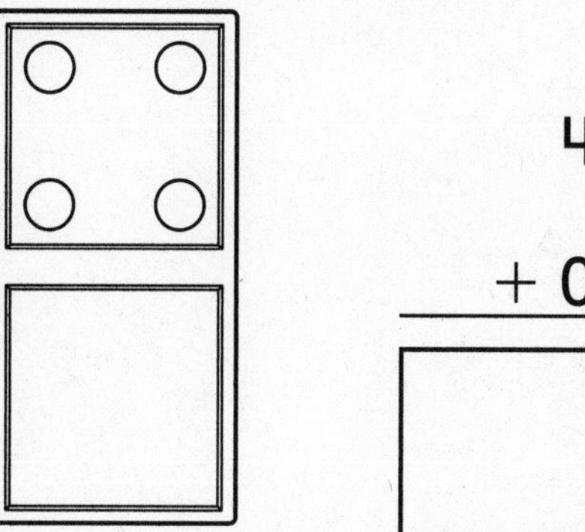

$$\begin{array}{r} 4 \\ +\ 0 \\ \hline \end{array}$$

Number Sense

5. 2 more than 7 is ___.

6. ___ more than 9 is 10.

Name ______________________

Practice
4-1

Adding with 0, 1, 2

Write the sum.

1. 7 + 0 = ______

2. 1 + 6 = ______

3. 4 + 2 = ______

4. 0 + 5 = ______

5. 4 + 1 = ______

6. 1 + 1 = ______

7. 2 + 7 = ☐

8. 1 + 8 = ☐

9. 0 + 9 = ☐

10. 7 + 0 = ☐

11. 6 + 1 = ☐

12. 5 + 2 = ☐

Algebra

13. 2 + 9 = ______ + 2

Ⓐ 11

Ⓑ 10

Ⓒ 9

Ⓓ 2

14. 1 + 2 = 0 + ______

Ⓐ 1

Ⓑ 2

Ⓒ 3

Ⓓ 4

Name ____________________

Doubles

You can use a double to add.

Both addends are the same. They are doubles.

2 + 2 = 4

3 + 3 = 6

Write an addition sentence for each double.

1. 

4 + 4 = 8

2. 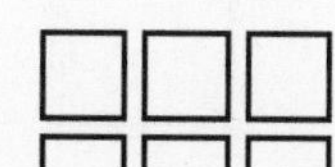 

6 + ____ = ____

3. 

____ + ____ = ____

4.  

____ + ____ = ____

5. 

How many coins are there in all?

____ + ____ = ____

6. 

How many coins are there in all?

____ + ____ = ____

Name ______________________

Doubles

Write the sum.

1. 4 + 4 = 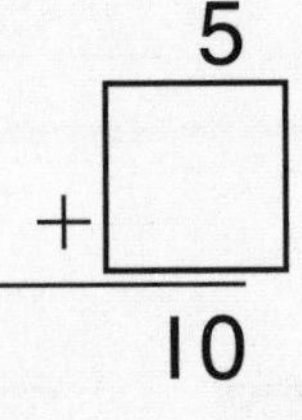

2. 6 + ☐ = 12

3. 1 + 1 = ☐

4. 3 + 3 = ☐

5. 5 + ☐ = 10

6. 0 + 0 = ☐

7. 2 + 2 = ☐

8. 7 + 7 = ☐

9. ☐ + ☐ = 16

10. ☐ + 9 = 18

Algebra

11. 1 + 1 + 2 + 2 = ______

Ⓐ 3

Ⓑ 4

Ⓒ 5

Ⓓ 6

Name ______________________

Near Doubles

We can use doubles to add other numbers.

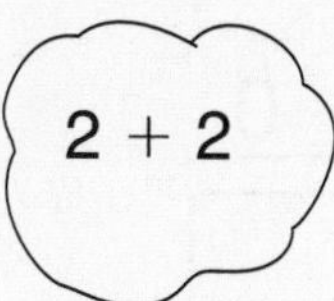

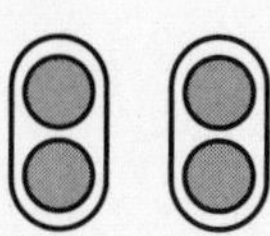

$2 + 2 = 4$

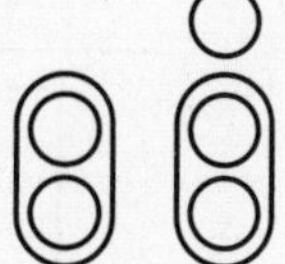

$2 + 3 = 5$

2 + 2 and
1 more

Find each sum. Use counters if you like.

1.

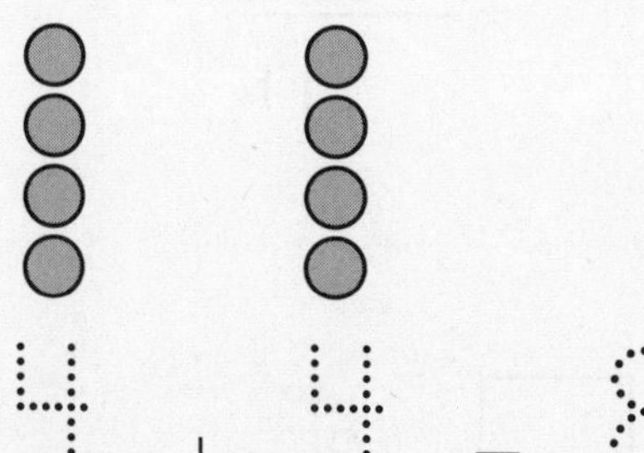

4 + 4 = 8

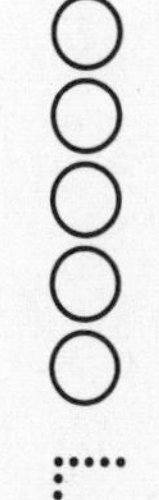

____ + 5 = ____

2.

____ + ____ = 8

____ + 5 = ____

Write a double or a near double for each sum.

3.

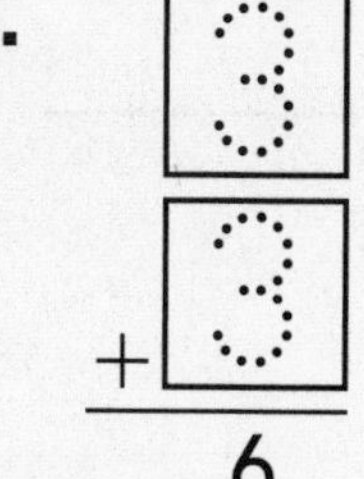

3 + 3 = 6

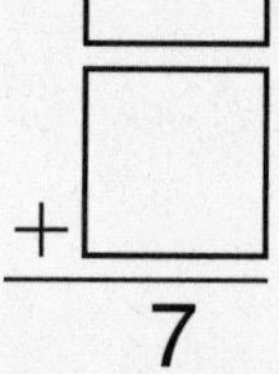

3 + ____ = 7

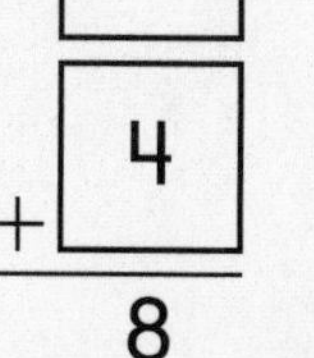

____ + 4 = 8

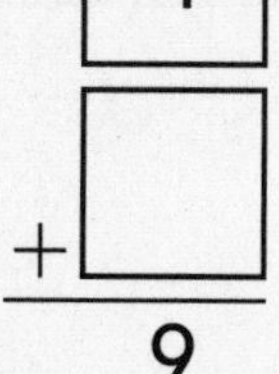

4 + ____ = 9

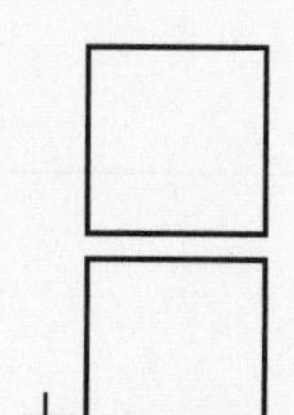

____ + ____ = 10

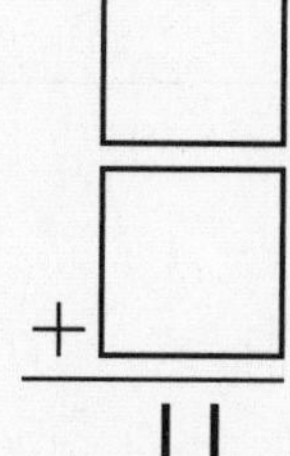

____ + ____ = 11

Name ____________________

Practice
4-3

Near Doubles

Add.

1. $\begin{array}{r} 3 \\ +\ 2 \\ \hline \boxed{5} \end{array}$

2. $\begin{array}{r} 3 \\ +\ 4 \\ \hline \boxed{} \end{array}$

3. $\begin{array}{r} 1 \\ +\ 0 \\ \hline \boxed{} \end{array}$

4. $\begin{array}{r} 4 \\ +\ 5 \\ \hline \boxed{} \end{array}$

5. $\begin{array}{r} 1 \\ +\ \boxed{} \\ \hline 3 \end{array}$

6. $\begin{array}{r} 5 \\ +\ \boxed{} \\ \hline 11 \end{array}$

7. $4 + \boxed{} = 7$

8. $5 = \boxed{} + 3$

Journal

9. How does knowing the double $6 + 6 = 12$ help you solve the near double $6 + 7 = 13$?

____

____

____

Name ______________________

Facts with 5 on a Ten-Frame

You can use a ten-frame to learn facts with 5.
Look at the addition sentence.
Draw counters in the frame.

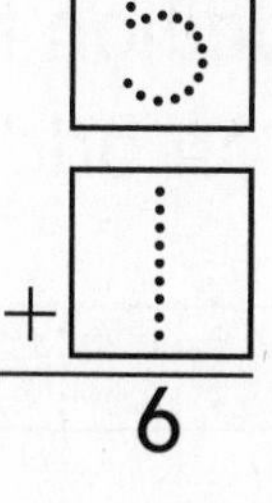

5 + 1 = 6

Draw counters and fill in the missing numbers.

1. 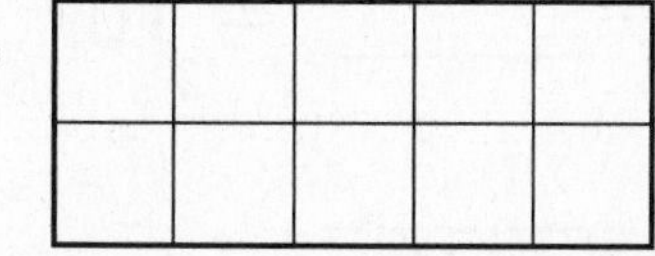

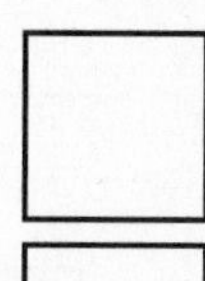

5 + 2 = 7

2. 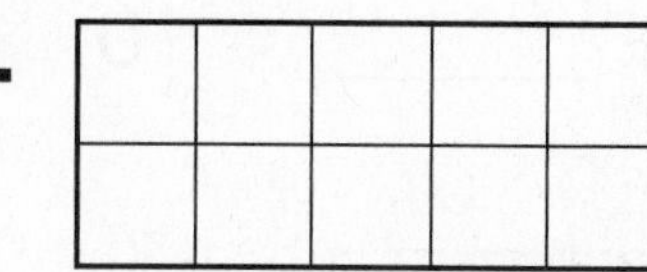

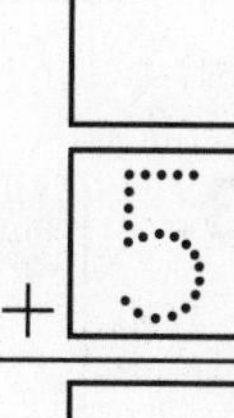

4 + 5 = ______

3. 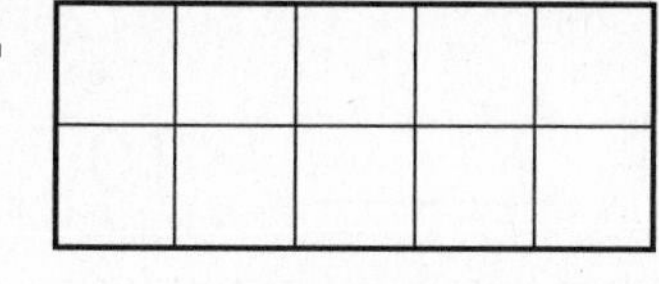

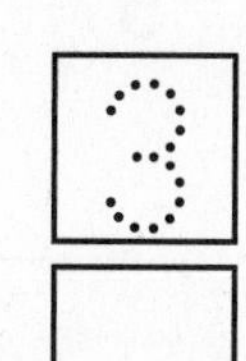

3 + 5 = ______

4. 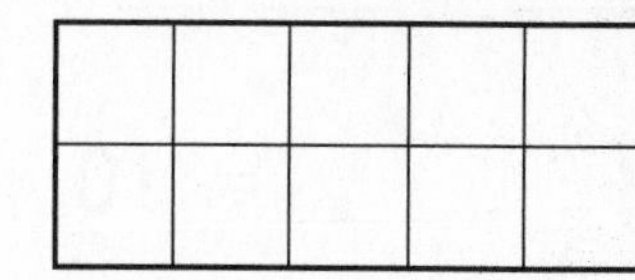

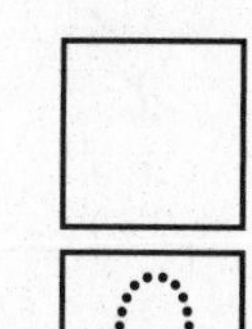

5 + 0 = ______

Number Sense

5. Nessa has 5 gray counters.
How many white counters does Nessa need to have 10 counters in all?

10	9	6	5

Name ______________________

Facts with 5 on a Ten-Frame

Look at the ten-frames.
Write an addition fact with 5.
Then write an addition fact for 10.

1. 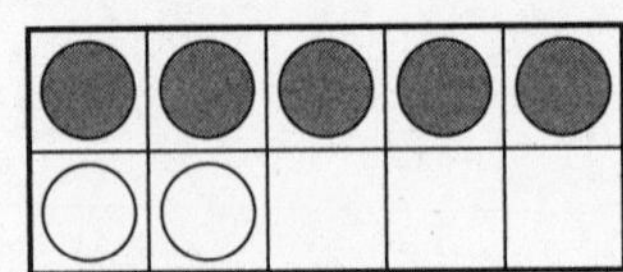

5 + 2 = 7

7 + ______ = 10

2. 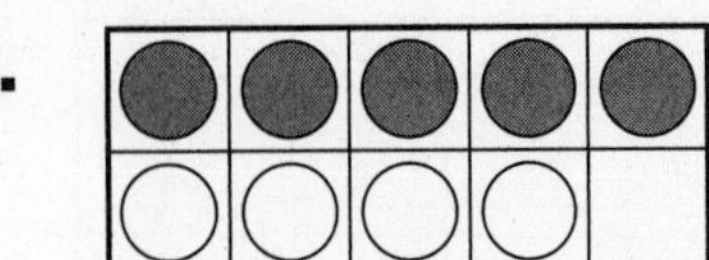

5 + ______ = ______

______ + ______ = 10

3. 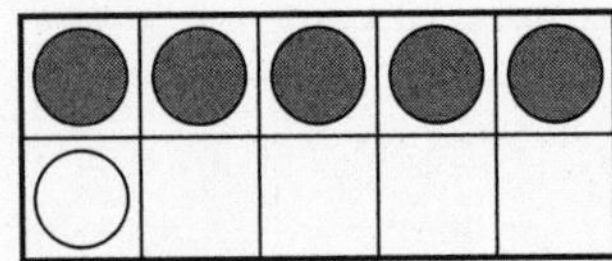

5 + ______ = ______

______ + ______ = 10

4. 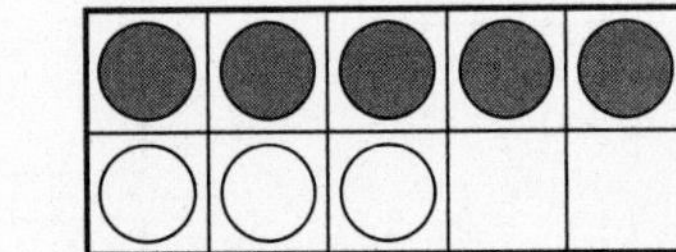

5 + ______ = ______

______ + ______ = 10

Algebra

5. 15 + 2 = 17

17 + ______ = 20

Ⓐ 2
Ⓑ 3
Ⓒ 5
Ⓓ 17

6. 15 + 4 = 19

19 + ______ = 20

Ⓐ 15
Ⓑ 4
Ⓒ 2
Ⓓ 1

Name ______________________________

Making 10 on a Ten-Frame

You can make 10 to add.
There are 7 white squares and 4 shaded squares. How many squares are there in all?

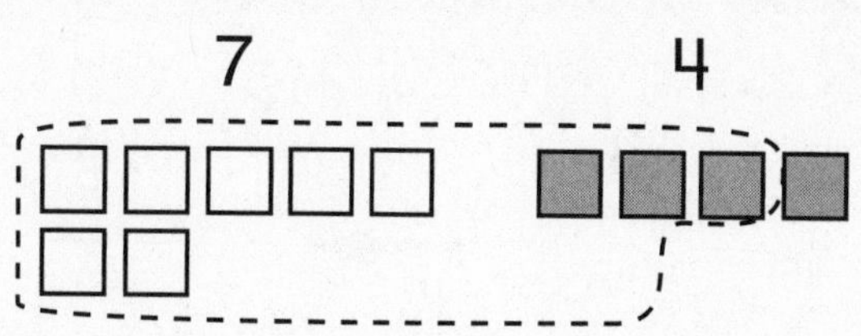

Circle a group of 10 squares.
Count the squares left over.
Then complete the number sentence.

10 + 1 = 11, so 7 + 4 = 11.

Circle a group of 10.
Write two addition sentences.

1. Hank has 9 black socks and 3 white socks. How many socks does Hank have in all?

10 + ______ = 12, so 9 + 3 = ______.

2. Pedro has 8 marbles in the left pocket of his pants. He has 7 marbles in the right pocket. How many marbles does Pedro have in all?

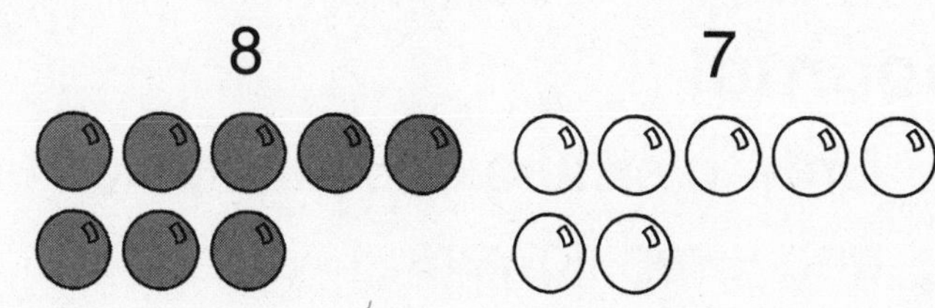

10 + ______ = ______, so 8 + 7 = ______.

Name ______________________________

Making 10 on a Ten-Frame

Draw counters to solve. Write the missing numbers.

1. 8 + 3 = ☐ → 10 + ☐ = ☐

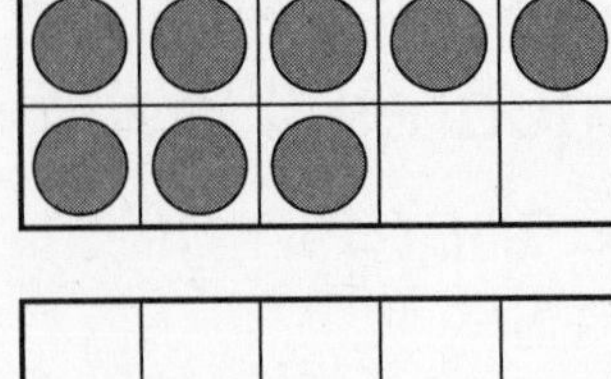

2. 9 + 3 = ☐ → 10 + ☐ = ☐

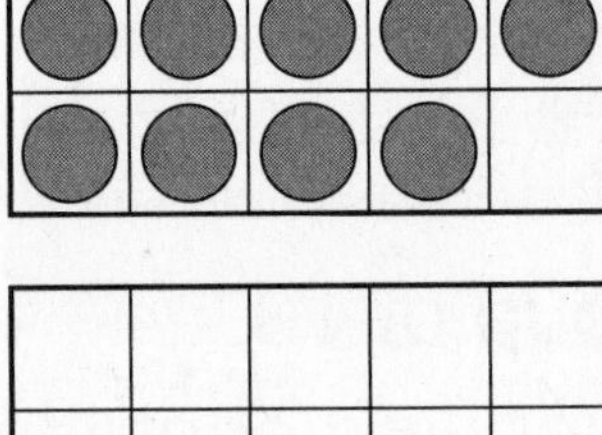

3. 7 + 4 = ☐ → 10 + ☐ = ☐

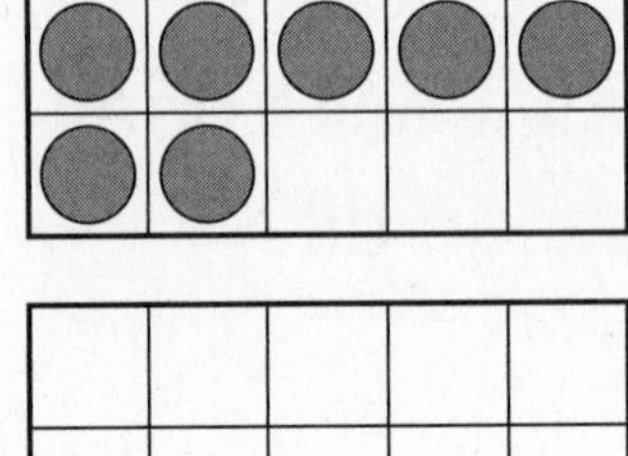

Journal

4. Draw a picture of 8 purple flowers and 4 red flowers.
Draw a picture of 10 red squares and 2 purple squares.
Write two addition sentences.

_____ + _____ = _____   _____ + _____ = _____

Name ______________________

Subtracting with 0, 1, 2

Reteaching
4-6

You can count back to subtract 0, 1, or 2.

Remember when you subtract 2, think "2 less than."

4 − 2 = ______

Start at 4.

Count back 2.

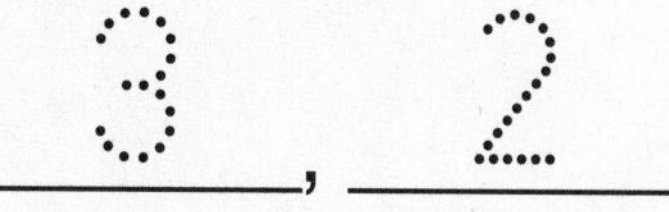

Write the number.

4 − 2 = 2

Count back to subtract 0, 1, or 2.
Use counters if you like.

1. 6

Count back 2.

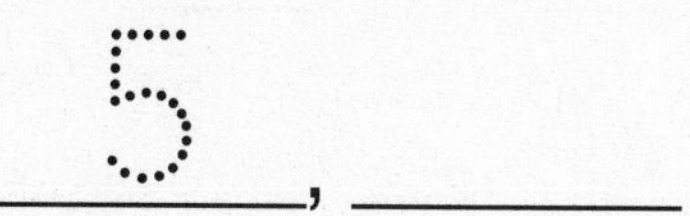

Write the number.

6 − 2 = ______

2. 9

Count back 1.

______

Write the number.

9 − 1 = ______

3.

Count back 0.

______

Write the number.

10 − 0 = ______

Name ______________________________

Subtracting with 0, 1, 2

Count back to subtract. Use counters if you like.

1. 

$$\begin{array}{r} 7 \\ -\ 1 \\ \hline 6 \end{array}$$

Start at 7.
Count back 1.

2.

11	6	1	7	3	8
− 2	− 1	− 1	− 0	− 2	− 1

3.

5	10	9	3	6	10
− 1	− 2	− 1	− 1	− 2	− 1

4.

2	4	12	8	11	9
− 1	− 0	− 2	− 2	− 1	− 2

Algebra

5. Three cats are asleep in a basket.
If no cats wake up, which tells how many are asleep?

Ⓐ 0

Ⓑ 1

Ⓒ 2

Ⓓ 3

Journal

6. Draw a picture that shows 2 less than.
Write a subtraction sentence for your story.

_____ − _____ = _____

Name ______________________________

Reteaching
4-7

Thinking Addition

Doubles help you to subtract.

Think: 3 + 3 = 6, so 6 − 3 = 3.

Add the doubles.
Then use the doubles to help you subtract.

1.

1 + 1 = 2, so 2 − 1 = ______.

2.

4 + 4 = ______, so 8 − 4 = ______.

Visual Thinking

Complete the addition and subtraction sentences.

3. 2 + 2 = ______

4 − 2 = ______

Name ______________________________

Practice
4-7

Thinking Addition

Add the doubles.
Then use the doubles to help you subtract.

1. 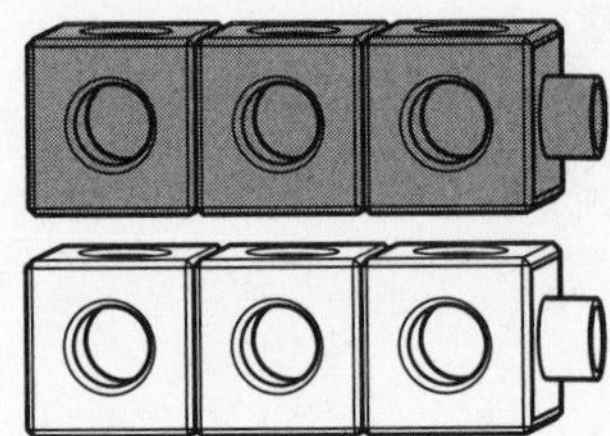

$$\begin{array}{r} 3 \\ +\,3 \\ \hline 6 \end{array} \qquad \begin{array}{r} 6 \\ -\,3 \\ \hline 3 \end{array}$$

If 3 + 3 = 6,
then 6 − 3 = 3.

2. 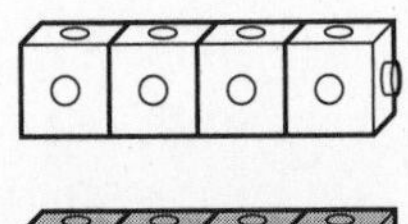

$$\begin{array}{r} 4 \\ +\,4 \\ \hline \end{array} \qquad \begin{array}{r} 8 \\ -\,4 \\ \hline \end{array}$$

3.

$$\begin{array}{r} 6 \\ +\,6 \\ \hline \end{array} \qquad \begin{array}{r} 12 \\ -\,6 \\ \hline \end{array}$$

4.

$$\begin{array}{r} 2 \\ +\,2 \\ \hline \end{array} \qquad \begin{array}{r} 4 \\ -\,2 \\ \hline \end{array}$$

5. 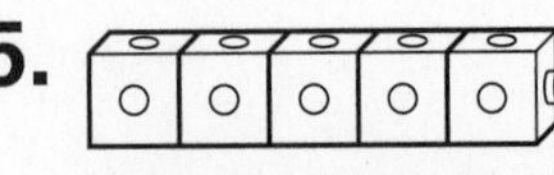

$$\begin{array}{r} 5 \\ +\,5 \\ \hline \end{array} \qquad \begin{array}{r} 10 \\ -\,5 \\ \hline \end{array}$$

Number Sense

6. Mark the double that will help you subtract.

8 − 4 = ______

Ⓐ 3 + 3

Ⓑ 4 + 4

Ⓒ 5 + 5

Ⓓ 8 + 8

Name ______________________

Thinking Addition to 8 to Subtract

You can think addition to help you subtract.

Think: I know 2 + 6 = 8, so 8 – 6 = 2.

2 + 6 = 8
8 – 6 = 2

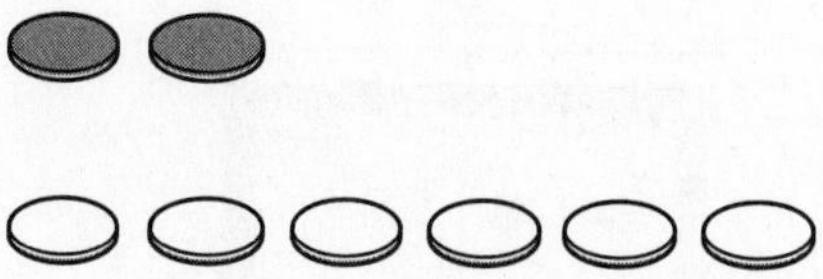

Write an addition fact. Think of the addition fact to help you write and solve the subtraction fact.

1.

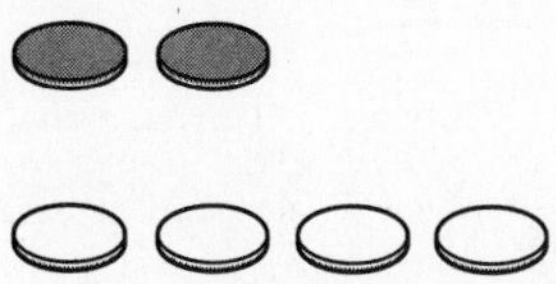

2 + 4 = 6
6 – 4 = 2

2.

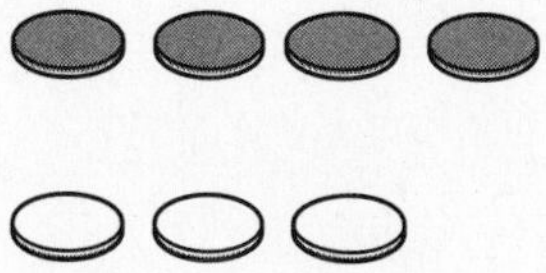

___ + ___ = 7
7 – ___ = ___

3.

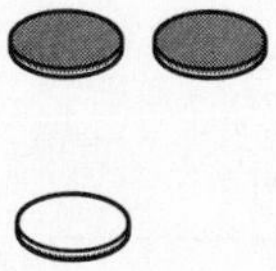

___ + ___ = ___
___ – ___ = ___

4.

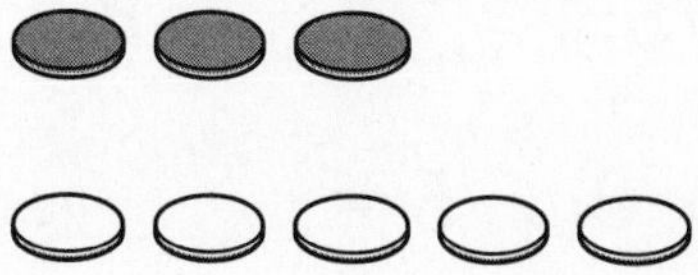

___ + ___ = ___
___ – ___ = ___

Algebra

5. If △ + ○ = □, then ___ – ___ = ___.

Name ______________________________

Practice
4-8

Thinking Addition to 8 to Subtract

Think addition to help you subtract.
Draw the missing part. Write the numbers.

1. 6

Think 4 + ______ = 6.

So, 6 − 4 = ______.

2. 6

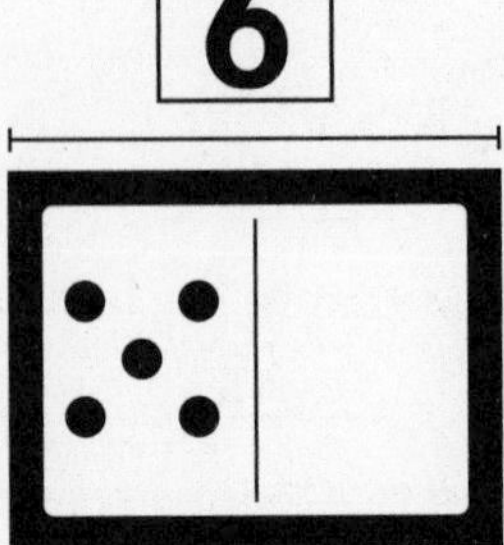

Think 5 + ______ = 6.

So, 6 − 5 = ______.

3. 8

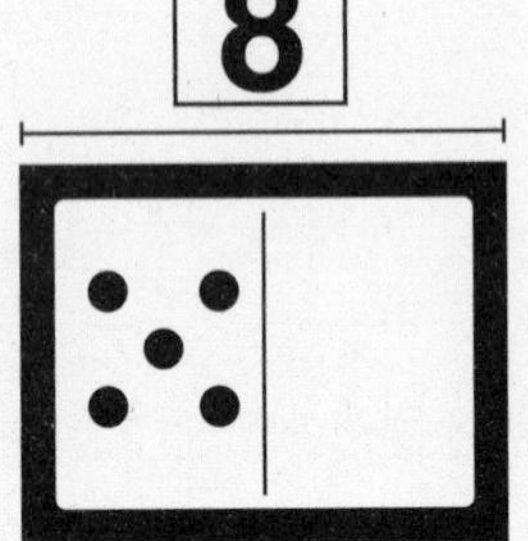

Think 5 + ______ = 8.

So, 8 − 5 = ______.

4. 7

Think 4 + ______ = 7.

So, 7 − 4 = ______.

Algebra

5. Tia needs to make 8 baskets. She makes 2 baskets.
How many more baskets does Tia need to make?
Which addition fact can help you subtract?

Ⓐ 8 + 6 = 14

Ⓑ 6 + 6 = 12

Ⓒ 2 + 8 = 10

Ⓓ 2 + 6 = 8

Name ____________________

Reteaching
4-9

Thinking Addition to 12 to Subtract

You can use addition facts to help you subtract.

8 + 1 = 9

9 − 1 = 8

8 + 1 = 9 and 9 − 1 = 8 are related facts.

Use the addition fact to help you subtract.

1. 10 − 2 = ______ 8 + 2 = 10

2. 11 − 4 = ______ 7 + 4 = 11

3. 12 − 9 = ______ 3 + 9 = 12

4. 11 − 6 = ______ 5 + 6 = 11

Name ______________________________

Practice
4-9

Thinking Addition to 12 to Subtract

Think addition to help you subtract.

1. 11

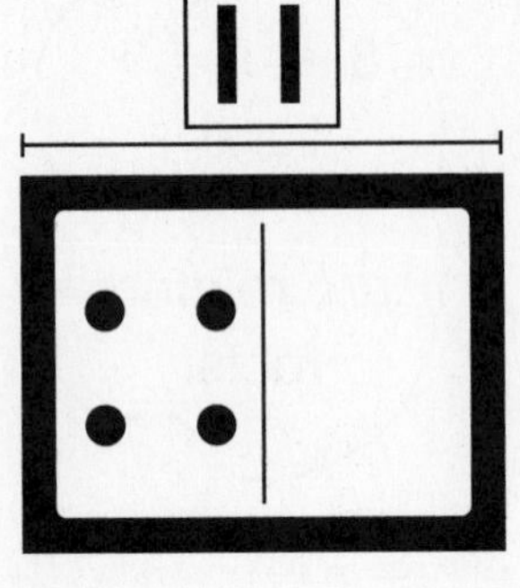

Think: 4 + ______ = 11

So, 11 − 4 = ______.

2. 12

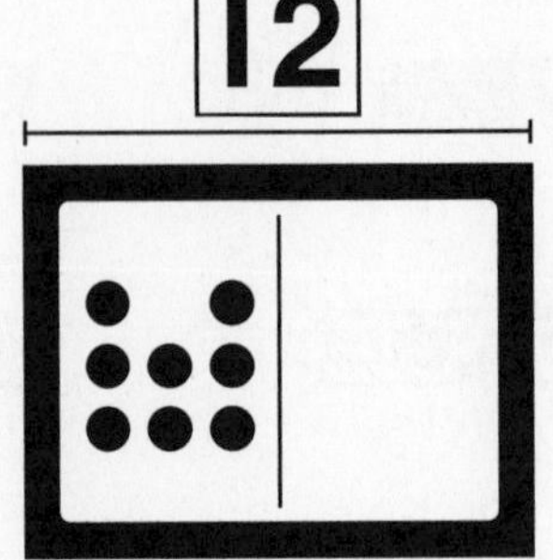

Think: 8 + ______ = 12

So, 12 − 8 = ______.

3. 12

Think: 9 + ______ = 12

So, 12 − 9 = ______.

4. 10

Think: 4 + ______ = 10

So, 10 − 4 = ______.

Problem Solving

5. Mark scores 6 points. Amy scores 11 points.
How many points does Mark need to tie the game?
Write a number sentence to solve.

______ ◯ ______ = ______

______ points

Name ______________________

Reteaching
4-10

Problem Solving: Draw a Picture and Write a Number Sentence

There are 4 blue butttons.
There are 3 red buttons.
How many buttons are there?

Blue Buttons	Red Buttons
◎	◎
◎	◎
◎	◎
◎	

You need to find how many buttons there are in all.

You can draw a picture of the buttons. 4 + ____ = ____
Then you can write a number sentence.
Count the buttons in your picture to find the sum.

____ buttons

You can also draw a picture to help you solve a subtraction problem.

Mia has 7 grapes.
First, draw a picture of all the grapes.

Mia eats 3 grapes.
Cross out the grapes she eats.

Count how many grapes are left. ____ grapes

Write a number sentence that tells about the picture.

7 − ____ = ____

Check your work.
Does the number sentence match the picture?

Name ______________________

Practice
4-10

Problem Solving: Draw a Picture and Write a Number Sentence

Write a number sentence to solve.
Draw a picture to check.

1. Abby has 8 apples.
Judy gives her 3 more apples.
How many apples does
Abby have in all?

8 + ______ = ______

2. Maya has 9 pears.
3 pears are green.
The rest are yellow.
How many pears are yellow?

______ − ______ = ______

Reasoning

3. There are 7 birds. 3 birds fly away.
How many birds are left?
Which number sentence can
help you find the answer?

Ⓐ 7 − 2 = 5

Ⓑ 7 − 3 = 4

Ⓒ 9 − 7 = 2

Ⓓ 7 − 6 = 1

Name ______________________

Reteaching
5-1

Doubles

When you add the same number to itself, you are using doubles.

$$\begin{array}{r} 1 \\ +\,1 \\ \hline 2 \end{array} \quad \begin{array}{r} 2 \\ +\,2 \\ \hline 4 \end{array} \quad \begin{array}{r} 3 \\ +\,3 \\ \hline 6 \end{array} \quad \begin{array}{r} 4 \\ +\,4 \\ \hline 8 \end{array}$$

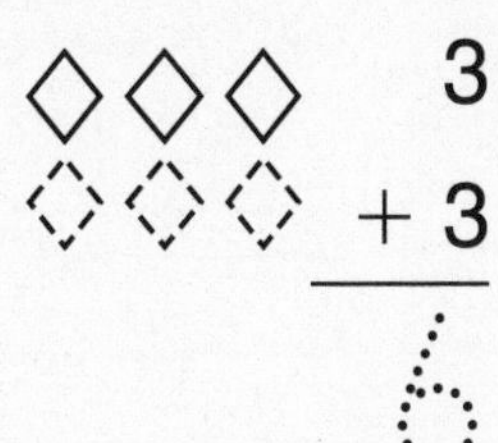

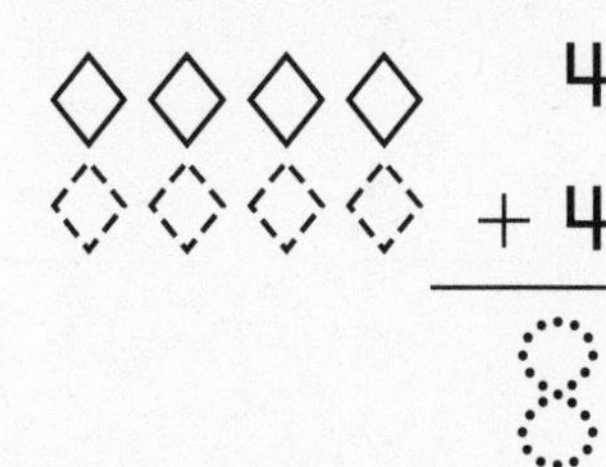

Use doubles to add. Draw doubles to help you.

1. $\begin{array}{r} 5 \\ +\,5 \\ \hline 10 \end{array}$

2. $\begin{array}{r} 6 \\ +\,6 \\ \hline \end{array}$

3. $\begin{array}{r} 7 \\ +\,7 \\ \hline \end{array}$

4. $\begin{array}{r} 10 \\ +\,10 \\ \hline \end{array}$

Visual Thinking

5. For each picture write an addition sentence that tells how many buttons there are.

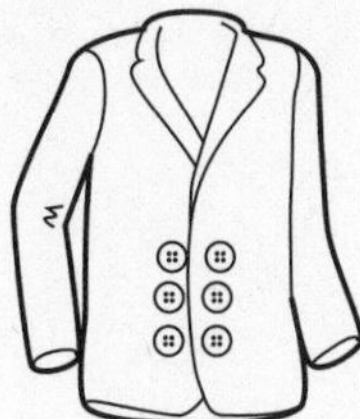

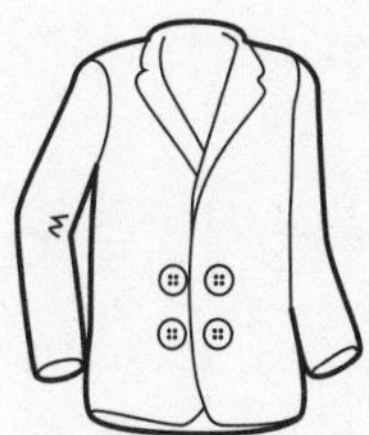

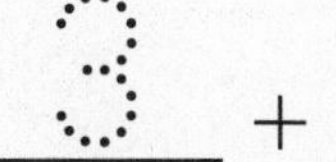

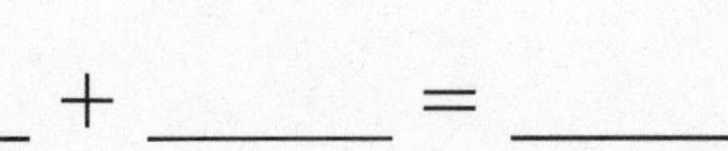

3 + ______ = ______   ______ + ______ = ______

Name ____________________

Doubles

Add to solve. Then circle the doubles.

1.	5	6	6	8	5	2
	+ 5	+ 7	+ 3	+ 8	+ 8	+ 2

2.	4	2	7	8	4	5
	+ 2	+ 7	+ 7	+ 1	+ 4	+ 2

3.	10	5	3	6	9	4
	+ 10	+ 0	+ 3	+ 9	+ 2	+ 4

4.	6	5	6	9	5	1
	+ 6	+ 7	+ 8	+ 9	+ 4	+ 1

Reasoning

5. Jack has 5 toy cars. Sam has 5 toy cars. Which doubles fact shows how many cars they have in all?

- Ⓐ $4 + 4 = 8$
- Ⓑ $5 + 5 = 10$
- Ⓒ $6 + 6 = 12$
- Ⓓ $7 + 7 = 14$

Name ____________________

Doubles Plus 1

You can use doubles facts to add 4 + 5.
Because 5 = 4 + 1, you can write 4 + 5 as

4 + 4 + 1

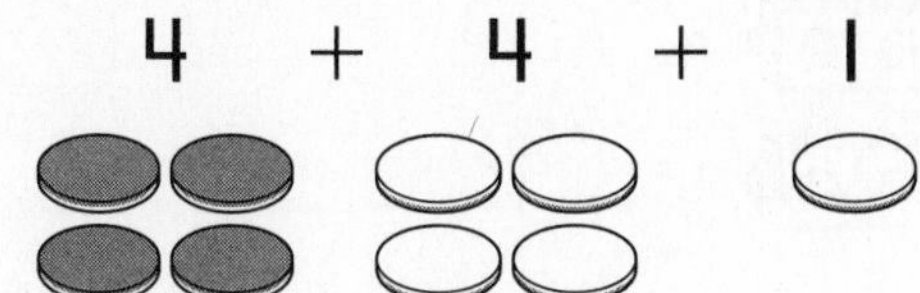

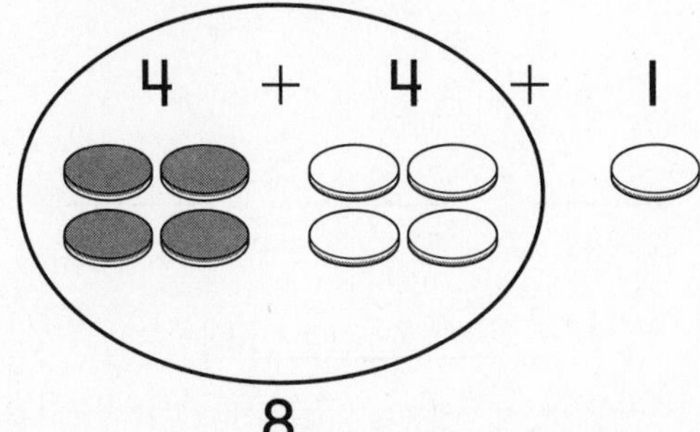

I know 4 + 4 = 8.
I know 8 and 1 more is 9.
So 4 + 5 = 9.

Add to find the doubles and doubles-plus-1 facts.

1. 3 + 3 = 6    3 + 4 = 7 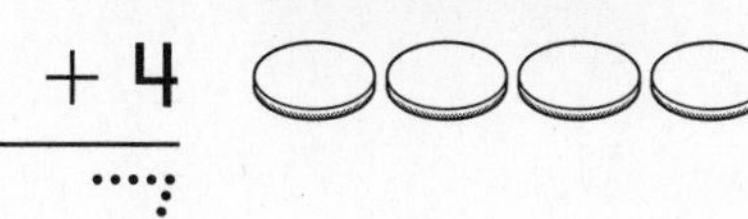

2. Bill has 6 trucks.
Ashley has 7 trucks.
How many trucks do they have in all?

_______ trucks

3. Peter read 7 books.
Kira read 8 books.
How many books did they read in all?

_______ books

Name ______________________

Practice 5-2

Doubles Plus 1

Add the doubles.
Then use the doubles to help you add.

1. Think 5 + 5 = 10.

So, 5 + 6 = ______.

2. Think ____ + ____ = ____.

So, 3 + 4 = ______.

3. Think ____ + ____ = ____.

So, 7 + 8 = ______.

4. Think ____ + ____ = ____.

So, 9 + 10 = ______.

Number Sense

5. Paco has 5 model cars.
He gets 6 more cars for his birthday.
How many cars does he have now?

Ⓐ 12
Ⓑ 11
Ⓒ 10
Ⓓ 9

Name ______________________

Reteaching
5-3

Doubles Plus 2

You can use doubles facts to add 6 + 8.
Because 8 = 6 + 2, you can write 6 + 8 as

6 + 6 + 2

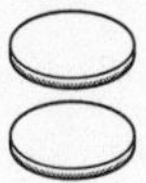

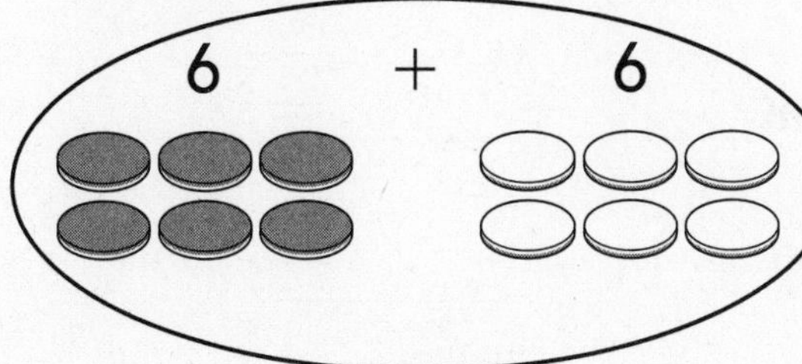

I know 6 + 6 = 12.
I know 12 and 2 more is 14.
So 6 + 8 = 14.

Add to find the doubles and doubles-plus-2 facts.

1. 3 + 3 = 6  3 + 5 = 8 

2. 4 + 6 = ______

3. 7 + 9 = ______

4. Max scored 9 runs on Monday and 11 runs on Tuesday. How many runs did he score in all?

What doubles fact will you use?

______ + ______ = ______

So, 9 + 11 = ______ runs.

Name ______________________

Practice **5-3**

Doubles Plus 2

Draw 2 more cubes. Use a doubles fact to help you add.

1.

Think 8 + 8 = 16.

So, 8 + 10 = ______.

2.

Think ____ + ____ = ____.

So, 9 + 11 = ______.

3.

Think ____ + ____ = ____.

So, 3 + 5 = ______.

4.

Think ____ + ____ = ____.

So, 2 + 4 = ______.

Journal

5. Write a story about the doubles-plus-2 fact 5 + 7 = 12.

____

____

____

____

Name ______________________

Reteaching
5-4

Problem Solving: Two-Question Problems

Jill has 6 marbles. She gets 5 more. How many marbles does she have in all?

6 + 5 = 11 marbles

I know Jill has 11 marbles in all.
I know she gives Sal 8.
I can subtract to find how many she has left.

Jill gives 8 marbles to Sal. Now how many marbles does Jill have?

11 − 8 = 3

Jill has 3 marbles left.

1. Jack has 4 model cars. He gets 3 more model cars. How many model cars does Jack have in all?

3 + 4 = 7 model cars

For his birthday Jack gets 5 model cars. How many model cars does he have now?

______ + ______ = ______ model cars

2. Nicky has 6 charms on her bracelet. She buys 8 more. How many charms does Nicky have in all?

______ + ______ = ______ charms

On the way home 4 charms are lost. How many charms does Nicky have now?

______ − ______ = ______ charms

Name ____________________

Problem Solving: Two-Question Problems

Write number sentences to solve both parts.

1. Peter read 7 books about dinosaurs.
He read 8 books about sharks.
How many books did Peter read in all?

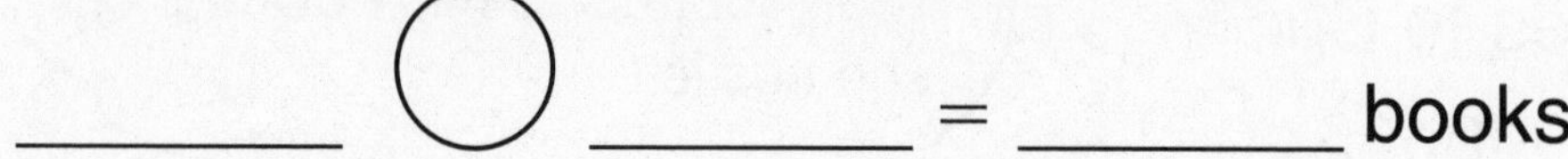

Peter did not like 6 of the books he read.
How many books did Peter like?

_______ ◯ _______ = _______ books

Journal

Write a second problem to go with the first problem.
Solve your problem.

2. Nate counts dogs at the dog park.
He sees 9 small dogs and 7 big dogs.
How many dogs does he see in all?

$9 + 7 = 16$

____

____

____

____

Name ______________________

Making 10 to Add

Making 10 can help you add.

Add 7 + 4. | Make a 10.

7 and 4 more

10 and 1 more

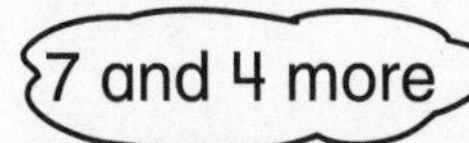

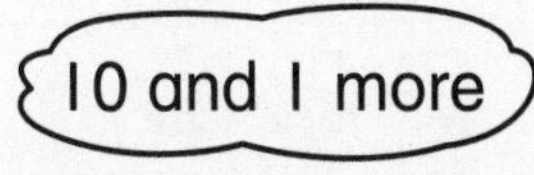

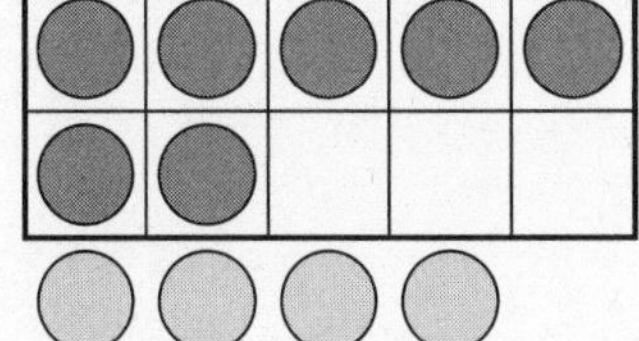

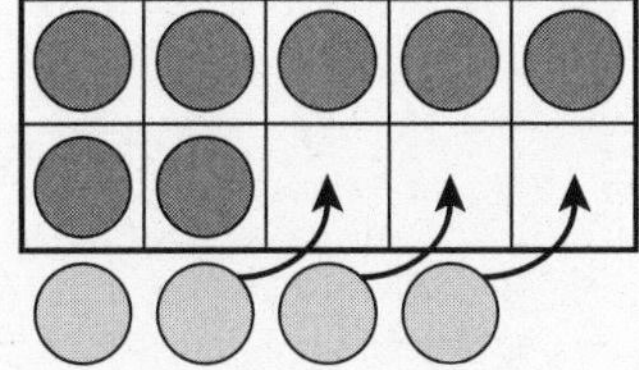

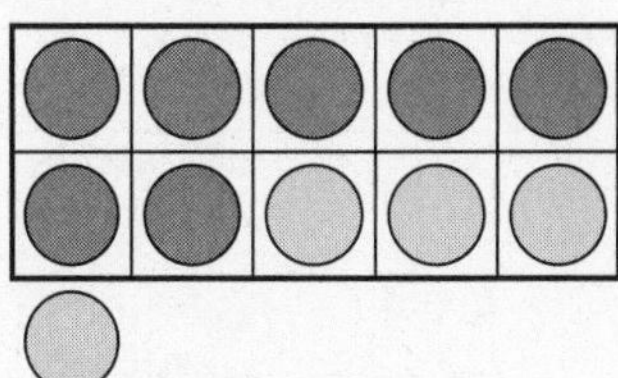

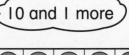

So 7 + 4 and 10 + 1 have the same sum.

7 + 4 = 11 and 10 + 1 = 11.

Draw the missing counters. Then write the sums.

1.

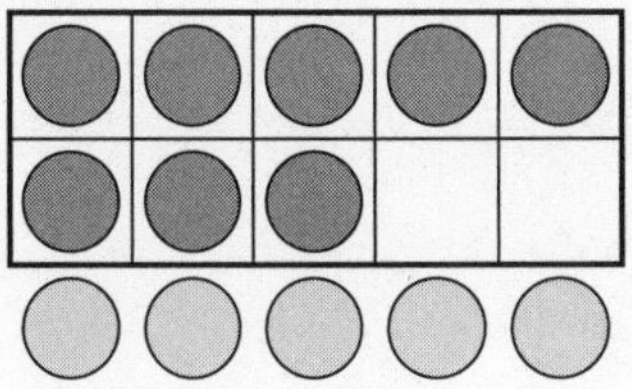

$$\begin{array}{r} 8 \\ +\,5 \\ \hline 13 \end{array}$$

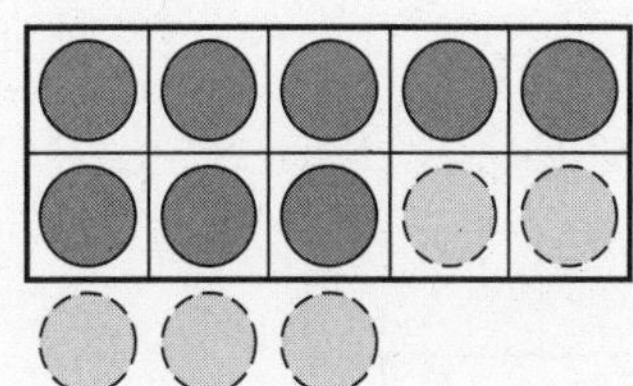

$$\begin{array}{r} 10 \\ +\,3 \\ \hline 13 \end{array}$$

2.

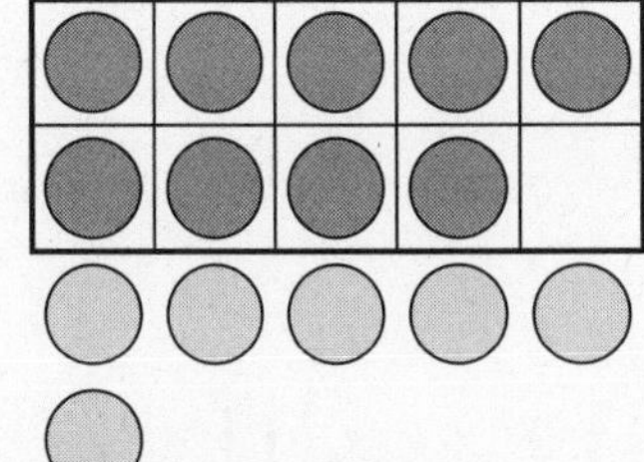

$$\begin{array}{r} 9 \\ +\,6 \\ \hline \end{array}$$

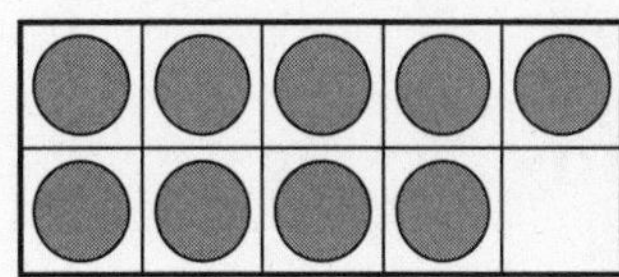

$$\begin{array}{r} 10 \\ +\,5 \\ \hline \end{array}$$

3.

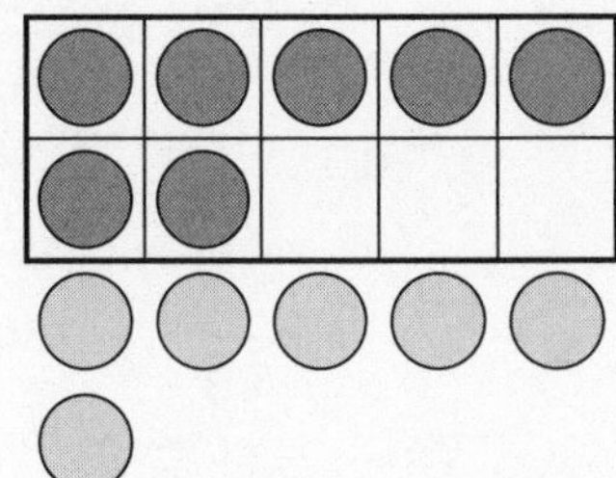

$$\begin{array}{r} 7 \\ +\,6 \\ \hline \end{array}$$

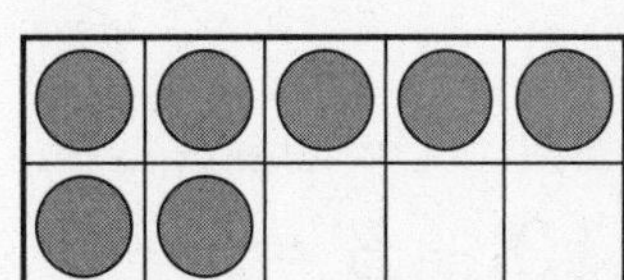

$$\begin{array}{r} 10 \\ +\,3 \\ \hline \end{array}$$

Name ______________________

Making 10 to Add

Draw the counters. Then write the sums.

1. 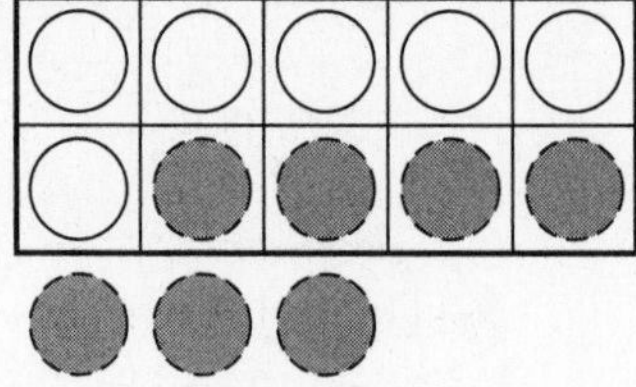

```
  6      10
+ 7     + 3
----    ----
 13      13
```

2. 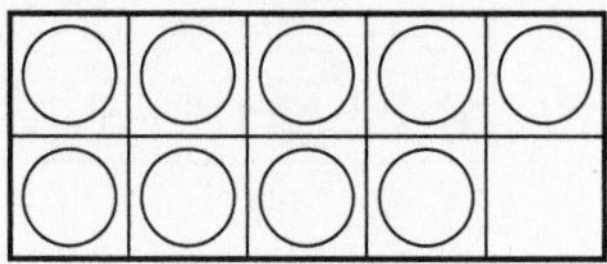

```
  9      10
+ 5     + 4
----    ----
```

3. 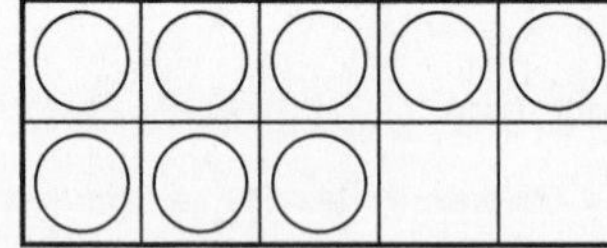

```
  8      10
+ 3     + 1
----    ----
```

4. 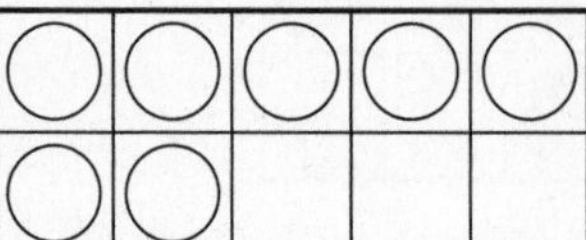

```
  7      10
+ 5     + 2
----    ----
```

Algebra

Find the sum.

5. 6 + 5 = 10 + 1 = ______

14	13	12	11
Ⓐ	Ⓑ	Ⓒ	Ⓓ

6. 9 + 9 = 10 + 8 = ______

16	17	18	19
Ⓐ	Ⓑ	Ⓒ	Ⓓ

Name ______________________

Making 10 to Add 9

You can make 10 to find 9 + 7.
Draw 9 white triangles and 7 gray triangles.
Circle a group of 10. Count the leftover triangles.
Then complete the number sentence.

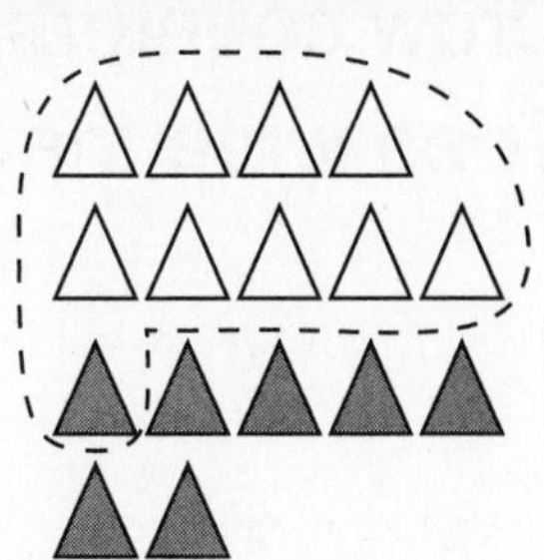

10 + __6__ = 16, so 9 + 7 = __16__.

Circle a group of 10. Then write 2 addition sentences.

1. Alice picked 9 flowers.
Tanisha picked 5 flowers.
How many flowers were picked altogether?

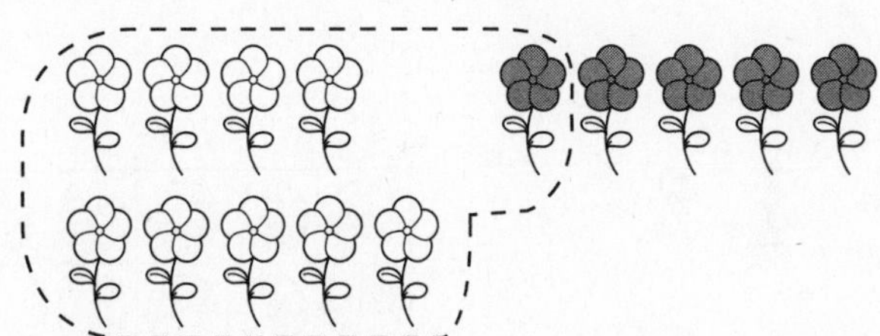

10 + ________ = 14, so 9 + 5 = ________.

2. Paul caught 9 ladybugs.
Cecil caught 3 ladybugs.
How many ladybugs were caught altogether?

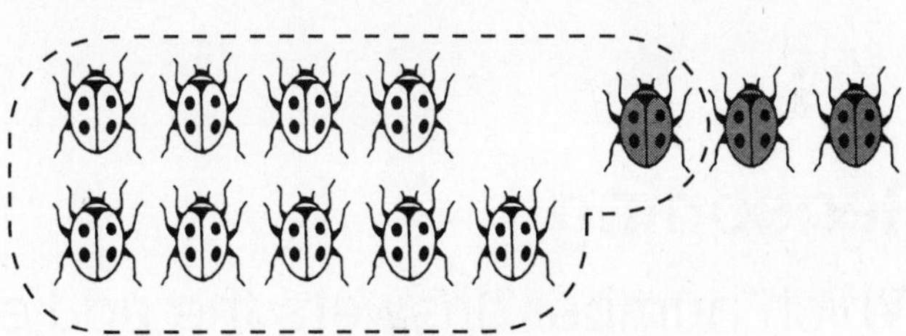

10 + ________ = ________, so 9 + 3 = ________.

Algebra

3. Sam has 9 red pens and 8 blue pens. Circle all the ways to show how many pens Sam has in all.

9 + 8   9 + 8 + 7   1 + 8 + 8   10 + 7   10 + 8

Name ______________________________

Making 10 to Add 9

Draw counters to help you add. Write the missing addend. Then write the sums.

1.

$$\begin{array}{r} 9 \\ +\ 3 \\ \hline ? \end{array}$$

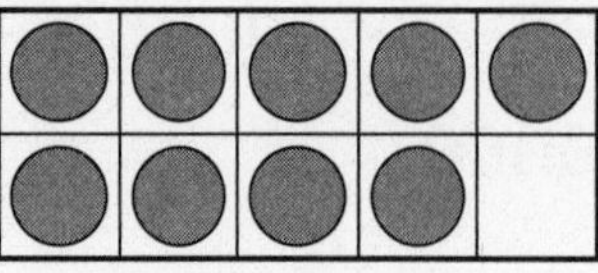

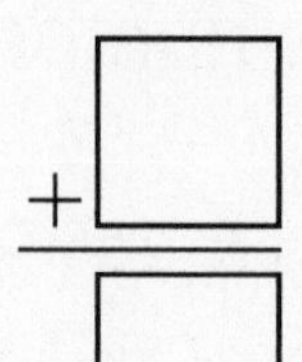

$$\begin{array}{r} 10 \\ +\ \square \\ \hline \square \end{array} \quad \text{so} \quad \begin{array}{r} 9 \\ +\ 3 \\ \hline \square \end{array}$$

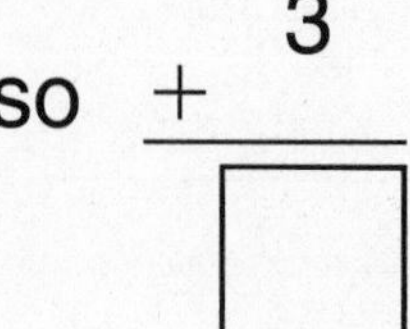

2.

$$\begin{array}{r} 9 \\ +\ 6 \\ \hline ? \end{array}$$

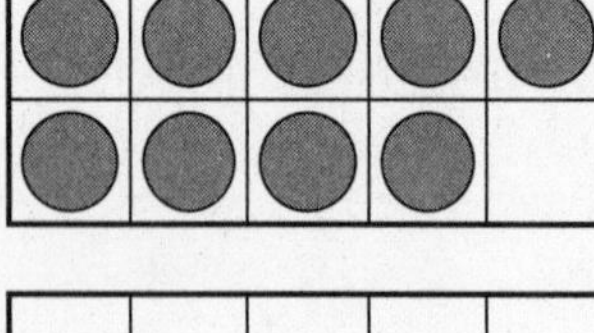

$$\begin{array}{r} 10 \\ +\ \square \\ \hline \square \end{array} \quad \text{so} \quad \begin{array}{r} 9 \\ +\ 6 \\ \hline \square \end{array}$$

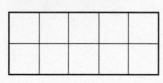

Reasoning

Which number answers the riddle?

3. When you add 9 to me, the sum is the same as 10 + 10.

Ⓐ 8

Ⓑ 9

Ⓒ 10

Ⓓ 11

Name ___________________

Making 10 to Add 8

You can make 10 to find 8 + 6.
Draw 8 white marbles and 6 black marbles.

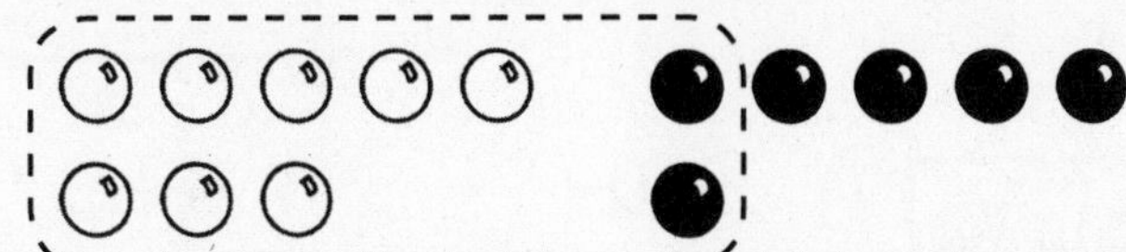

Circle a group of 10. Count the leftover marbles.
Then complete the number sentence.

10 + 4 = 14, so 8 + 6 = 14.

Circle a group of 10. Then write 2 addition sentences.

1. Kim has 8 white toy bears.
Tia has 4 gray toy bears.
How many bears do they have in all?

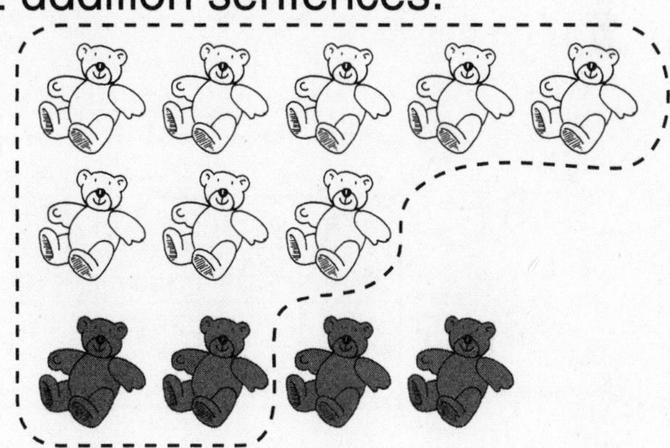

10 + _______ = 12, so 8 + 4 = _______.

2. Tamika caught 8 butterflies.
Cecil caught 7 butterflies.
How many butterflies were caught altogether?

10 + _______ = _______, so 8 + 7 = _______.

Name ______________________________

Making 10 to Add 8

Draw counters to help you add.
Write the missing addend.
Then write the sums.

1. 8 + 6 = ?

10 + ☐ = ☐ so 8 + 6 = ☐

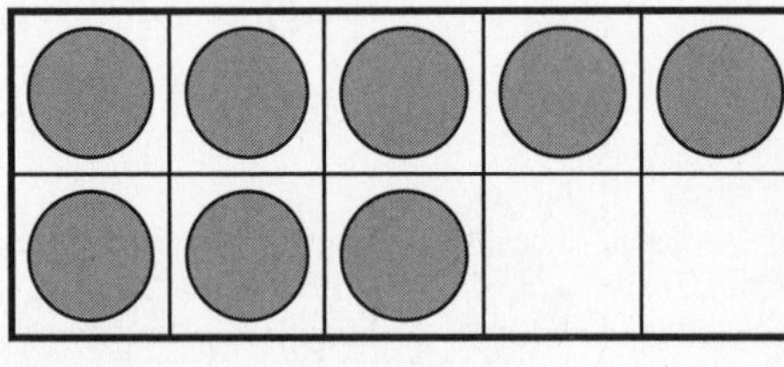

2. 8 + 3 = ?

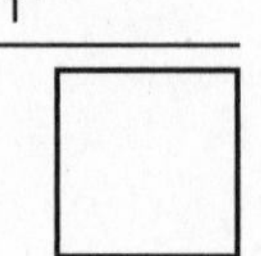

10 + ☐ = ☐ so 8 + 3 = ☐

Algebra

Find the sum.

3. 8 + 4 = 10 + 2 = ______

Ⓐ 11 Ⓑ 12 Ⓒ 13 Ⓓ 14

Name ______________________________

Adding Three Numbers

When you add 3 numbers, look for facts you know.
Then add the other number.

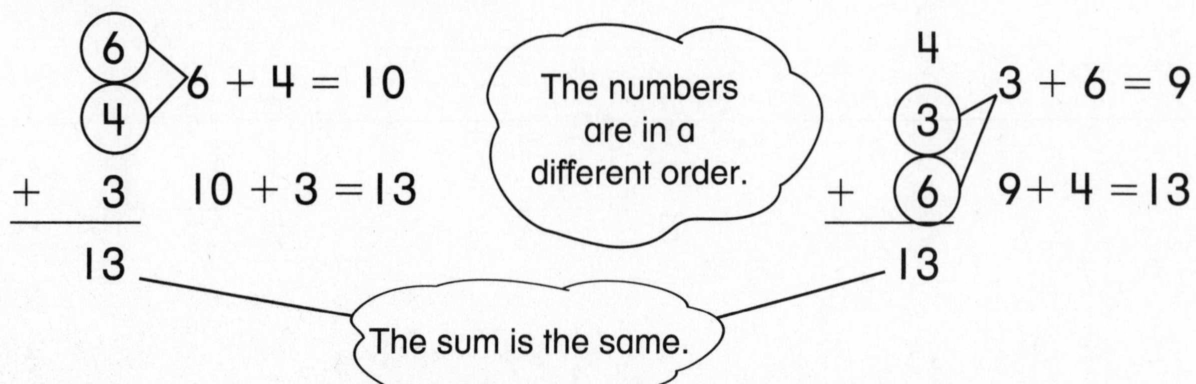

Find each sum. Add the circled numbers first.
Then add the other number.

1.

$$\begin{array}{r} (5) \\ 2 \\ + (5) \\ \hline 12 \end{array}$$

5 + 5 = 10

10 + 2 = 12

$$\begin{array}{r} 5 \\ (2) \\ + (5) \\ \hline 12 \end{array}$$

2 + 5 = 7

7 + 5 = 12

2.

$$\begin{array}{r} (3) \\ (6) \\ + 4 \\ \hline \end{array}$$

3 + 6 = ____

____ + 4 = ____

$$\begin{array}{r} 3 \\ (6) \\ + (4) \\ \hline \end{array}$$

6 + 4 = ____

____ + 3 = ____

3.

$$\begin{array}{r} (9) \\ (4) \\ + 7 \\ \hline \end{array}$$

9 + 4 = ____

____ + 7 = ____

$$\begin{array}{r} 9 \\ (4) \\ + (7) \\ \hline \end{array}$$

4 + 7 = ____

____ + 9 = ____

Name ______________________________

Adding Three Numbers

Circle 2 numbers to add first.
Write their sum in the box.
Then write the sum of all 3 numbers.

1.

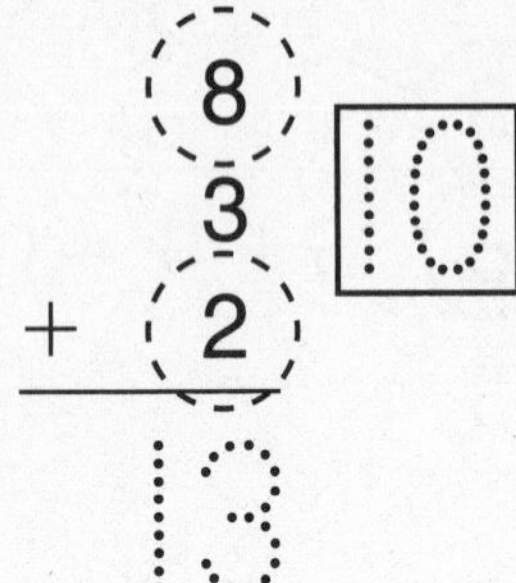

7
4
+ 3

9
1
+ 5

2.

6
3
+ 4

5
5
+ 7

2
8
+ 7

Spatial Thinking

Add the dots on the dominoes.
What is the sum?

3. 

Ⓐ 17

Ⓑ 15

Ⓒ 13

Ⓓ 11

Algebra

Find the missing number.

4. 8 + ____ + 7 = 19

Ⓐ 2

Ⓑ 3

Ⓒ 4

Ⓓ 5

Name ______________________________

Word Problems with Three Addends

Sally has some fruit.
She has 3 apples, 5 bananas, and 5 pears.
How many pieces of fruit does she have in all?

   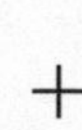 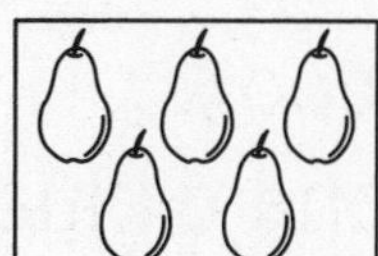

Way 1: First, add the apples and bananas. Complete the number sentence.

3 + ________ = ________

Next, add the pears.

8 + ________ 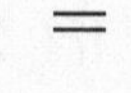 ________

and  

   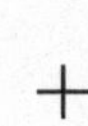 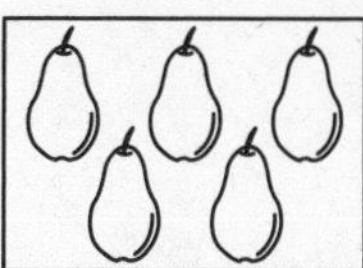

Way 2: First, add the bananas and pears. Complete the number sentence.

5 + ________  ________

 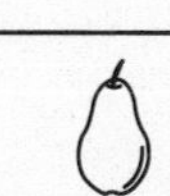 

Next, add the apples.

________ + ________ = ________

and

, , and

Name ______________________________

Practice
5-9

Word Problems with Three Addends

Write a number sentence. Find the best way to group the addends.

1. There are some books on the shelf.
There are 3 red books,
3 brown books, and 6 blue books.
How many books are there in all?

____ ◯ ____ ◯ ____ = ____ ____ books

2. Hal has some beads.
He has 7 green beads,
4 purple beads, and 6 yellow beads.
How many beads does he have in all?

____ ◯ ____ ◯ ____ = ____ ____ beads

Algebra

3. Terry sees 12 flowers.
He sees 7 roses, 3 tulips,
and some daisies.
How many daisies does he see?

7 + 3 + ____ = 12 ____ daisies

Name ______________________

Making 10 to Subtract

Making a 10 can help you subtract.
Subtract 14 − 6.

14 altogether

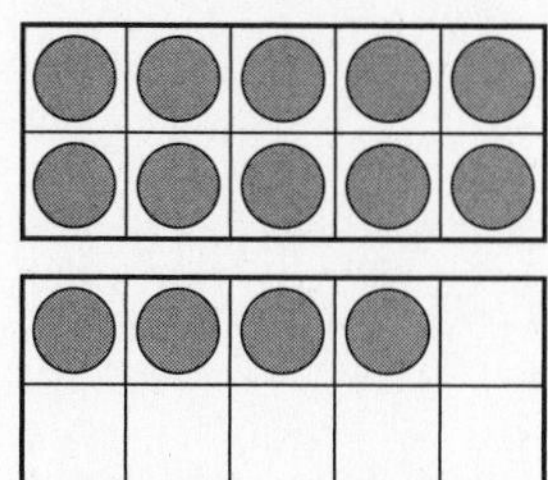

Subtract 4.

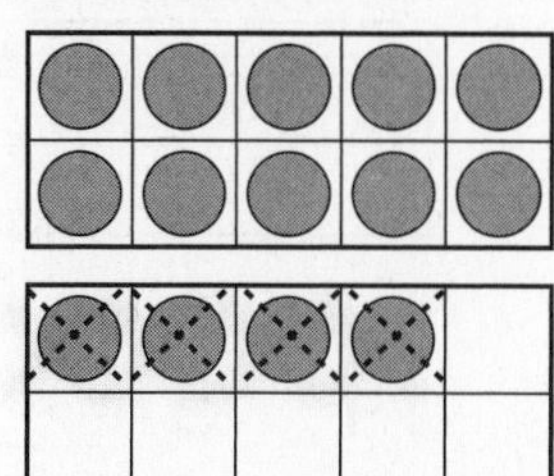

There are 10 left.

Subtract 2 more.

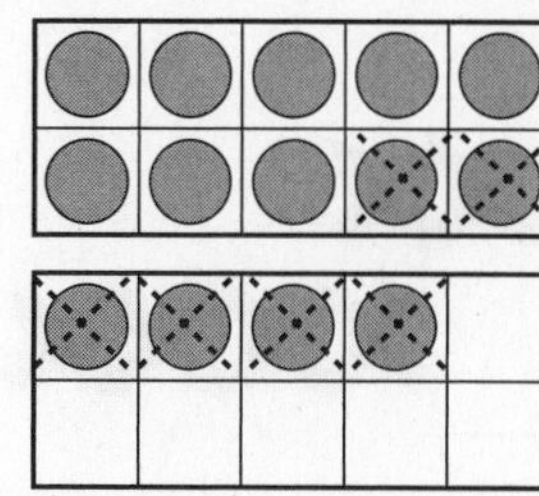

There are 8 left.

You subtracted 6 altogether.

14 − 6 = 8

Make a 10.
Cross out the counters to help you subtract.
Complete the subtraction fact.

1. 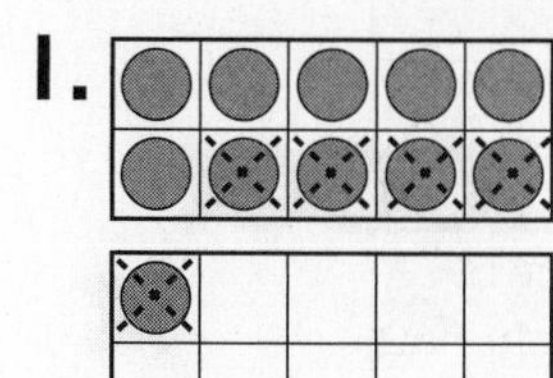 11 − 5 = 6

2. 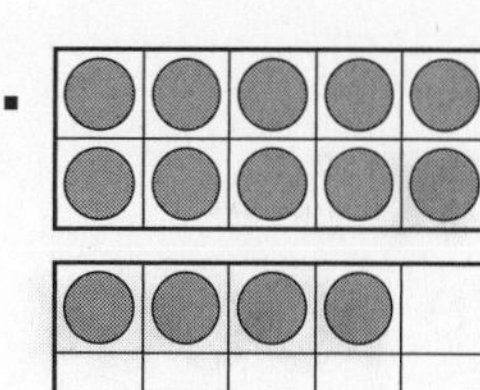 14 − 5 = ____

3. 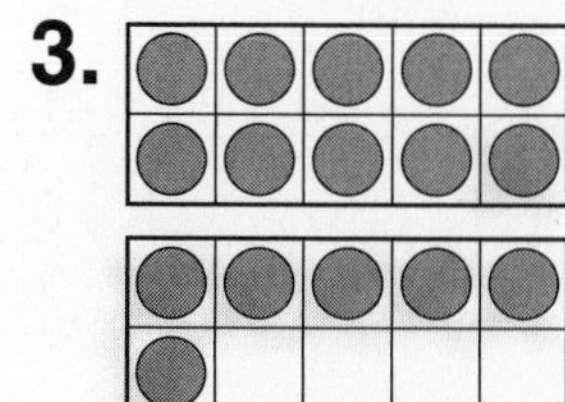 16 − 7 = ____

4. 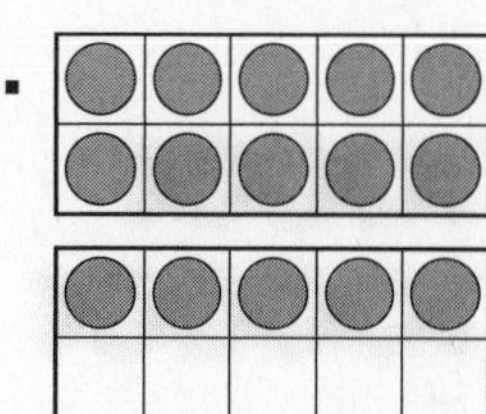 15 − 9 = ____

Name ______________________

Practice
6-1

Making 10 to Subtract

Make a 10 to subtract.
Complete the subtraction fact.

1.

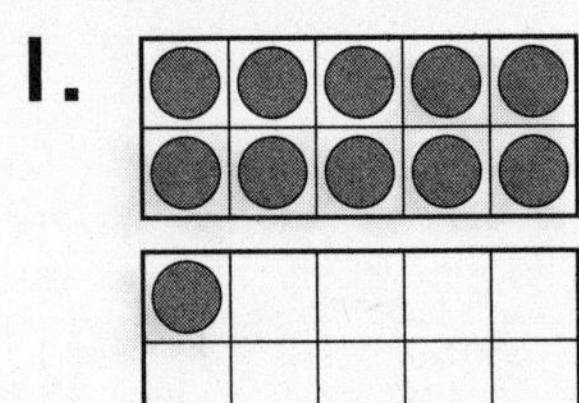

11 − 8 = _____

2.

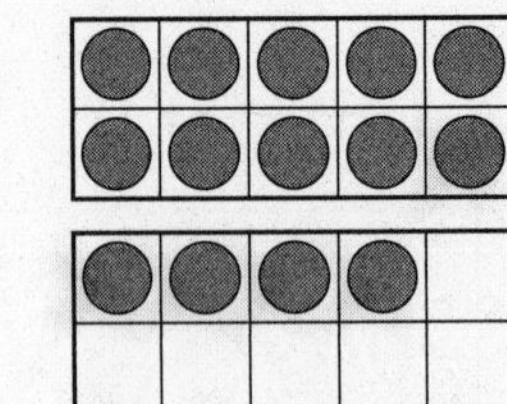

14 − 5 = _____

3.

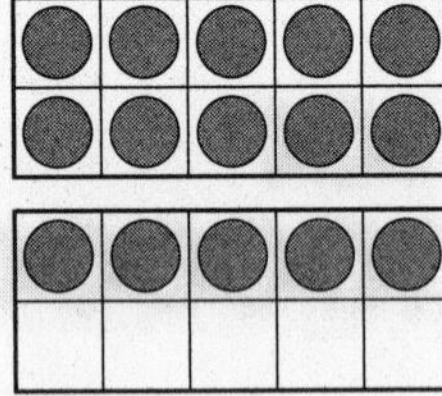

15 − 7 = _____

4.

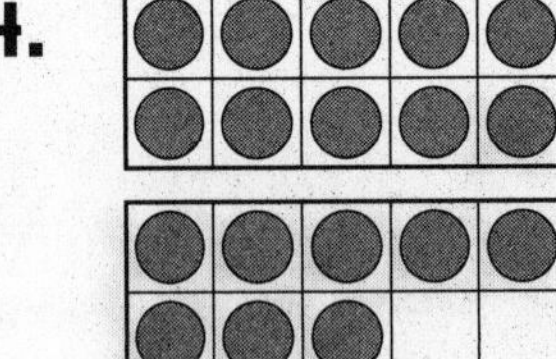

18 − 9 = _____

Reasoning

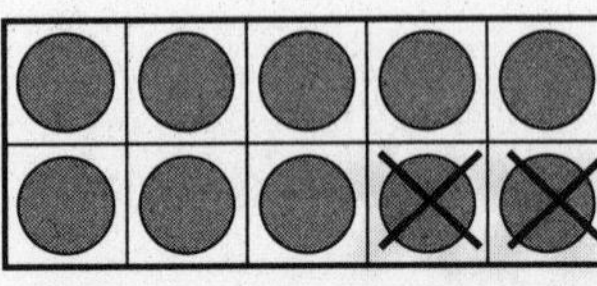

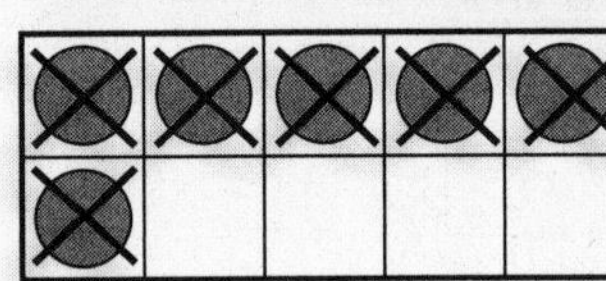

5. Which subtraction fact does this picture show?

Ⓐ 17 − 8 = 9

Ⓑ 16 − 10 = 6

Ⓒ 16 − 9 = 7

Ⓓ 16 − 8 = 8

Name ______________________

More with Making 10 to Subtract

Reteaching
6-2

Here are some different ways to make 10.

There are 12 pears on a tree.
4 pears fall off.
How many pears are left?

12 – 4 = 8

So, 8 pears are left.

Use a counter for each pear.

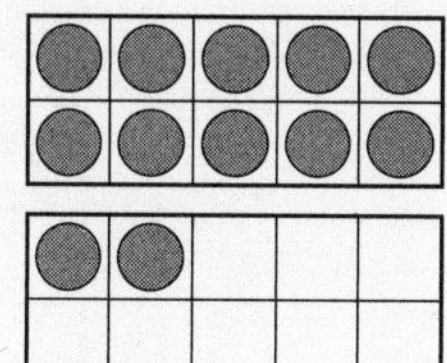

Cross out 2 counters to make a 10.

Cross out 2 more.

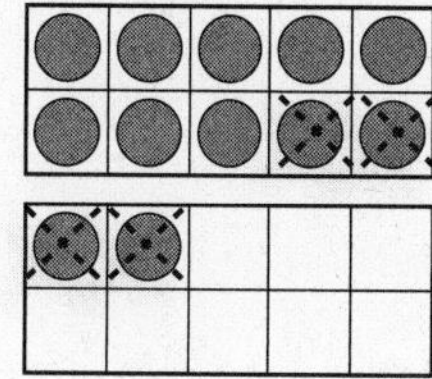

2 + 2 = 4

Cross out counters to help you subtract.
Write a subtraction sentence.

1. Maria buys 13 tubes of paint.
She uses 7 tubes of paint.
How many tubes does she have left?

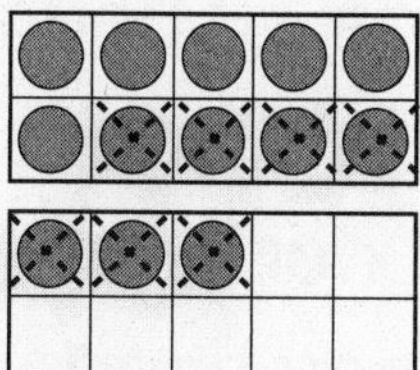

____ – ____ = ____

2. Max has 16 buttons on his shirt.
8 buttons fall off.
How many buttons are left on his shirt?

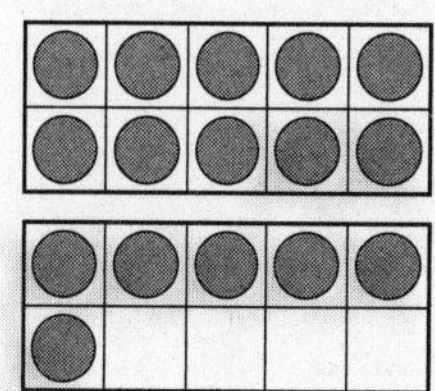

____ – ____ = ____

Name ______________________________

More with Making 10 to Subtract

Make a 10 to solve.
Write a subtraction sentence.

1. Nick has 13 sports cards.
He loses 4 cards.
How many sports cards
does Nick have left?

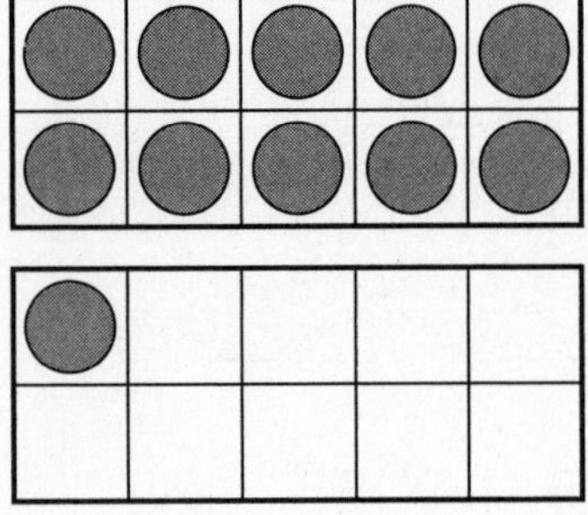

_____ − _____ = _____

2. Jay picks 11 flowers.
He gives 8 to his grandmother.
How many flowers
does Jay have left?

_____ − _____ = _____

Algebra

3. Anita has 18 beads.
She uses 9 beads to
make a necklace.
How many beads does
Anita have left?
Which subtraction sentence
tells about the story?

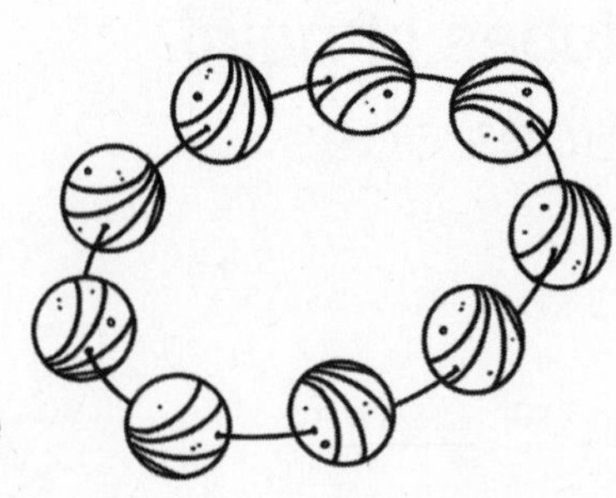

Ⓐ 19 − 9 = 10

Ⓑ 18 − 10 = 8

Ⓒ 18 − 8 = 10

Ⓓ 18 − 9 = 9

Name ____________________

Reteaching
6-3

Using Related Facts

These two facts are related.

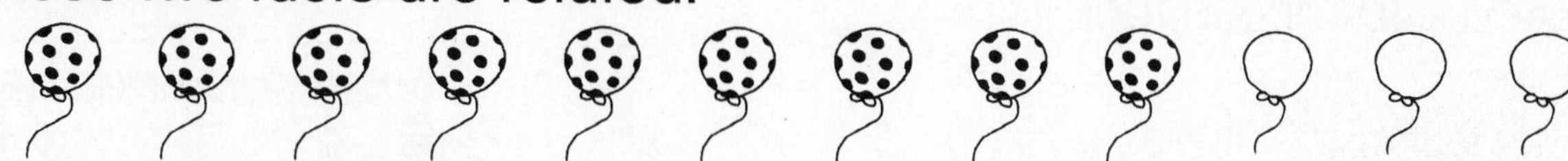

The addition sentence and the subtraction sentence have the same 3 numbers.

$9 + 3 = 12$

$12 - 3 = 9$

The sum of the addition sentence is the first number in the subtraction sentence.

Add. Then write a related subtraction fact.

1. $8 + 4 =$ 12

12 − 4 = 8

2. $7 + 6 =$ 13

13 − 6 = ______

3. $9 + 2 =$ ______

______ − 9 = ______

4. $8 + 5 =$ ______

______ − 8 = ______

5. $8 + 6 =$ ______

______ − 8 = ______

6. $8 + 7 =$ ______

______ − 8 = ______

Name ____________________

Using Related Facts

Write an addition fact and a related subtraction fact.

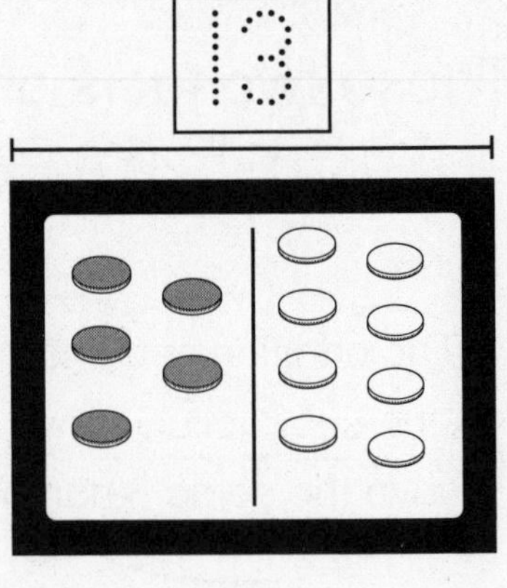

1. 5 + 8 = 13

13 – 8 = 5

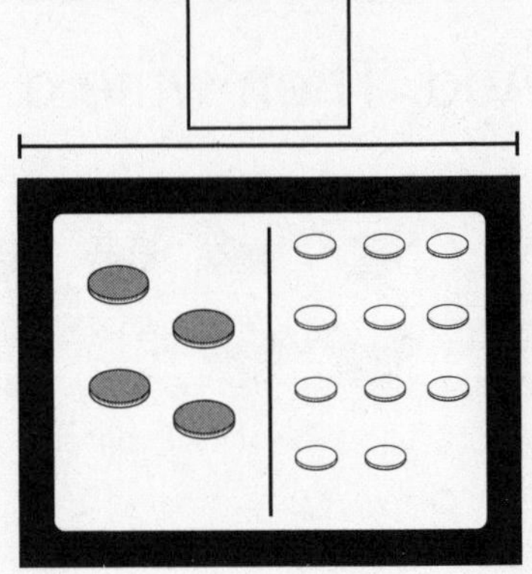

2. ______ + ______ = ______

______ – ______ = ______

Reasoning

Solve the problem.

3. Abby's dad wrote this addition sentence on a piece of paper.

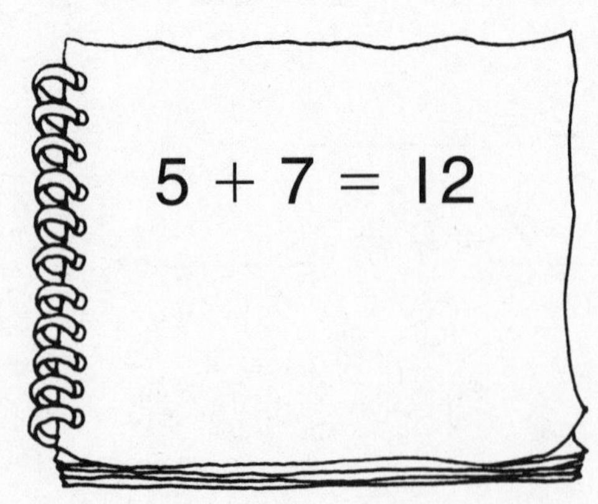

Which subtraction sentence is related?

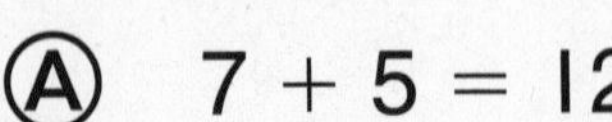

Ⓐ 7 + 5 = 12
Ⓑ 12 – 7 = 5
Ⓒ 12 – 9 = 3
Ⓓ 7 – 5 = 2

Name ______________________

Reteaching
6-4

Fact Families

This is a fact family.

8 + 4 = 12
4 + 8 = 12
12 − 8 = 4
12 − 4 = 8

Each number sentence has the same 3 numbers.

Complete each fact family. Use counters to help you.

1. | 6 | 11 | 5 |

6 + 5 = 11
5 + 6 = 11
11 − 5 = 6
11 − 6 = 5

2. | 9 | 5 | 14 |

9 + 5 = ______
5 + ______ = 14
14 − 5 = ______
14 − ______ = 5

3. | 7 | 6 | 13 |

7 + 6 = ______
6 + ______ = 13
13 − 6 = ______
13 − ______ = 6

Name ___________________________

Fact Families

Write the fact family for the model.

1\. 

7 + 8 = 15

8 + 7 = ____

15 − 8 = ____

15 − ____ = ____

2\.

18

10 | 8

____ + ____ = ____

____ + ____ = ____

____ − ____ = ____

____ − ____ = ____

Reasoning

Solve the problem.

 Which related facts describe this picture?

Ⓐ 4 + 11 = 15, 15 − 4 = 11

Ⓑ 11 − 4 = 7, 7 + 4 = 11

Ⓒ 3 + 7 = 10, 10 − 3 = 7

Ⓓ 7 − 4 = 3, 7 − 3 = 4

Name ______________________

Using Addition to Subtract

Reteaching
6-5

6 + 5 = 11

11 − 5 = 6

You can use an addition fact to help you write a subtraction fact with the same numbers.

Add. Then use the addition fact to help you subtract. Use cubes if you like.

1. 4 + 9 = 13

13 − 9 = 4

2. 8 + 7 = ______

15 − 7 = ______

3. 7 + 4 = ______

11 − 4 = ______

4. 6 + 7 = ______

13 − 7 = ______

Name ____________________

Practice 6-5

Using Addition to Subtract

Complete the model.
Then complete the number sentences.

1. 

18 − 8 = 10

8 + ______ = 18

2. 

15 − 6 = ______

6 + ______ = 15

Algebra

3. Which addition fact will help you solve 14 − 9?

Ⓐ 5 + 14 = 19

Ⓑ 5 + 9 = 14

Ⓒ 4 + 9 = 13

Ⓓ 5 + 7 = 12

Algebra

4. Draw the missing shape. Then explain how you know.

If ⏢ + ○ = △

Then △ − ⏢ = ☐

Explain: ____________________

____

____

Name ______________________

Subtraction Facts

There are many ways to learn and remember subtraction facts. One way is to think about a related addition fact.

$12 - 8 = ?$

Think: What plus 8 equals 12?
$? + 8 = 12$

Then you can use a number line to help you add.

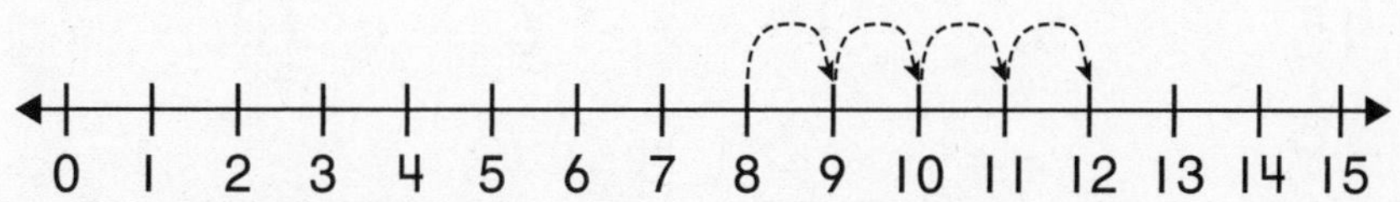

By using the line, I know that $8 + 4 = 12$

Complete the addition fact. Then solve the subtraction fact. Use the number line to help you.

1. $5 + 6 = \square$ $\qquad 11 - 5 = \square$

4 5 6 7 8 9 10 11 12 13 14 15 16 17

2. $9 + \square = 16$ $\qquad 16 - 9 = \square$

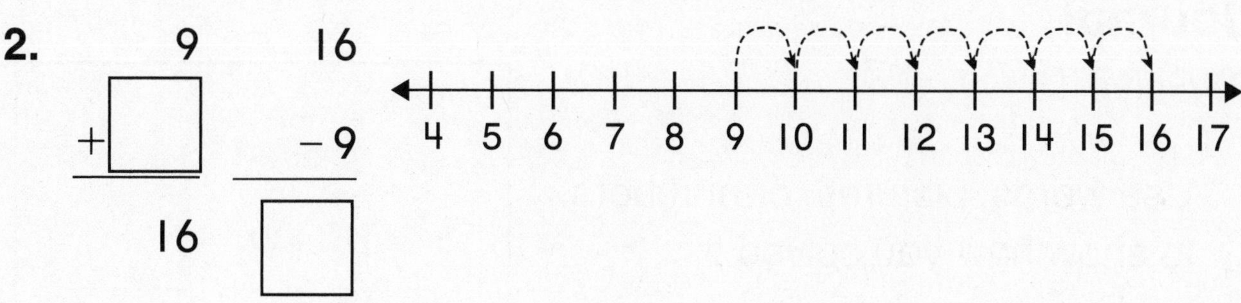

Name ______________________

Subtraction Facts

Complete the addition fact.
Then solve the subtraction fact.

1. $16 - 7 = \square$

$7 + \square = 16$

2. $14 - 6 = \square$

$6 + \square = 14$

Subtract.

3. $17 - 8 = \square$

4. $15 - 9 = \square$

5. $14 - 6 = \square$

6. $13 - 7 = \square$

Reasonableness

7. Can the addition fact help you solve the subtraction problem?

$9 + 9 = 18$
$18 - 9 = ?$

Circle **yes** or **no**.

yes **no**

Journal

8. Solve $15 - 9$.

Use words, pictures, or numbers to show how you solved it.

Name ____________________

Problem Solving: Draw a Picture and Write a Number Sentence

You can write a number sentence to solve problems.

Avi played 2 games of basketball.
He scored 8 points in the first game.
He scored 6 points in the second game.
How many points did Avi score in all?

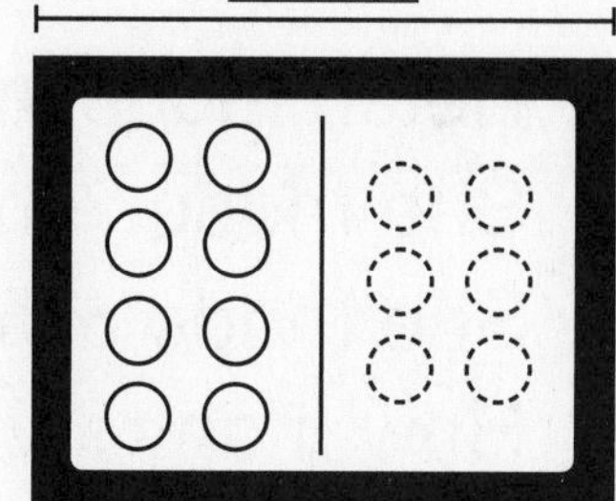

You can draw a picture to help you solve the problem.
Then you can write a number sentence.

8 + 6 = 14

Complete the model.
Then write a number sentence.

1. Gina has 9 books.
She buys 4 more books.
How many books
does Gina have now?

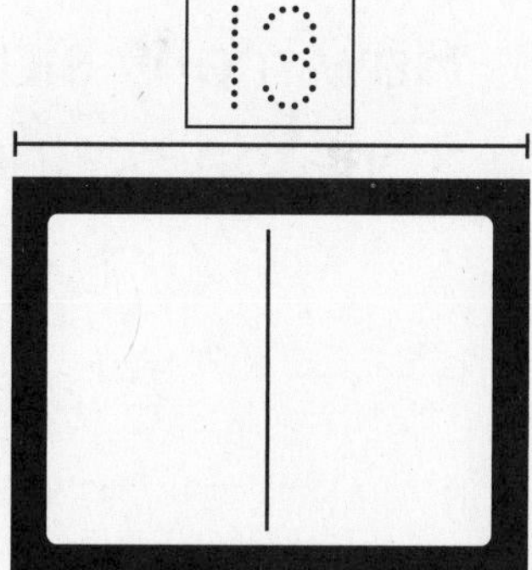

2. Metta sees 15 frogs.
7 frogs hop away.
How many frogs
are left?

Name ______________________________

Practice
6-7

Problem Solving: Draw a Picture and Write a Number Sentence

Write a number sentence to solve.
Draw a picture to check your answer.

1. Helen made invitations for her party.
She made 7 invitations on Monday.
She made 6 invitations on Tuesday.
How many invitations
did Helen make in all?

_____ ◯ _____ = _____ invitations

2. Joe started at the bottom
of the stairs.
He hopped up 9 stairs.
Then he hopped down 3 stairs.
How many stairs is Joe
from the bottom?

_____ ◯ _____ = _____ stairs

Reasoning

3. Which number sentence
tells how many apples in all?

Ⓐ $8 - 7 = 1$

Ⓑ $8 - 1 = 7$

Ⓒ $7 + 1 = 8$

Ⓓ $7 + 8 = 15$

Name ____________________

Reteaching 7-1

Making Numbers 11 to 19

Write each number as 10 and some left over.

This shows 10.

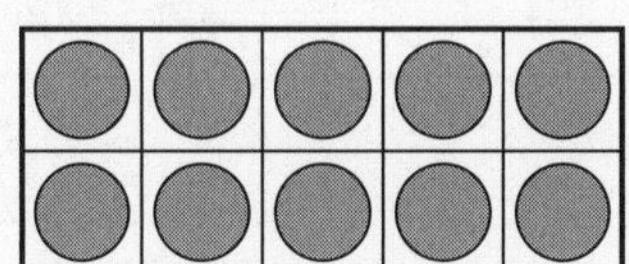

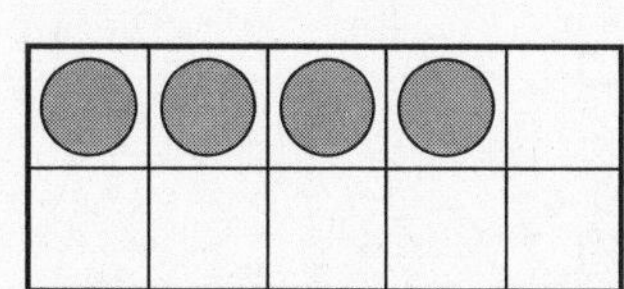

This shows 4 left over.

14 is __10__ and __4__.

1.

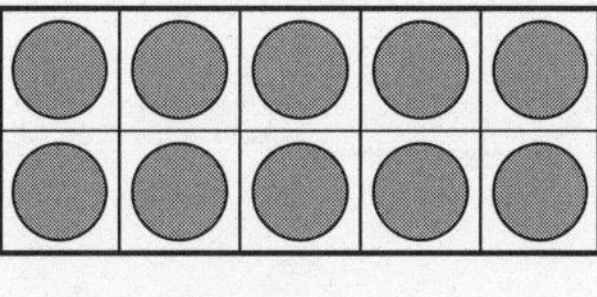

17 is __10__ and __7__.

2.

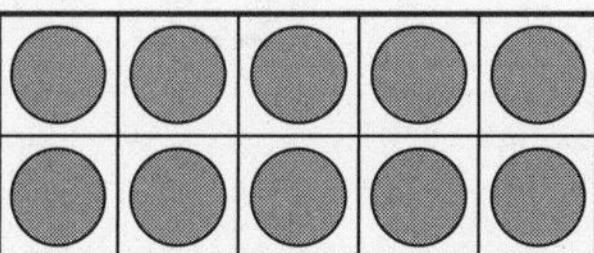

16 is ______ and __6__.

3.

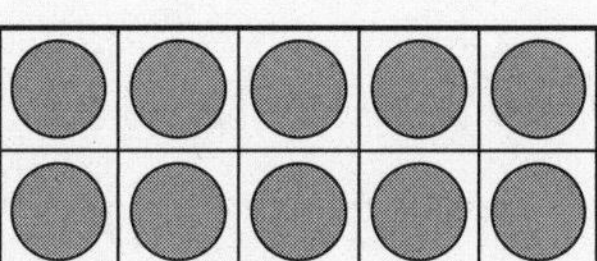

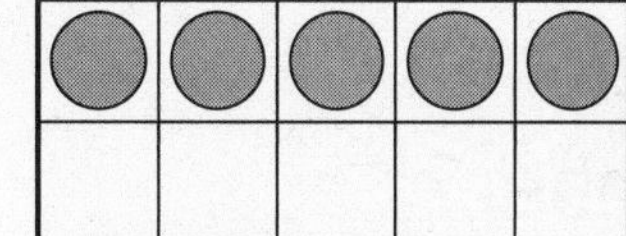

15 is ______ and ______.

4.

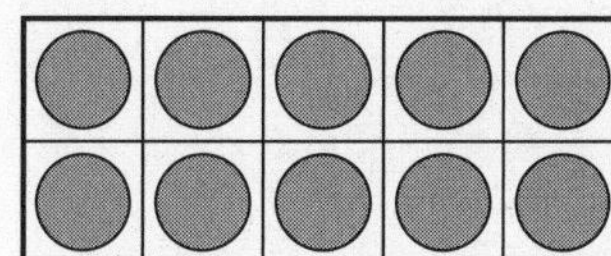

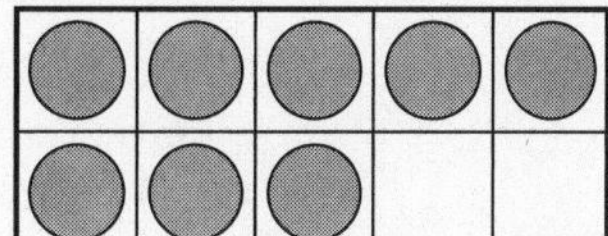

18 is ______ and ______.

Name ____________________

Practice
7-1

Making Numbers 11 to 19

Write each number as 10 and some ones.

1. twelve — 12 is 10 and 2.

2. eighteen — 18 is _______ and _______.

3. fourteen — 14 is _______ and _______.

4. eleven — 11 is _______ and _______.

5. seventeen — 17 is _______ and _______.

6. nineteen — 19 is _______ and _______.

7. sixteen — 16 is _______ and _______.

Algebra

8. Which is the missing number?

13 is 10 and _______.

Ⓐ 1
Ⓑ 2
Ⓒ 3
Ⓓ 10

9. Which is the missing number?

15 is _______ and 5.

Ⓐ 10
Ⓑ 5
Ⓒ 3
Ⓓ 1

Name ____________________

Using Numbers 11 to 19

This shows 12.

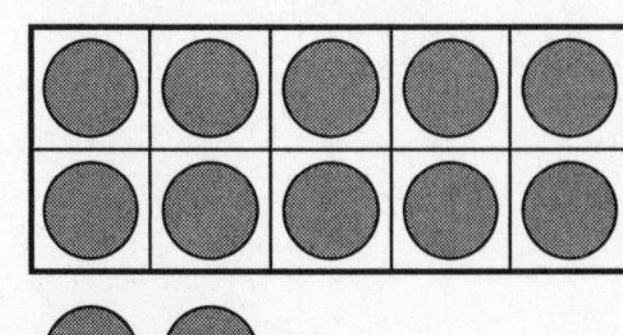

Count 10, 11, 12.

This shows **2 more** than 12.

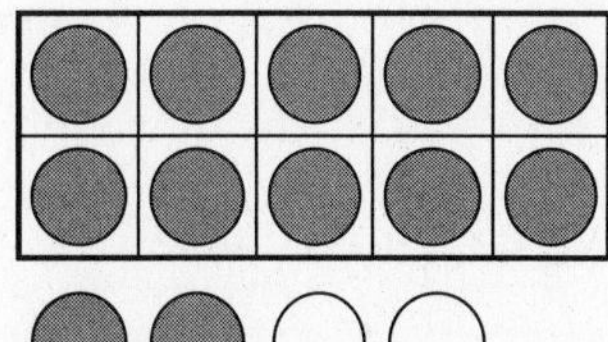

Count 10, 11, 12, 13, 14.
2 more than 12 is 14.

This shows 13.

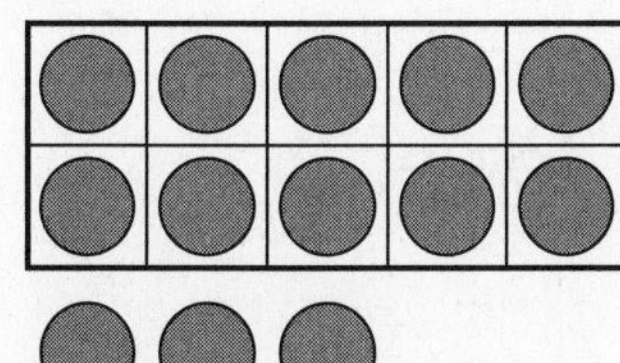

Count 10, 11, 12, 13.

This shows **2 fewer** than 13.

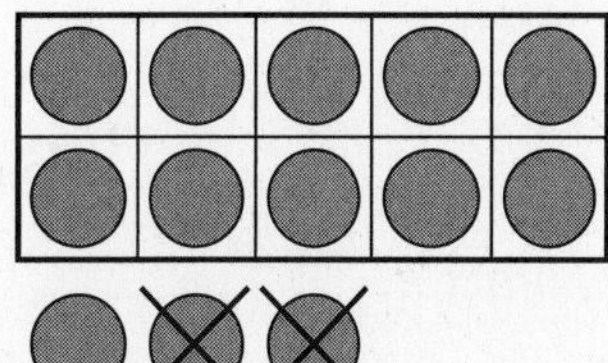

Count 10, 11.
2 fewer than 13 is 11.

Write the numbers.

1.

2 more than 13 is 15.

2. 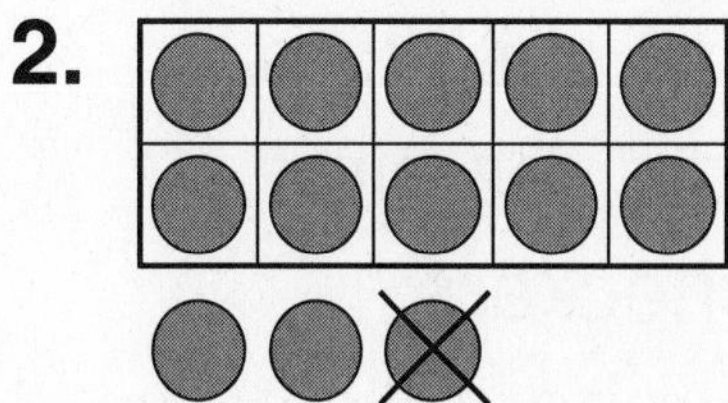

1 fewer than 13 is ______.

3. 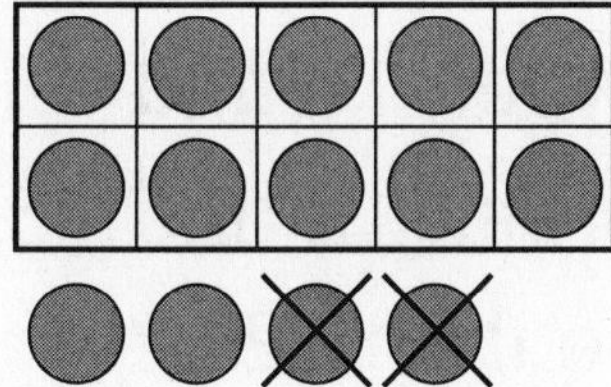

2 fewer than 14 is ______.

4. 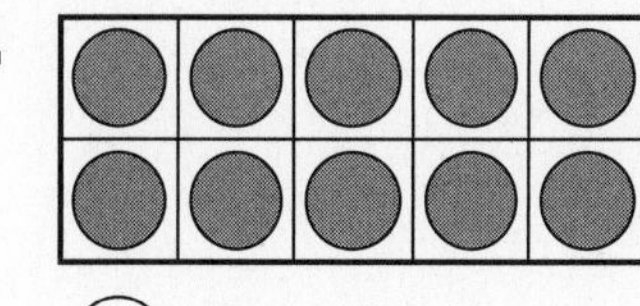

1 more than 10 is ______.

Name ______________________

Practice
7-2

Using Numbers 11 to 19

Write the numbers.

1. twelve _____ 1 more _____ 1 fewer _____

2. seventeen _____ 2 more _____ 2 fewer _____

3. fifteen _____ 2 more _____ 2 fewer _____

4. seventeen _____ 1 more _____ 1 fewer _____

5. thirteen _____ 2 more _____ 2 fewer _____

Number Sense

6. Jeff has 16 checkers. His friend gives him 2 more checkers. Which number tells how many checkers he has now?

   Ⓐ 14
   Ⓑ 15
   Ⓒ 17
   Ⓓ 18

Reasonableness

7. There are 12 birds in the tree. 1 bird flies away. Which tells how many birds are left in the tree?

   Ⓐ less than 10
   Ⓑ between 10 and 12
   Ⓒ between 12 and 15
   Ⓓ more than 12

Name ______________________

Counting by 10s to 120

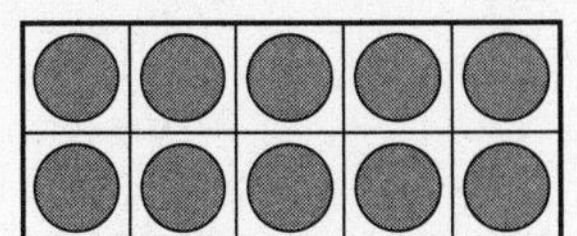 stands for one group of ten.

10, ten,	20, twenty,	30, thirty,	40, forty,	50, fifty,	60, sixty,
70, seventy,	80, eighty,	90, ninety,	100, one hundred	110, one hundred ten	120, one hundred twenty

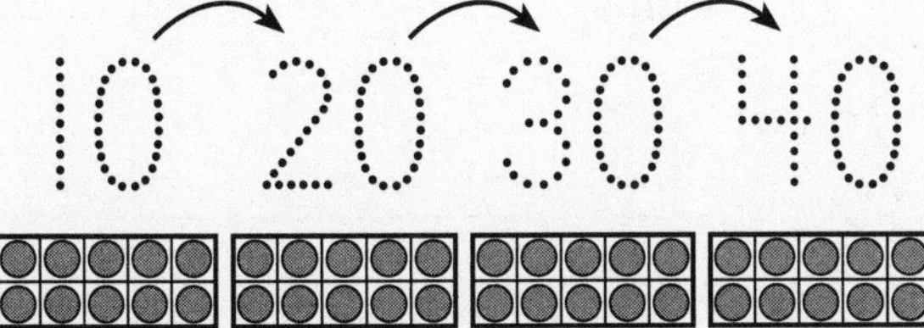

4 groups of ten

40 forty

Count by 10s. Then write the numbers.

1. 10 20 30 40 50

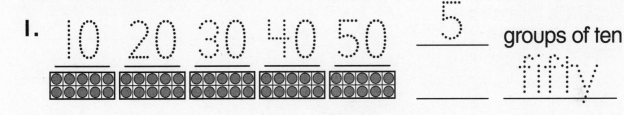

5 groups of ten

fifty

2. ____ ____ ____ ____ ____

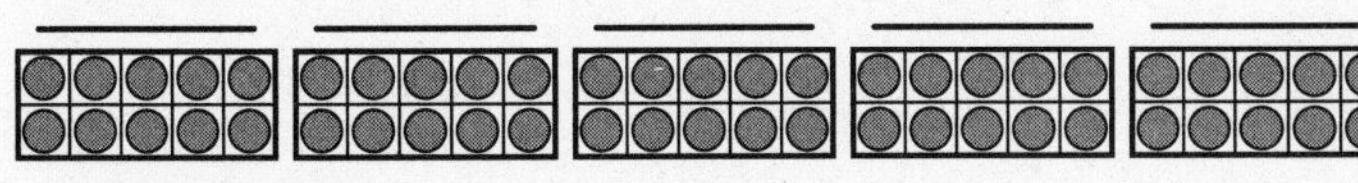

____ groups of ten

____

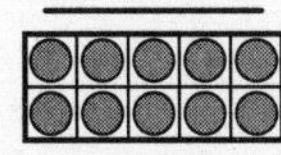

____ ________

3. ____ ____ ____ ____ ____

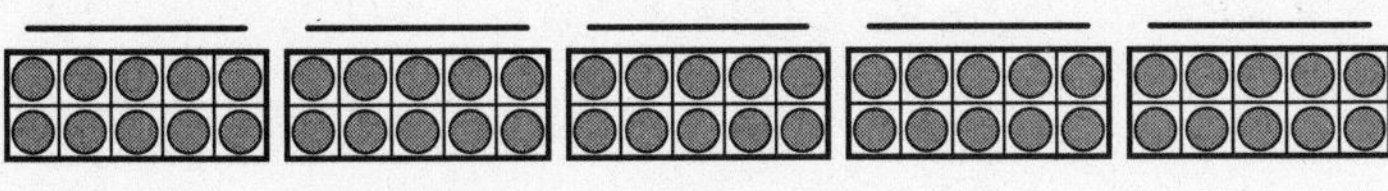

____ groups of ten

____ ____ ____

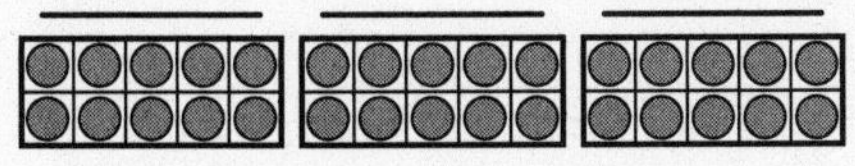

____ ________

Name ____________________

Practice **7-3**

Counting by 10s to 120

10, ten,	20, twenty,	30, thirty,	40, forty,	50, fifty,	60, sixty,
70, seventy,	80, eighty,	90, ninety,	100, one hundred	110, one hundred ten	120, one hundred twenty

Count by tens. Then write the numbers.

1. 4 tens = 40

forty

2. ______ tens = ______

____

3. ______ tens = ______

____

Journal

4. Laura wants to show 70 in tens.
How many tens will she draw?
How do you know?

____

____

Name ___________________

Reteaching 7-4

Counting on a Hundred Chart

Use the hundred chart to count forward. Start at 13. Then count forward by 1s.

13, 14, 15, 16

Start at 62. Then count forward by 1s.

62, 63, 64, 65

1	2	3	4	5	6	7	8	9	10
11	12	13	14	15	16	17	18	19	20
21	22	23	24	25	26	27	28	29	30
31	32	33	34	35	36	37	38	39	40
41	42	43	44	45	46	47	48	49	50
51	52	53	54	55	56	57	58	59	60
61	62	63	64	65	66	67	68	69	70
71	72	73	74	75	76	77	78	79	80
81	82	83	84	85	86	87	88	89	90
91	92	93	94	95	96	97	98	99	100

1. Write the missing numbers. Look for patterns.

81				85			88		90
	92		94		96			99	100

Count by 1s. Write the numbers.

2. 40, ______, ______, ______, ______, ______

3. 78, ______, ______, ______, ______, ______

Name ______________________________

Practice
7-4

Counting on a Hundred Chart

Count by 1s. Write the numbers.

1. 33, ______, ______, ______, ______

2. 71, ______, ______, ______, ______

3. 58, ______, ______, ______, ______

4. 46, ______, ______, ______, ______

5. 39, ______, ______, ______, ______

Reasoning

6. Which shows the numbers the way they look on the hundred chart?

Ⓐ 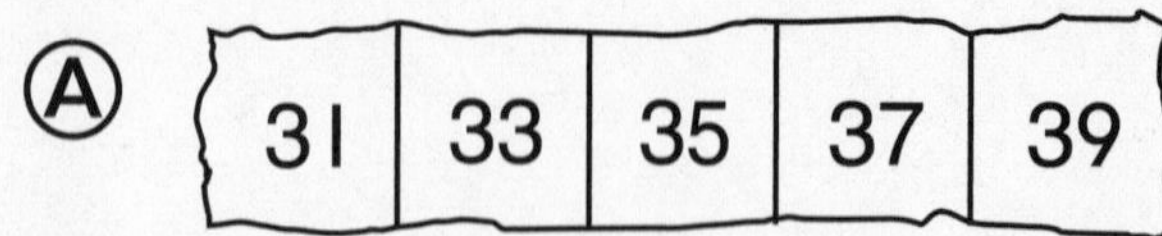

31	33	35	37	39

Ⓑ 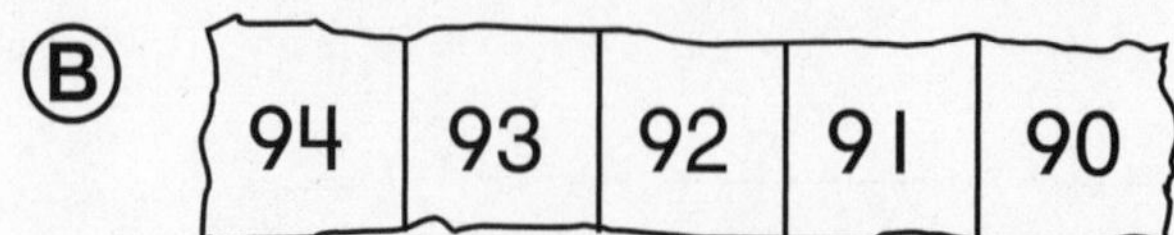

94	93	92	91	90

Ⓒ 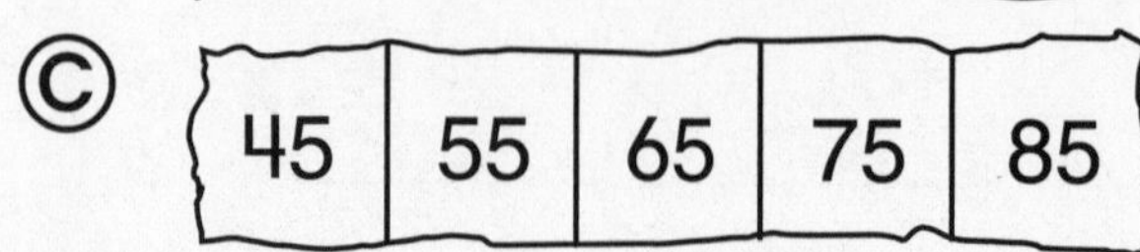

45	55	65	75	85

Ⓓ

66	67	68	69	70

Name ______________________

Using Skip Counting

Skip count to find how many.

Skip count by 2, or add 2 to the last number.

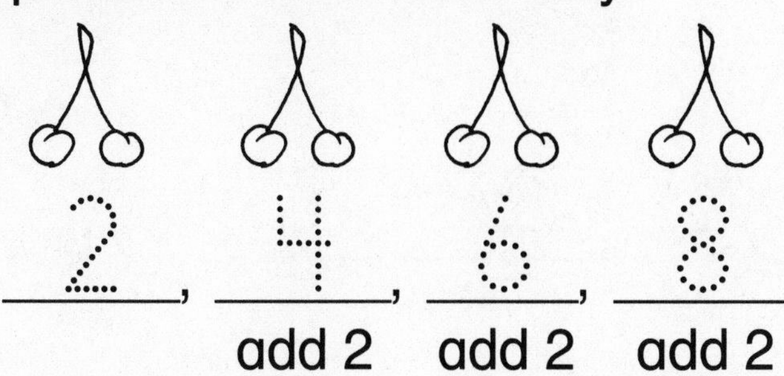

2, 4, 6, 8

add 2 add 2 add 2

There are 8 cherries.

1. Skip count by 2s.

2, 4, ____, ____, ____, ____

2. Skip count by 5s.

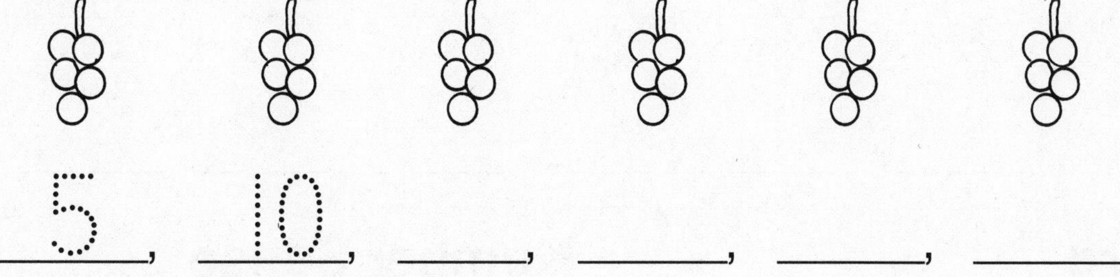

5, 10, ____, ____, ____, ____

3. Skip count by 10s.

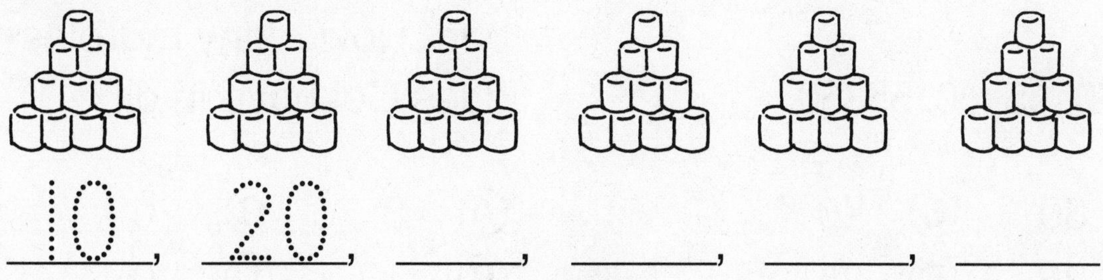

10, 20, ____, ____, ____, ____

Name ___________________________________

Practice
7-5

Using Skip Counting

Use the pictures to skip count.

1. How many ears are there?
Count by twos.

__2__, ______, ______, ______, ______, ______, ______

2. How many cans are there?
Count by fives.

______, ______, ______, ______, ______, ______, ______

3. How many balls are there?
Count by tens.

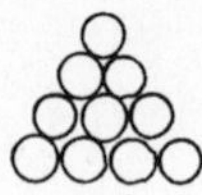 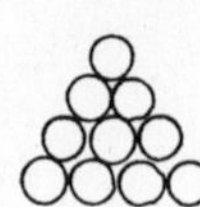 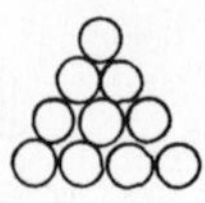  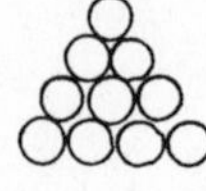 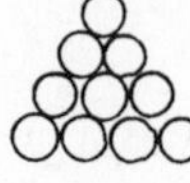 

______, ______, ______, ______, ______, ______, ______

Algebra

4. Look for a pattern.
Find the missing number.

75, 70, 65, 60, 55, 50, ______

Ⓐ 30 Ⓒ 40
Ⓑ 35 Ⓓ 45

Number Sense

5. Cal has 8 bags.
He puts 5 marbles in each bag. How many marbles does Cal have in all?

Ⓐ 3 Ⓒ 20
Ⓑ 13 Ⓓ 40

Name ______________________

Reteaching
7-6

Problem Solving: Look for a Pattern

The children need mittens.
Each child has two hands.
How many mittens are needed for all of the children?

You need to find how many hands the children have altogether.

Make a table to show a pattern.
Write the numbers.

Number of Children	1	2		
Number of Mittens	2	4		

Count the children by 1s.
Count the mittens by 2s.

8 mittens will be needed for all of the children.
Does your answer make sense?

Find the pattern. Write the numbers.

1. There are 4 boxes.
Each box has 5 crayons.
How many crayons are there in all?

Number of Boxes	1	2		
Number of Crayons	5			

There are _______ crayons in all.

Name ____________________

Practice
7-6

Problem Solving: Look for a Pattern

Find the pattern.
Write the numbers.

1. There are 6 dragonflies.
Each dragonfly has 4 wings.
How many wings are there in all?

Number of Dragonflies	1					
Number of Wings	4					

2. There are 5 tricycles.
Each tricycle has 3 wheels.
How many wheels are there in all?

Number of Tricycles					
Number of Wheels					

Reasoning

3. There are 7 boxes.
Each box has 10 balls in it.
How many balls are there in all?

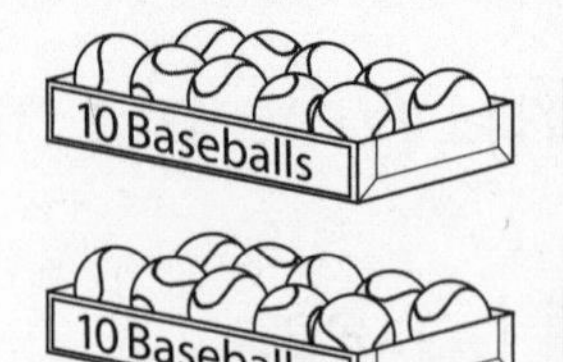

Ⓐ 3
Ⓑ 7
Ⓒ 10

Ⓓ 70

Name ______________________

Counting with Groups of 10 and Leftovers

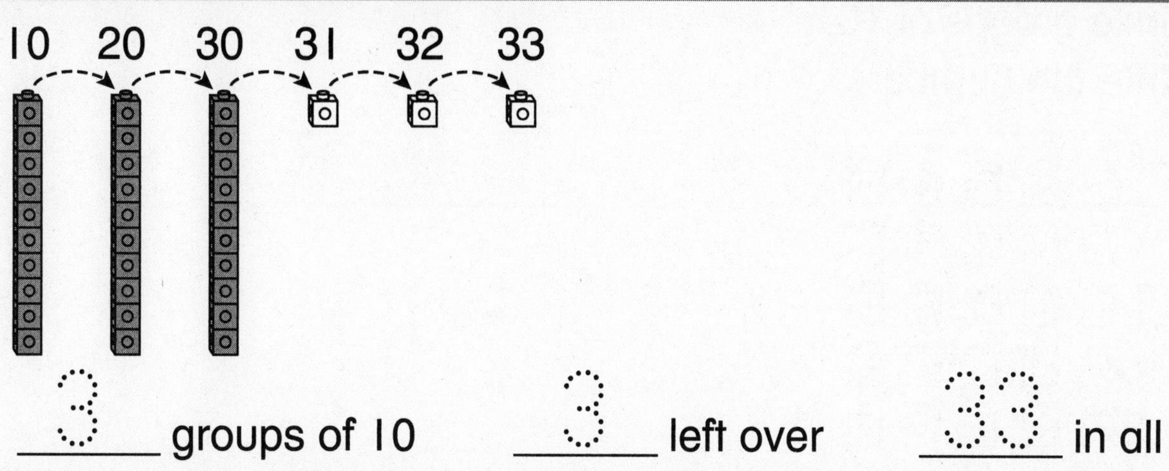

3 groups of 10 3 left over 33 in all

Use counters to show the snap cubes.
Make groups of 10.
Then write the numbers.

1. 10 20 21 22 23 24 25 26 27

2 groups of ten

7 left over

______ in all

2. ______ ______ ______ ______ ______ ______

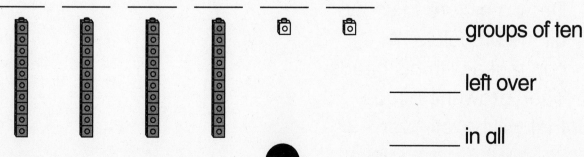

______ groups of ten

______ left over

______ in all

Name ______________________________

Counting with Groups of 10 and Leftovers

Circle groups of 10.
Write the numbers.

1.

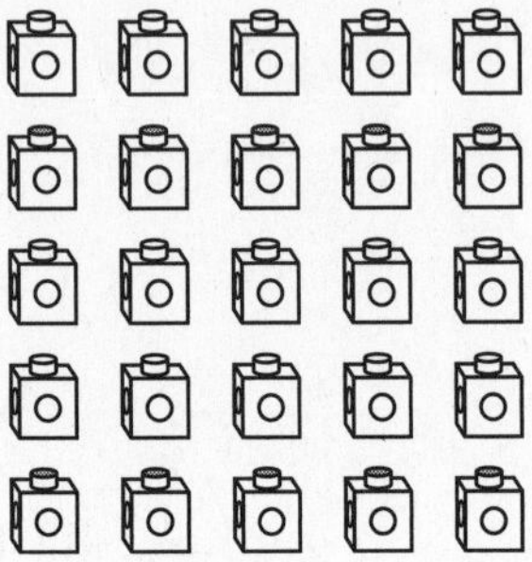

______ is ______ groups of 10 and ______ left over.

2.

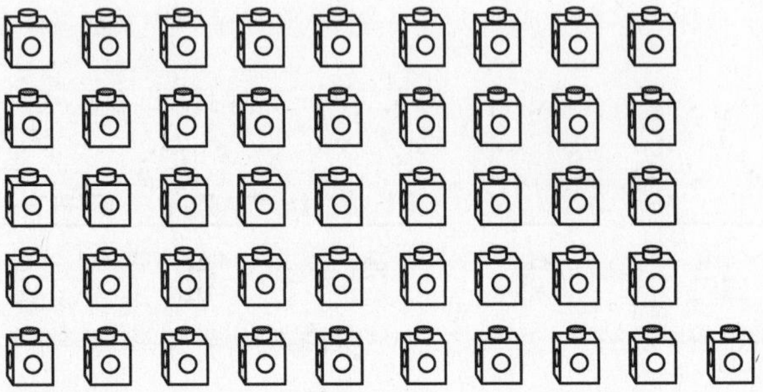

______ is ______ groups of 10 and ______ left over.

Journal

3. 10 beads fit on a bracelet.
Ben has 34 beads.
Draw a picture to show all the bracelets he can make with his beads.
Then draw the beads that will be left over.

Name ______________________

Reteaching
8-2

Numbers Made with Tens

You can count the models to find out how many groups of ten.

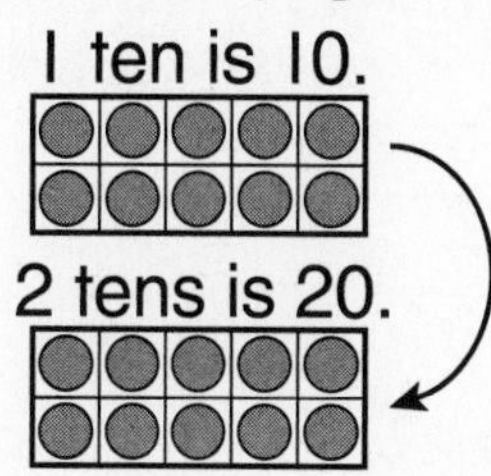

1 ten is 10.
2 tens is 20.
3 tens is 30.

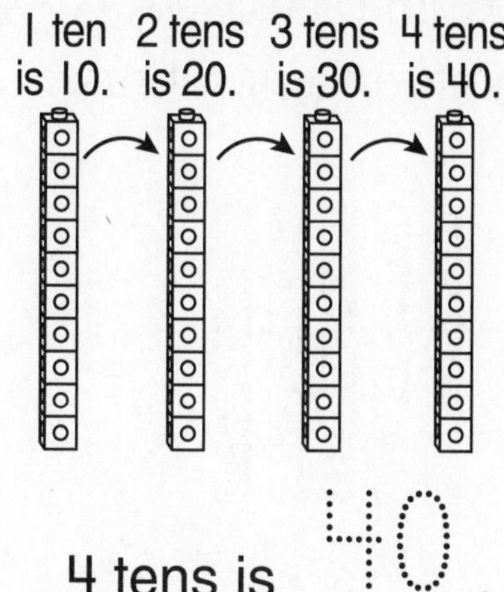

2 tens is 20.   3 tens is 30.   4 tens is 40.

Count the models. Write how many. Then write the number.

1.

1 ten is 10.

2 tens is 20.

3 tens is 30.

3 tens is 30.

2.

_____ ten is _____.

_____ tens is _____.

_____ tens is _____.

_____ tens is _____.

4 tens is _____.

3.

_____ ten is _____.

_____ tens is _____.

_____ tens is _____.

_____ tens is _____.

_____ tens is _____.

_____ tens is _____.

Name ______________________________

Practice
8-2

Numbers Made with Tens

Count by 10s.
Write the numbers.

1.

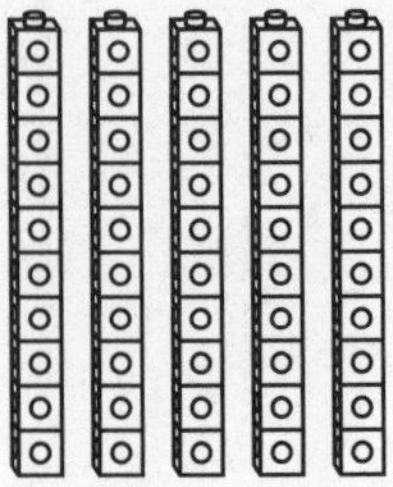

_____ tens is _____.

2.

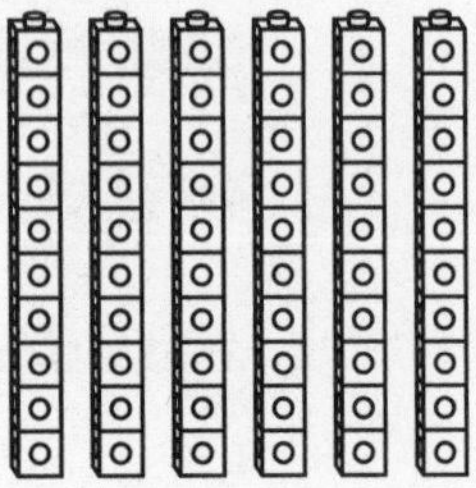

_____ tens is _____.

3.

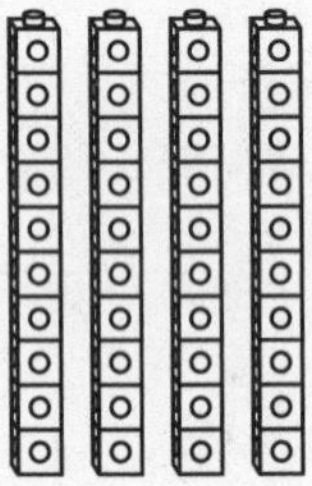

_____ tens is _____.

4.

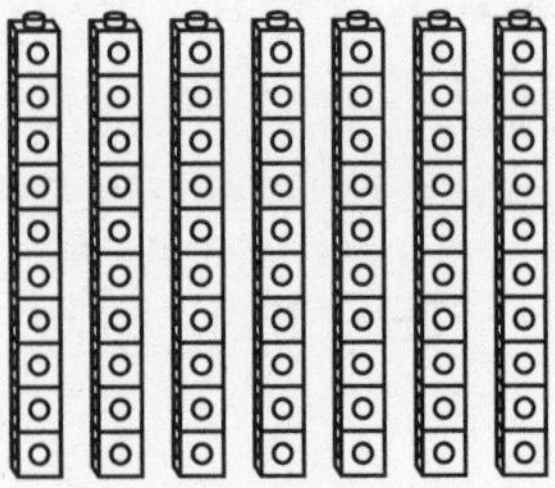

_____ tens is _____.

Reasonableness

5. What number is shown?

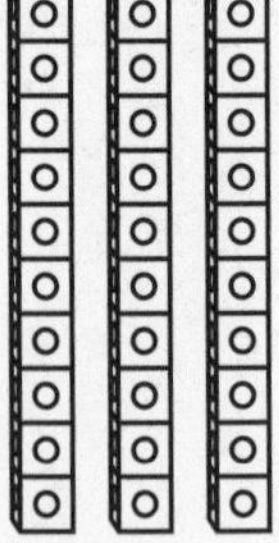

Ⓐ 3
Ⓑ 10
Ⓒ 12
Ⓓ 30

Algebra

6. Nancy has 50 marbles.
30 of the marbles are in one bag.
The rest are in another bag.
How many marbles are in the second bag?

Ⓐ 40
Ⓑ 30
Ⓒ 20
Ⓓ 10

Name ______________________

Reteaching 8-3

Tens and Ones

The chart shows

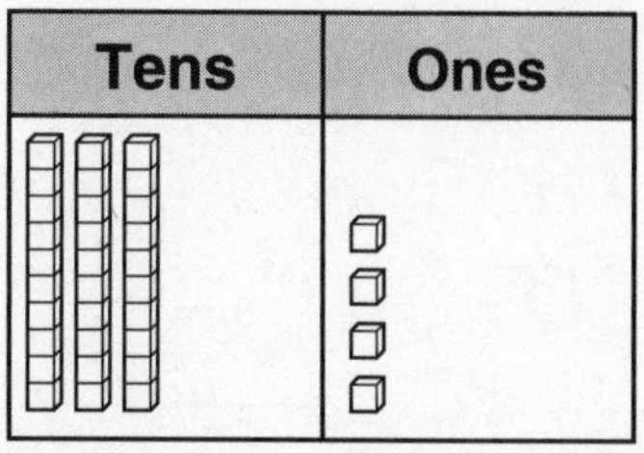

Tens	Ones
(3 tens)	(4 ones)

3 tens 4 ones

3 tens is 30.
4 ones is 4.
30 + 4 = 34

34 is the same as 3 tens and 4 ones.

Count the tens and ones. Then write the numbers.

1.

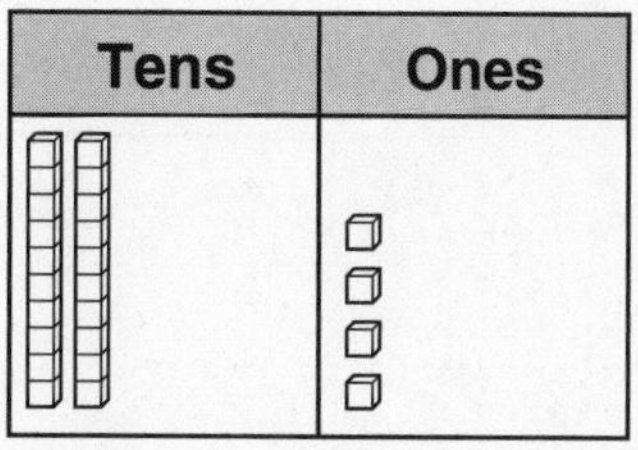

Tens	Ones
(2 tens)	(4 ones)

2 tens and 4 ones

2 tens is 20.

4 ones is 4.

20 + 4 = 24

2.

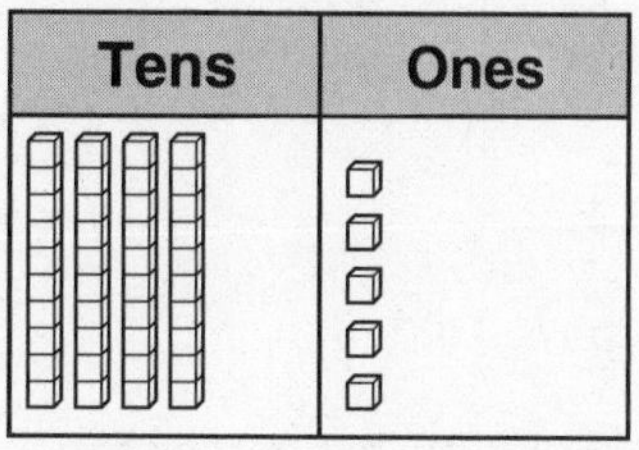

Tens	Ones
(4 tens)	(6 ones)

_____ tens and _____ ones

_____ tens is _____.

_____ ones is _____.

_____ + _____ = _____

3.

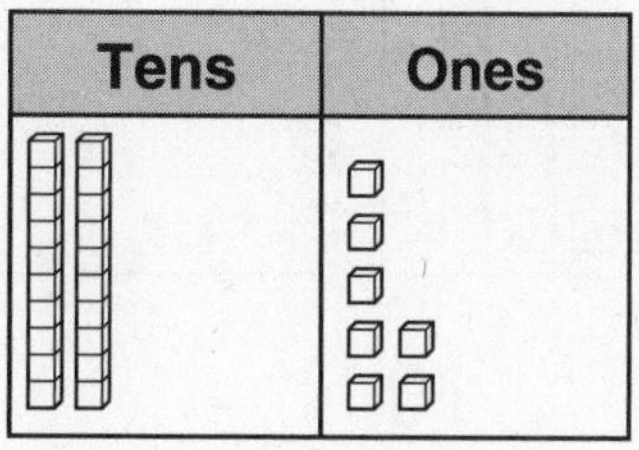

Tens	Ones
(2 tens)	(7 ones)

_____ tens and _____ ones

_____ tens is _____.

_____ ones is _____.

_____ + _____ = _____

Name ______________________

Tens and Ones

Count the tens and ones. Then write the numbers.

1.

Tens	Ones
4	5

45

2.

Tens	Ones

______

3.

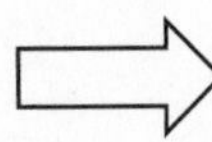

Tens	Ones

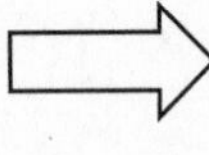

______

Estimation

4. About how many cubes are shown in the picture?

Tens	Ones

70 Ⓐ 50 Ⓑ 30 Ⓒ 10 Ⓓ

Name ______________________

Reteaching
8-4

Expanded Form

Two-digit numbers are made up of tens and ones.
27 is a two-digit number.

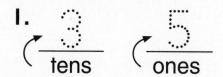

Tens	Ones

2 is in the tens column.
7 is in the ones column.

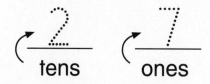

2 tens 7 ones

2 tens + 7 ones = 27

1. 3 tens 5 ones

Tens	Ones

3 tens + 5 ones = 35

2. ______ tens ______ ones

Tens	Ones

______ tens + ______ ones = ______

3. ______ ten ______ one

Tens	Ones

______ ten + ______ one = ______

Name ______________________

Practice 8-4

Expanded Form

Draw the tens and ones. Then write the numbers.

1.

Tens	Ones

3 tens + 6 ones = 36

30 + 6 = 36

2.

Tens	Ones

______ tens + ______ ones = ______

______ + ______ = ______

3.

Tens	Ones

______ tens + ______ ones = ______

______ + ______ = ______

Reasoning

4. The number in the tens place is greater than 6.
The digit in the ones place is between 3 and 7.
Which number matches the clues?

Ⓐ 98

Ⓑ 92

Ⓒ 85

Ⓓ 66

Name ______________________

Ways to Make Numbers

Reteaching **8-5**

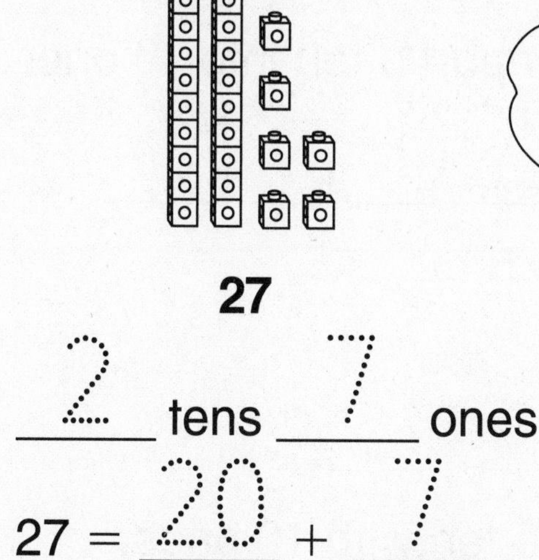

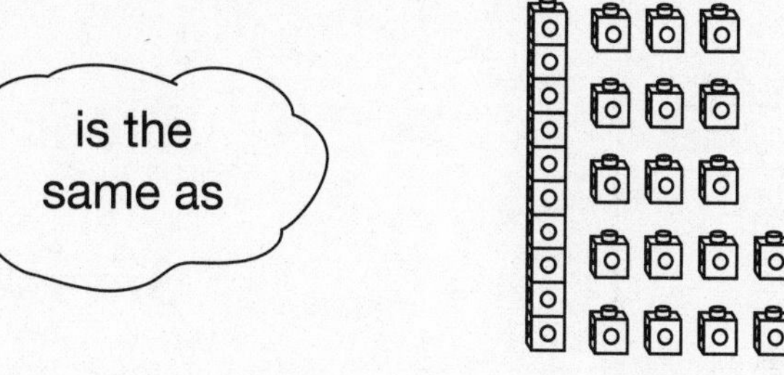

27 **27**

2 tens 7 ones

27 = 20 + 7

1 ten 17 ones

27 = 10 + 17

Use cubes to show a different way to make the number. Draw the ones.

1. **32**

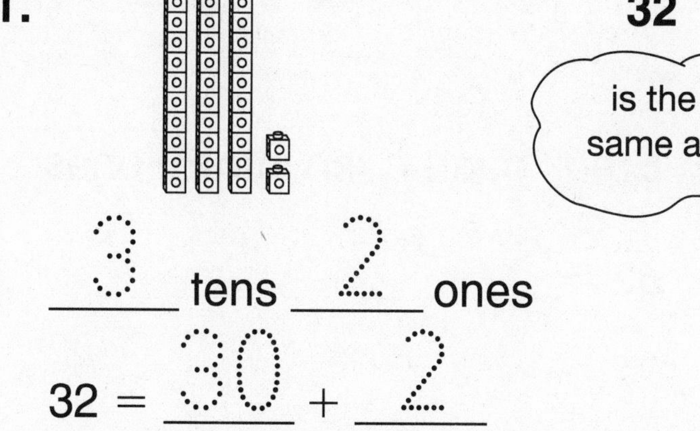

3 tens 2 ones

32 = 30 + 2

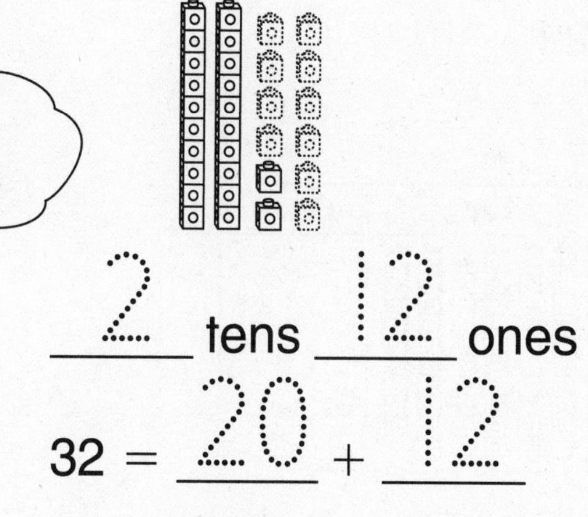

2 tens 12 ones

32 = 20 + 12

2.

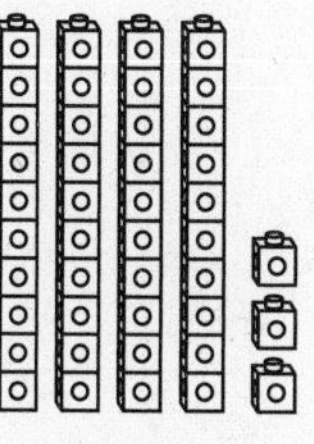

is the same as

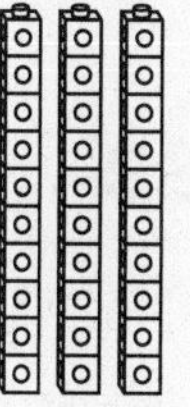

_____ tens _____ ones

43 = _____ + _____

_____ tens _____ ones

43 = _____ + _____

Name ______________________

Practice 8-5

Ways to Make Numbers

Use cubes. Show a different way to make the number.

1.

Tens	Ones
3 tens	7 ones

37 = 30 + 7

Break apart a ten into 10 ones.

37 = 20 + 17

2.

Tens	Ones
1 ten	14 ones

24 = 10 + 14

Make a ten with 10 ones.

24 = ______ + ______

3.

Tens	Ones
6 tens	2 ones

62 = 60 + 2

Break apart a ten into 10 ones.

62 = ______ + ______

Number Sense

4. On Mario's workmat, there are 4 tens and 8 ones. Which is another way to show this same number?

Ⓐ 6 tens and 6 ones
Ⓑ 3 tens and 9 ones
Ⓒ 3 tens and 18 ones
Ⓓ 1 ten and 28 ones

Name ____________________

Problem Solving: Make an Organized List

How many ways can you show 18 with tens and ones?

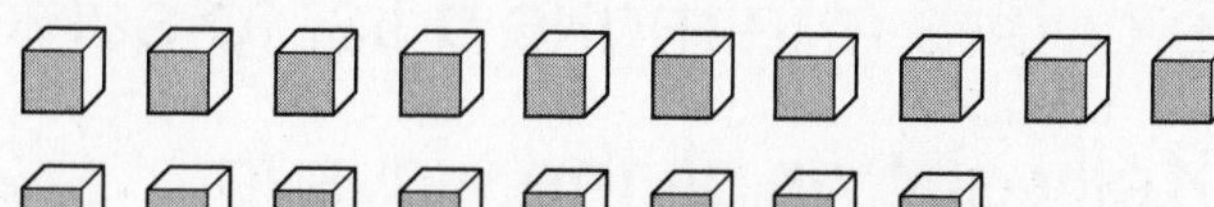

How many tens are in 18? 1

How many ones are left over? 8

Tens	Ones
1	8
0	18

Break apart a ten into 10 ones.

How many ones are there? 18

Make a list to show the ways.

1. Olivia wants to show 25 with tens and ones. Make a list to show the ways.

Tens	Ones
2	5

Reasonableness

2. Penny says there are 4 ways to make 26. Is she correct?

Yes   No

Name ______________________

Problem Solving: Make an Organized List

Use cubes and make a list to solve.

1. Kelly shows all the ways to make 49 as tens and ones. What ways does she show?

Tens	Ones

2. Marc wants to show 34 as tens and ones. What are all the ways he can show?

Tens	Ones

Reasoning

3. Hector's list shows ways to make 52, but he forgot one way. Which numbers are missing from his list?

Tens	Ones
5	2
?	?
3	22
2	32
1	42
0	52

Ⓐ 5 and 12

Ⓑ 4 and 12

Ⓒ 4 and 22

Ⓓ 3 and 12

Name ______________________

I More, I Less; 10 More, 10 Less

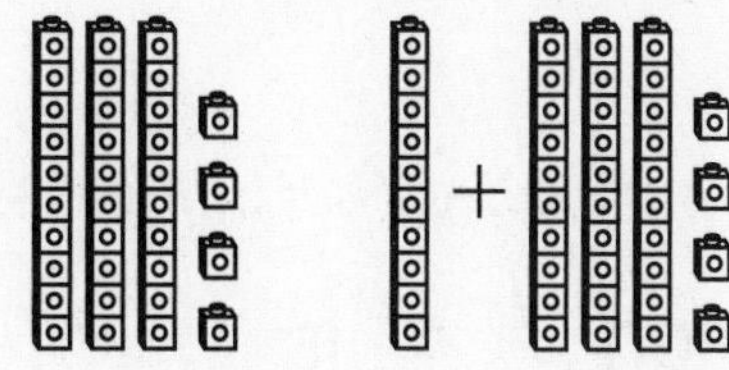

34 take away 10 is 24.

10 less than 34 is 24.

34 and 10 more is 44.

10 more than 34 is 44.

Use cubes. Write the numbers.

1.

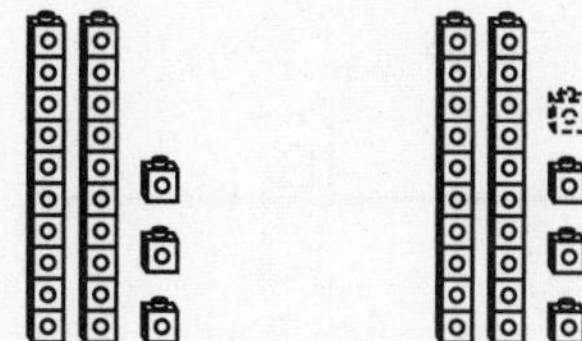

23 take away 1 is 22.

1 less than 23 is ______.

23 and 1 more is 24.

1 more than 23 is ______.

2.

1 less than 45 is ______.

1 more than 45 is ______.

3.

10 less than 68 is ______.

10 more than 68 is ______.

Name ____________________

Practice 9-1

1 More, 1 Less; 10 More, 10 Less

Use cubes. Write the numbers.

1. 72

1 more than 72 is 73.

1 less than ____ is ____.

10 more than ____ is ____.

10 less than ____ is ____.

2. 26

1 more than ____ is ____.

1 less than ____ is ____.

10 more than ____ is ____.

10 less than ____ is ____.

3. 70

1 more than ____ is ____.

1 less than ____ is ____.

10 more than ____ is ____.

10 less than ____ is ____.

4. 14

1 more than ____ is ____.

1 less than ____ is ____.

10 more than ____ is ____.

10 less than ____ is ____.

Reasoning

5. Tom is thinking of a number. His number is 10 more than 45. Which number is he thinking of?

Ⓐ 35
Ⓑ 44
Ⓒ 46
Ⓓ 55

6. Shay is thinking of a number. Her number is 1 less than 87. Which number is she thinking of?

Ⓐ 97
Ⓑ 88
Ⓒ 86
Ⓓ 77

Name ________________________

Reteaching
9-2

Making Numbers on a Hundred Chart

1	2	3
11	12	13
21	22	23

Go right to find 1 more.
1 more than 12 is 13.

1	2	3
11	12	13
21	22	23

Go left to find 1 less.
1 less than 12 is 11.

1	2	3
11	12	13
21	22	23

Go down to find 10 more.
10 more than 12 is 22.

1	2	3
11	12	13
21	22	23

Go up to find 10 less.
10 less than 12 is 2.

Write the missing numbers.

21	22	23	24	25	26	27	28	29	30
31	32	33	34	35	36	37	38	39	40

1. 1 more than 38 is 39.

2. 1 less than 27 is ________.

3. 10 more than 23 is ________.

4. 10 less than 35 is ________.

Name ___________________

Making Numbers on a Hundred Chart

Use the hundred chart to help.

1	2	3	4	5	6	7	8	9	10
11	12	13	14	15	16	17	18	19	20
21	22	23	24	25	26	27	28	29	30
31	32	33	34	35	36	37	38	39	40
41	42	43	44	45	46	47	48	49	50
51	52	53	54	55	56	57	58	59	60
61	62	63	64	65	66	67	68	69	70
71	72	73	74	75	76	77	78	79	80
81	82	83	84	85	86	87	88	89	90
91	92	93	94	95	96	97	98	99	100

1.

1 more than 77 is ______.

1 less than 77 is ______.

10 more than 77 is ______.

10 less than 77 is ______.

2.

1 more than 82 is ______.

1 less than 82 is ______.

10 more than 82 is ______.

10 less than 82 is ______.

3.

1 more than 73 is ______.

1 less than 73 is ______.

10 more than 73 is ______.

10 less than 73 is ______.

4.

1 more than 90 is ______.

1 less than 90 is ______.

10 more than 90 is ______.

10 less than 90 is ______.

Reasoning

5. Sara has 10 more freckles than Tim.
Tim has 1 less freckle than Hank.
Hank has 65 freckles.
How many freckles does Sara have?

76	74	66	55
Ⓐ	Ⓑ	Ⓒ	Ⓓ

Name ______________________________

Comparing Numbers with $>$, $<$, $=$

Write $>$, $<$, or $=$.

$23 < 33$ $33 > 23$ $23 = 23$

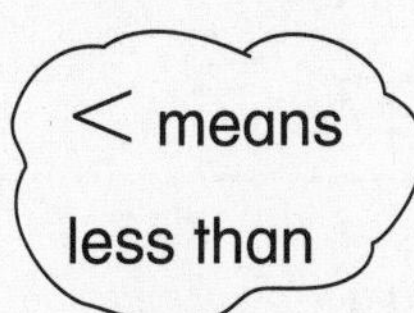
$<$ means
less than

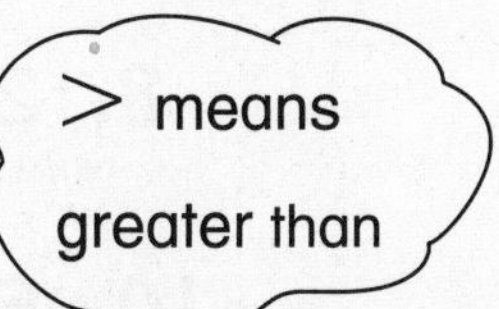
$>$ means
greater than

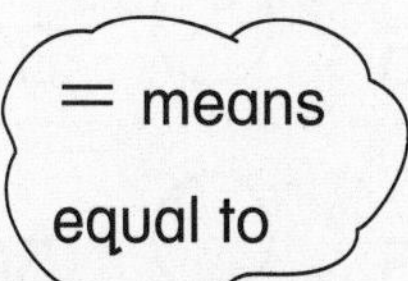
$=$ means
equal to

23 is **less than** 33 33 is **greater than** 23 23 is **equal to** 23

Circle **less than, greater than,** or **equal to.**
Write $<$, $>$, or $=$.

1. (less than) greater than equal to

17 ($<$) 24

2. less than greater than equal to

45 ◯ 32

3. less than greater than equal to

29 ◯ 29

Name ______________________________

Practice 9-3

Comparing Numbers with >, <, =

Write >, <, or =.

1. 43 ◯ 52 (<)
2. 17 ◯ 16
3. 48 ◯ 58
4. 29 ◯ 86
5. 31 ◯ 31
6. 92 ◯ 57
7. 65 ◯ 37
8. 27 ◯ 27
9. 45 ◯ 50
10. 59 ◯ 41
11. 35 ◯ 53
12. 21 ◯ 12

Number Sense

13. Which sentence is true?

38 < 30	38 > 30	38 = 30	30 > 38
Ⓐ	Ⓑ	Ⓒ	Ⓓ

Reasoning

14. Which is equal to 13?

Ⓐ 1 ten, 1 one

Ⓑ 1 ten, 3 ones

Ⓒ 2 tens, 3 ones

Ⓓ 3 tens, 1 one

Name ______________________

Reteaching 9-4

Ordering Three Numbers

The number line can help you put numbers in order.

Show 27, 14, 38 from **least** to **greatest.**

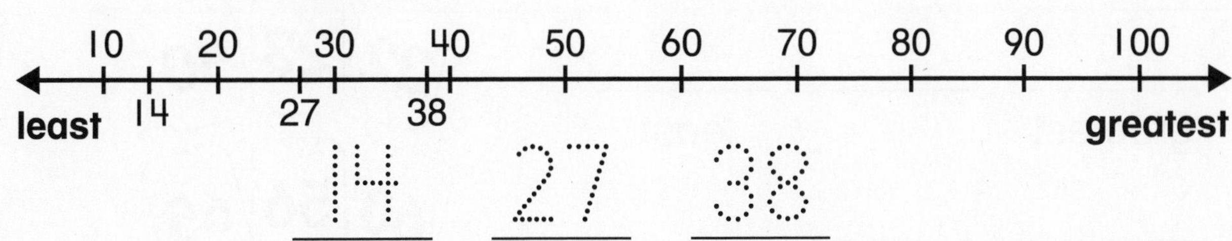

14 27 38

least **greatest**

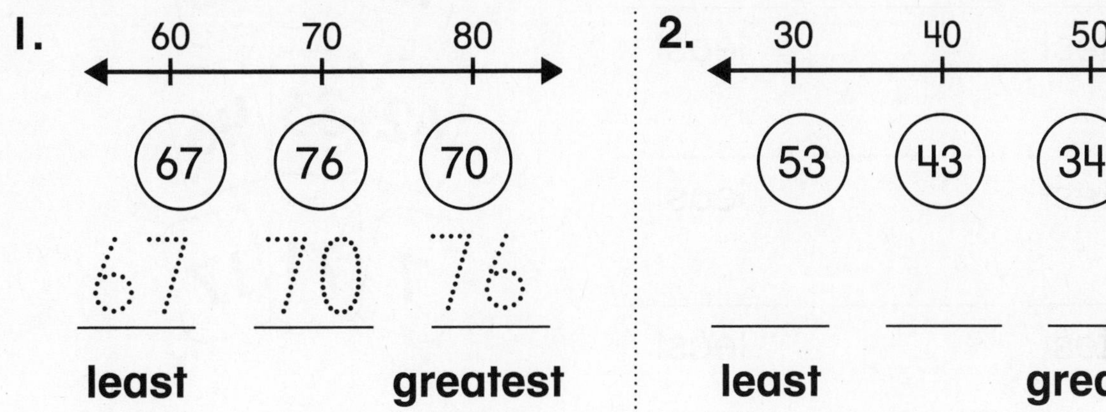

1. 67 76 70

67 70 76
least **greatest**

2. 53 43 34

_____ _____ _____
least **greatest**

Write the numbers in order from **greatest** to **least.**
Use the number line to help you.

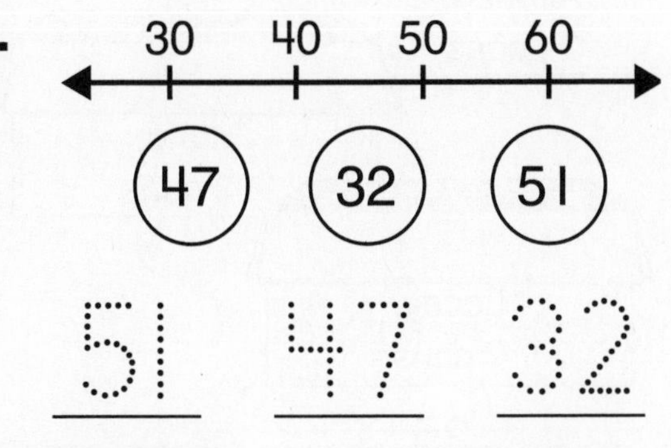

3. 47 32 51

51 47 32
greatest **least**

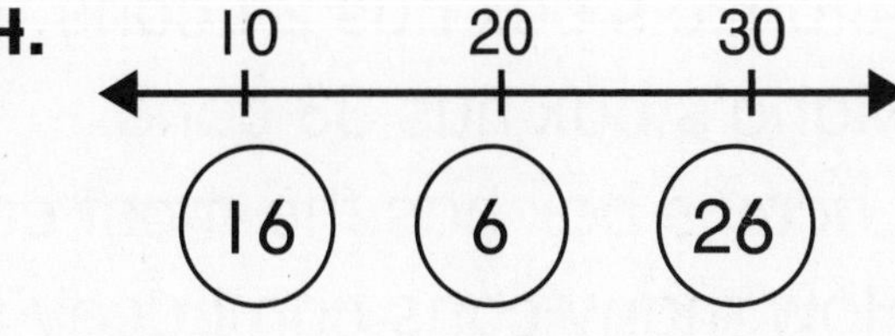

4. 16 6 26

_____ _____ _____
greatest **least**

Name ____________________

Practice 9-4

Ordering Three Numbers

Write the numbers in order from greatest to least.

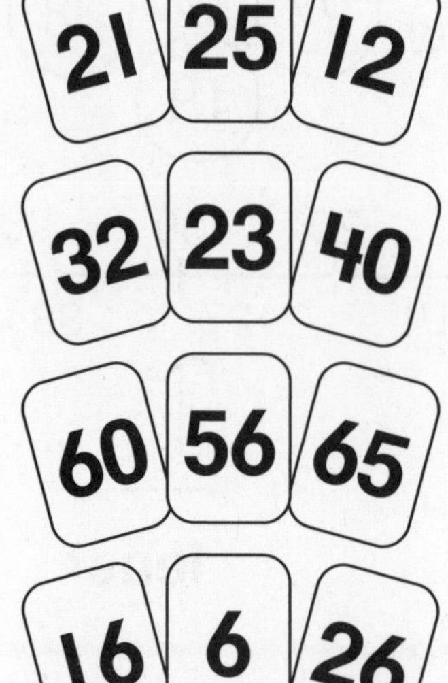

1. 25 21 12
greatest least

2. ______ ______ ______
greatest least

3. ______ ______ ______
greatest least

4. ______ ______ ______
greatest least

5. ______ ______ ______
greatest least

6. ______ ______ ______
greatest least

Number Sense

Order the numbers to solve.

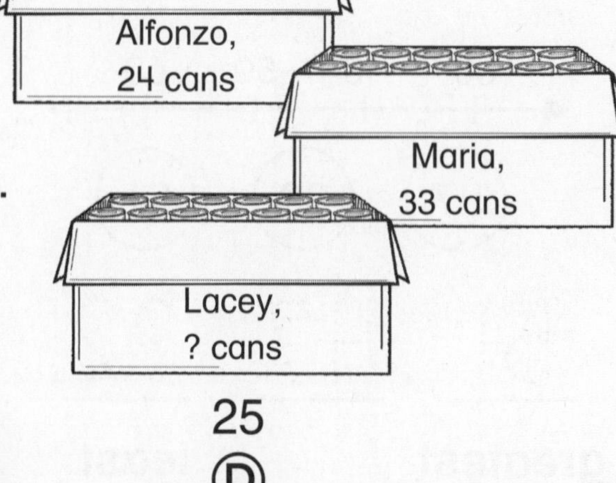

7. Alfonzo's box has 24 cans. Maria's box has 33 cans. Lacey's box has the most cans. How many cans can Lacey's box have?

42	33	32	25
Ⓐ	Ⓑ	Ⓒ	Ⓓ

Name ______________________________

Reteaching
9-5

Problem Solving: Make an Organized List

Kyla picks a number card.
Her number is less than 40.
It is greater than 35.
Which number does she pick?

Make a list to find Kyla's number.

Look at the first clue.
List the numbers on the cards
that are less than 40.

29
32
38

Kyla's number could be 29, 32, or 38.

Look at the second clue.
Circle the numbers on the list
that are greater than 35.
38 is greater than 35.

29
32
(38)

Kyla's number must be 38.

1. Ian picks a number card.
It is less than 60.
Ian says his number when
he counts by 2s.
Which number does Ian pick?

Make a list of the numbers less than 60.
Then circle the number on the list
that Ian says when he counts by 2s.

_____
_____
_____

Ian's number must be ________.

Name ______________________________

Practice
9-5

Problem Solving: Make an Organized List

Make a list. Write the color of the motorcycle.

red	pink	orange	yellow	green	blue	purple	black

1. This motorcycle is between numbers 3 and 6.

Which color could it be?

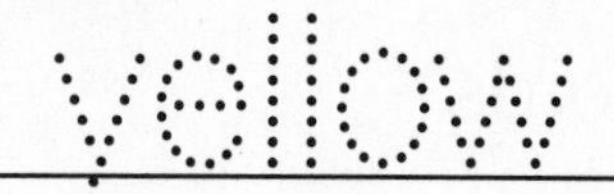

____

This motorcycle is the color of a banana. What color is the motorcycle?

____

2. This motorcycle is between numbers 1 and 4.

Which color could it be?

____

____

This motorcycle is the color of a pumpkin. What color is the motorcycle?

____

Reasoning

Make a list to find the secret number.

3. I am a number greater than 55.
I am in a square.
What number am I?

Ⓐ 28 Ⓒ 60
Ⓑ 63 Ⓓ 78

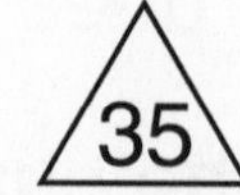

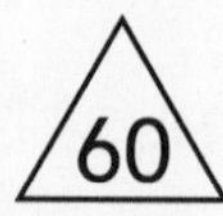

78

Name ______________________

Adding Groups of 10

You can use what you know about adding ones to add groups of ten.

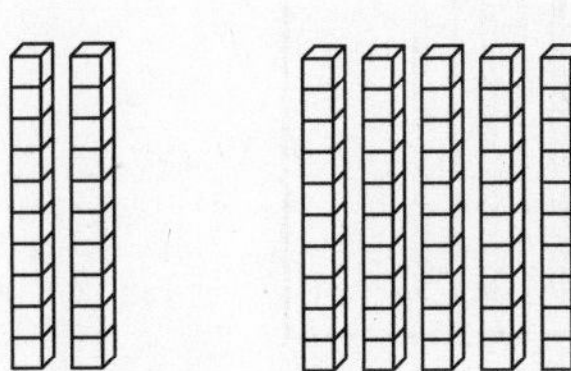

2 ones and 5 ones are 7 ones. 2 tens and 5 tens are 7 tens.

2 + 5 = 7 20 + 50 = 70

Write each number sentence.

1.

3 + 2 = 5

30 + 20 = 50

2.

____ + ____ = 6

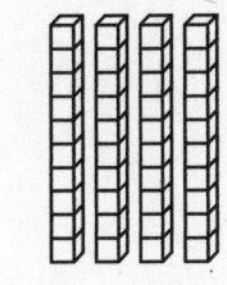

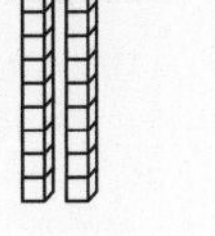

____ + ____ = 60

3.

____ + ____ = ____

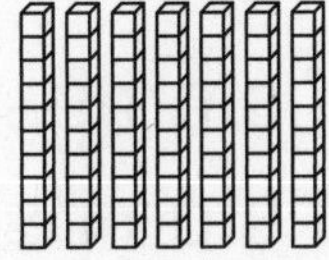

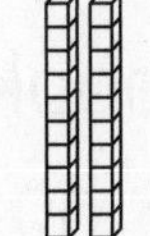

____ + ____ = ____

4.

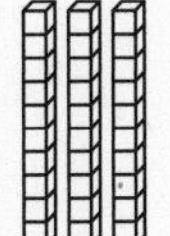

____ + ____ = ____

5.

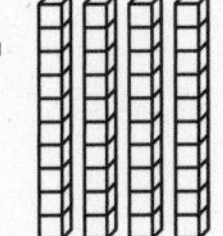

____ + ____ = ____

Name ______________________________

Practice
10-1

Adding Groups of 10

Write numbers to complete each number sentence.

1.

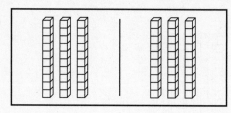

____ tens + ____ tens = ____ tens

____ + ____ = ____

Complete each number sentence.

2. 50 + 20 = ____

3. 30 + 40 = ____

4. 20 + 30 = ____

5. 70 + 20 = ____

6. 60 + 30 = ____

7. 10 + 80 = ____

Number Sense

8. David has 2 books of stamps.
The first book has 50 stamps.
The other book has 30 stamps.
How many stamps does David have in all?

Ⓐ 20
Ⓑ 70
Ⓒ 80
Ⓓ 90

Name ____________________

Reteaching
10-2

Adding Tens on a Hundred Chart

1	2	3	4	5	6	7	8	9	10
11	12	13	14	15	16	17	18	19	20
21	22	23	24	25	26	27	28	29	30
31	32	33	34	35	36	37	38	39	40
41	42	43	44	45	46	47	48	49	50
51	52	53	54	55	56	57	58	59	60
61	62	63	64	65	66	67	68	69	70
71	72	73	74	75	76	77	78	79	80
81	82	83	84	85	86	87	88	89	90
91	92	93	94	95	96	97	98	99	100

When you add tens on a hundred chart, you skip count by tens. The ones digit in each number is the same as the ones digit in the number you started from.

The tens digit of each number is one more than the tens digit of the number before it.

Use the hundred chart to add tens to 16.

1. 16 + 10 = 26

2. 16 + 20 = ____

3. 16 + 30 = ____

4. 16 + 40 = ____

5. What numbers did you skip count on the hundred chart to find the answers? ______

Algebra

6. Fill in the missing digits to complete the pattern.

5______, 62, ______2, ______2

Name ______________________

Adding Tens on a Hundred Chart

1	2	3	4	5	6	7	8	9	10
11	12	13	14	15	16	17	18	19	20
21	22	23	24	25	26	27	28	29	30
31	32	33	34	35	36	37	38	39	40
41	42	43	44	45	46	47	48	49	50
51	52	53	54	55	56	57	58	59	60
61	62	63	64	65	66	67	68	69	70
71	72	73	74	75	76	77	78	79	80
81	82	83	84	85	86	87	88	89	90
91	92	93	94	95	96	97	98	99	100

Use the hundred chart to add tens.

1. 24 + 30 = ______ 56 + 20 = ______ 13 + 70 = ______

2. 11 + 80 = ______ 67 + 10 = ______ 39 + 40 = ______

Algebra

3. Which number sentence is equal to 24 + 10?

Ⓐ 14 + 10

Ⓑ 14 + 20

Ⓒ 24 + 20

Ⓓ 34 + 10

Name ____________________

Adding Tens to Two-Digit Numbers

You can count on by tens to add.

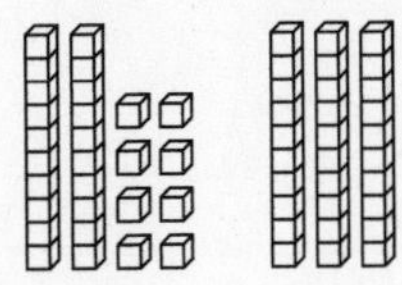

28 + 30 is 28 + 3 tens

3 tens

10 10 10

28, 38, 48, 58

28 + 30 = 58

Solve each number sentence.

1.

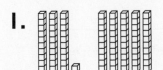

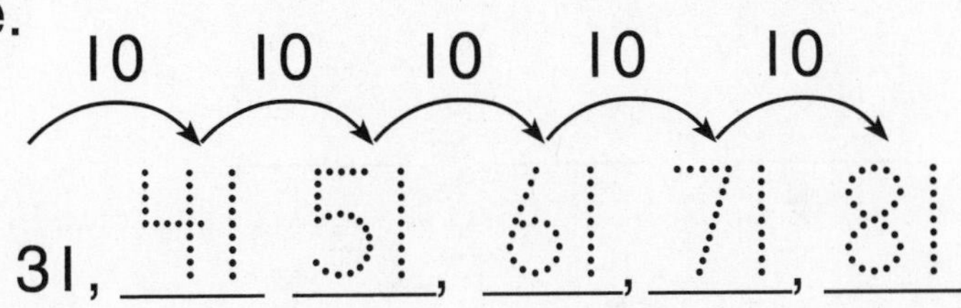

31, ____ ____, ____, ____, ____

31 + 50 is 31 + 5 tens

31 + 50 = 81

2.

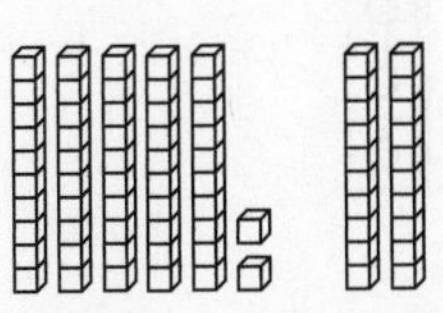

52, ____ ____

52 + 20 is 52 + ____ tens

52 + 20 = ____

3.

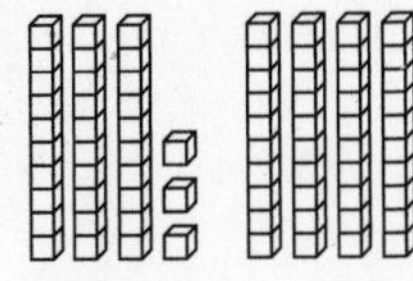

33, ____, ____, ____, ____

33 + 40 is 33 + ____ tens

33 + 40 = ____

Name ______________________________

Adding Tens to Two-Digit Numbers

Write each number sentence.

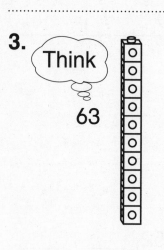

1. Think 36

_____ + _____ = _____

2. Think 54

_____ + _____ = _____

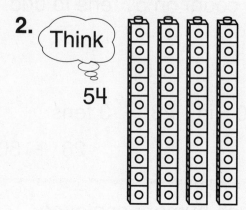

3. Think 63

_____ + _____ = _____

4.

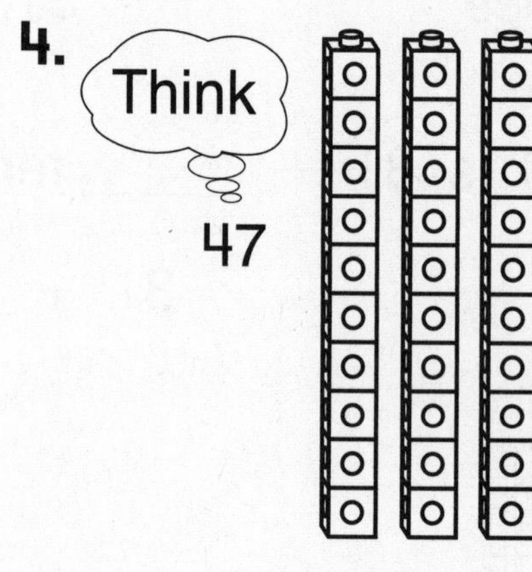

_____ + _____ = _____

Number Sense

5. Will has 24 crayons.
He gets 4 more boxes of crayons.
Each box has 10 crayons.
How many crayons does Will have now?

64	54	44	34
			Ⓓ

Name ______________________

Mental Math

Reteaching
10-4

Use mental math to add these two-digit numbers: 15 + 20.
You just need to add the tens.
Only the tens digit will change.

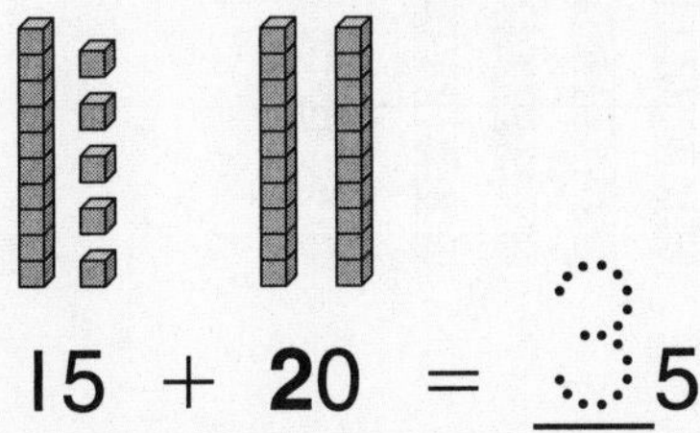

15 + **20** = 35

Add using mental math. Complete the addition sentence.

1. 32 + 20

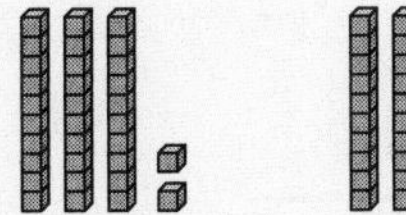

32 + 20 = 52

2. 28 + 40

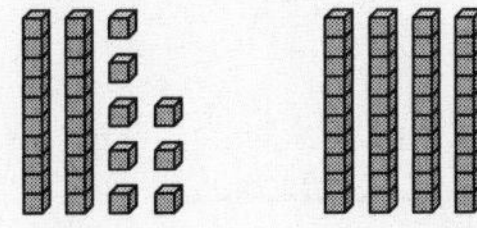

______ + 40 = ______

3. 33 + 50

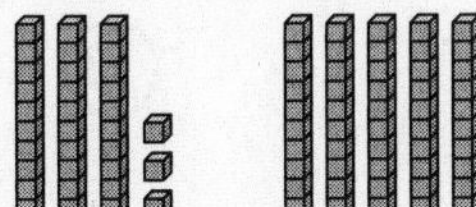

______ + 50 = ______

4. 47 + 30

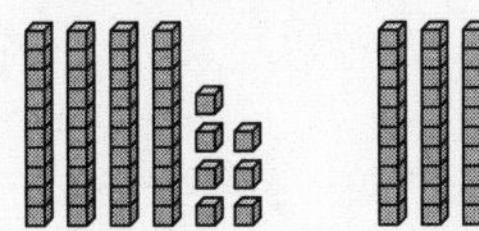

______ + 30 = ______

5. Add using mental math. Use models if needed.

56 + 30 = ______

Name ____________________

Practice
10-4

Mental Math

Add using mental math. Use models if you need to.

1. and 30

41 + 30 = 71

2. and 20

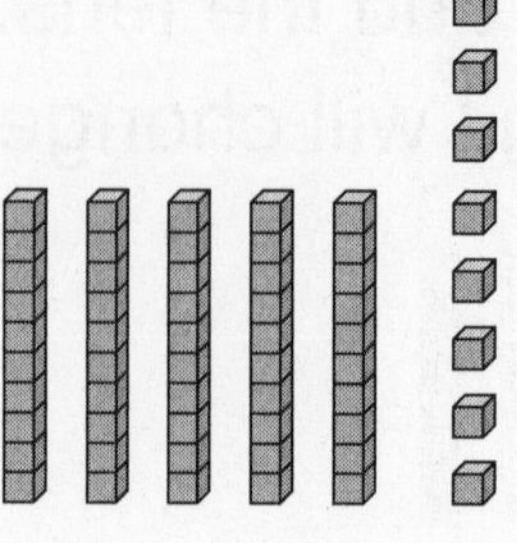

____ + ____ = ____

3. 71 + 20 = ____

4. 65 + 30 = ____

5. 40 + 23 = ____

6. 60 + 24 = ____

7. Tanner has 50 star stickers. She has 17 rainbow stickers. How many stickers does Tanner have in all?

47	50	57	67
Ⓐ	Ⓑ	Ⓒ	Ⓓ

8. Darrin has 27 basketball stickers. He has 30 football stickers. How many stickers does Darrin have in all?

63	27	57	68
Ⓐ	Ⓑ	Ⓒ	Ⓓ

9. **Algebra** Write the missing numbers that make these number sentences true.

40 + 50 = 60 + ____ ____ = 89 + 10

Name ______________________

Reteaching
10-5

Adding to a Two-Digit Number

Add 26 and 5.

Show 26. Add 5.

Regroup 10 ones as 1 ten.

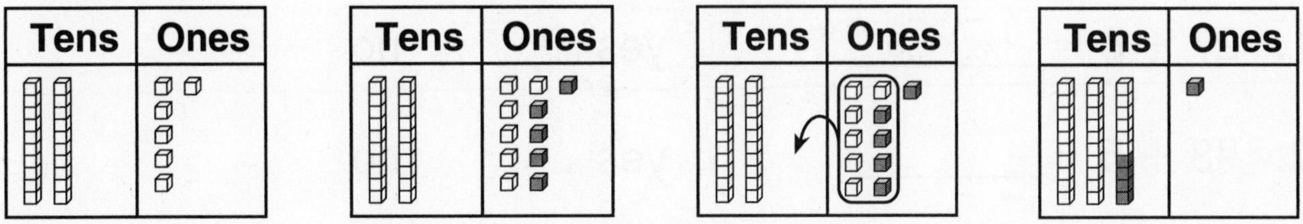
Tens
Ones
Tens
Ones
Tens
Ones
Tens
Ones

26 + 5 = 31

Find the sum.

1. Add 16 and 7.

Show 16. Add 7. Regroup. Find the sum.

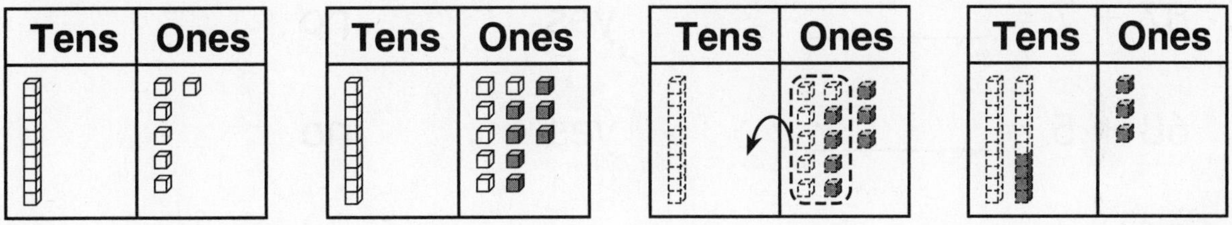
Tens
Ones
Tens
Ones
Tens
Ones
Tens
Ones

16 + 7 = 23

2. Add 28 and 5.

Show 28. Add 5. Regroup. Find the sum.

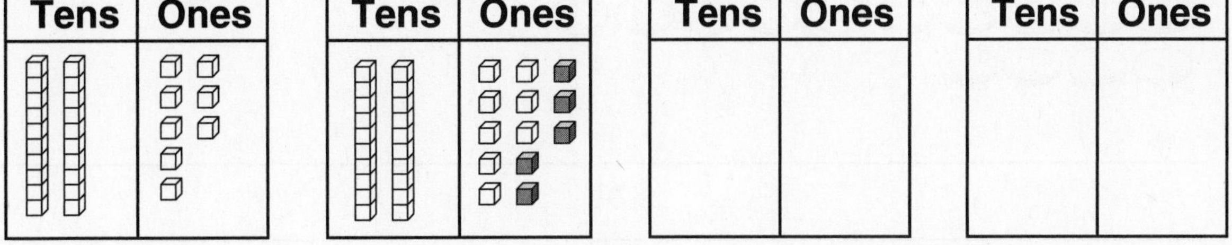
Tens
Ones
Tens
Ones
Tens
Ones
Tens
Ones

28 + 5 = ______

Name ___________________________

Practice
10-5

Adding to a Two-Digit Number

Write the sum.

Find the sum. **Do you need to regroup?**

1. 27 + 6 = 33 yes no

2. 43 + 5 = ______ yes no

3. 34 + 8 = ______ yes no

4. 17 + 4 = ______ yes no

5. 56 + 3 = ______ yes no

6. 93 + 2 = ______ yes no

7. 87 + 7 = ______ yes no

8. 68 + 5 = ______ yes no

9. 36 + 3 = ______ yes no

10. Journal There are 24 counters.
How many counters could you add without having to regroup? Why?

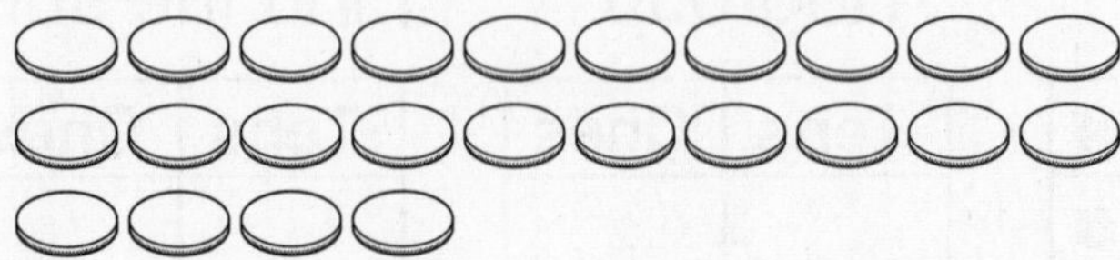

____

____

____

Name ______________________________

Reteaching
10-6

Problem Solving: Draw a Picture and Write a Number Sentence

Add multiples of ten to two-digit numbers. Look for clue words to help you decide.

Lois has 16 counters.
She gets 10 more counters.
How many counters does Lois have in all?

In all tells you that you need to add.

Draw a picture.

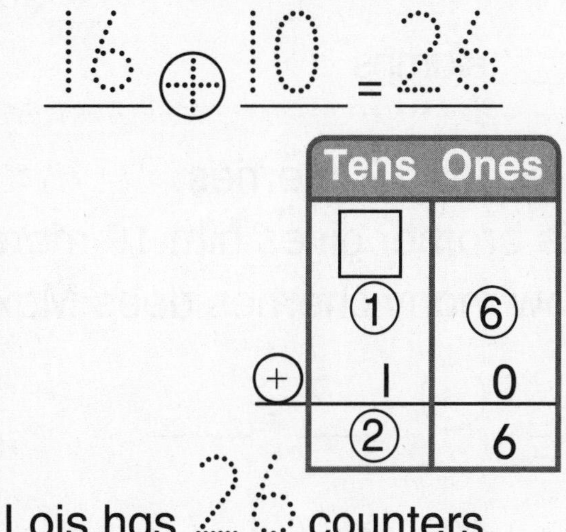

Write a number sentence.

16 + 10 = 26

	Tens	Ones
	1	6
+	1	0
	2	6

Lois has 26 counters.

Circle the words that tell you to add.
Draw a picture and write a number sentence to solve.
Use your workmat to help.

1. Carlos has 17 counters.
He gets 20 more counters.
How many counters does he have in all?

____ + ____ = ____

____ counters

Name ______________________________

Practice
10-6

Problem Solving: Draw a Picture and Write a Number Sentence

Write a number sentence.
Then solve the problem.

1. Jan has 14 stamps.
She gets 30 more stamps.
How many stamps does she have now?

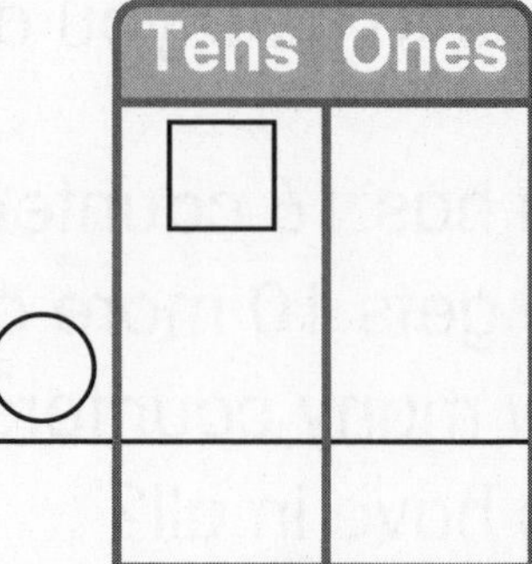

_____ stamps

2. Max has 19 cherries.
His brother gives him 10 more cherries.
How many cherries does Max have now?

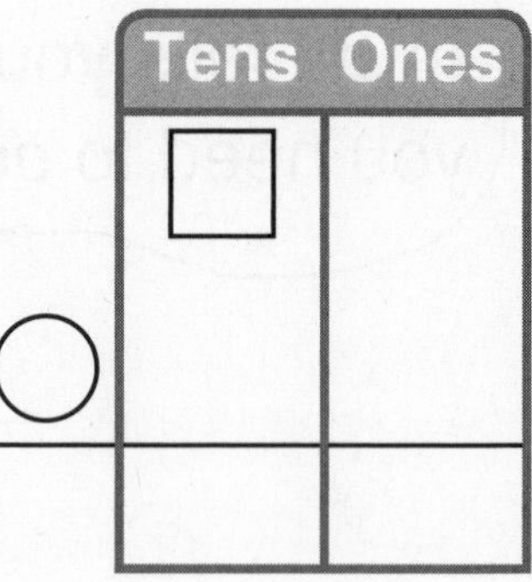

_____ ◯ _____ = _____

_____ cherries

Reasoning

3. Bill says that he can add 23 and 40 without regrouping.
Is Bill correct? How do you know?

____

____

____

____

Name ______________________

Reteaching
11-1

Subtracting Groups of 10

You can use what you know about subtracting ones to subtract groups of ten.

$7 - 2 = 5$

$70 - 20 = ?$

Show 7 tens. Take away 2 tens.
Count the tens left over.
Then complete the number sentence.

7 tens − __2__ tens = 5 tens, so 70 − 20 = __50__.

Write the numbers to complete each subtraction sentence.

1. _____ tens − _____ tens = _____ ten

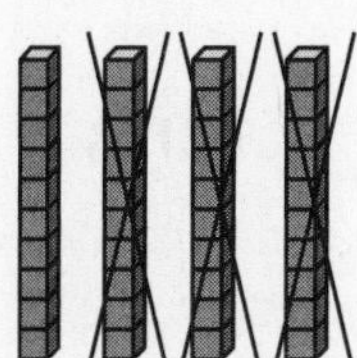

_____ − _____ = _____

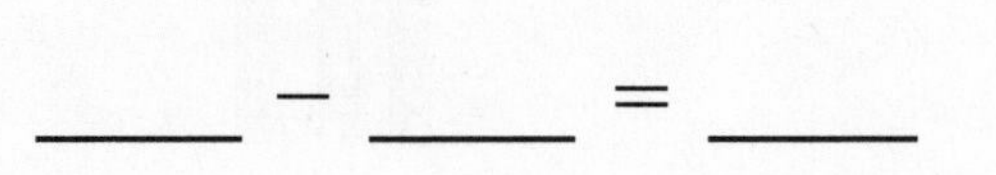

2. _____ tens − _____ tens = _____ tens

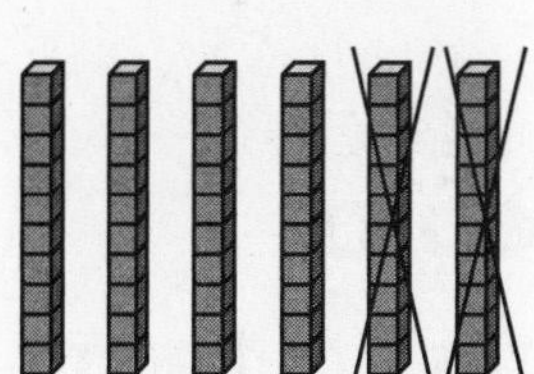

_____ − _____ = _____

3. _____ tens − _____ tens = _____ tens

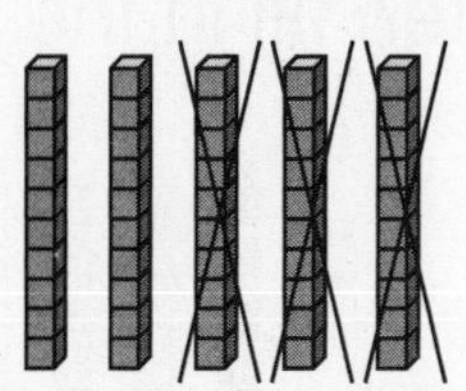

_____ − _____ = _____

Number Sense

4. Simon has 7 tens.
Can he take away 9 tens?
Circle Yes or No

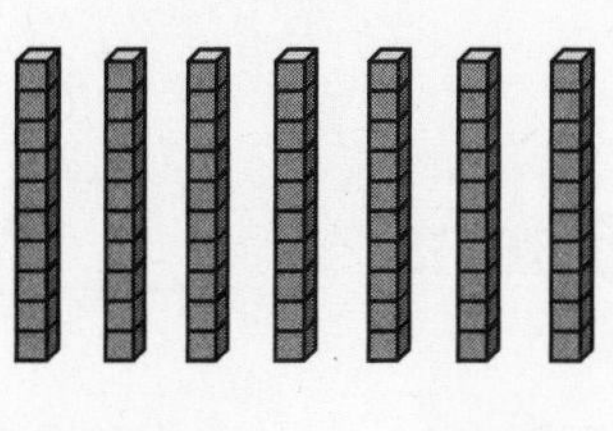

Yes No

Name ______________________

Practice
11-1

Subtracting Groups of 10

Write the numbers to complete each number sentence.

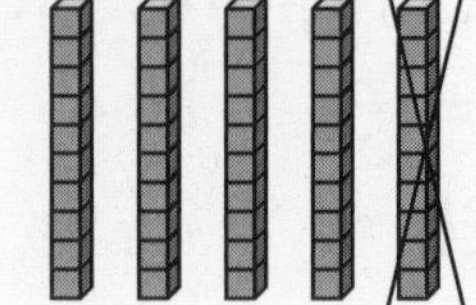

1. ____ tens − ____ ten = ____ tens

____ − ____ = ____

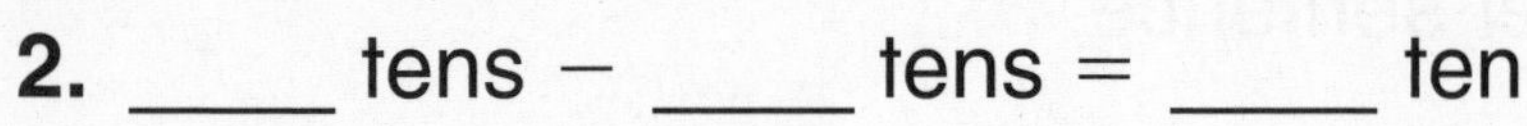

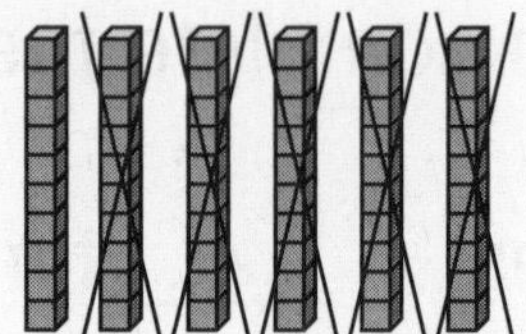

2. ____ tens − ____ tens = ____ ten

____ − ____ = ____

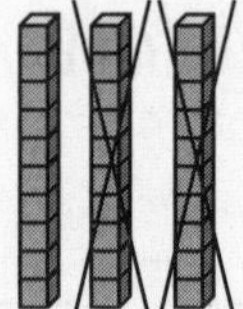

3. ____ tens − ____ tens = ____ ten

____ − ____ = ____

Algebra

4. Cross out some tens in the picture.
Then fill in the number sentence.

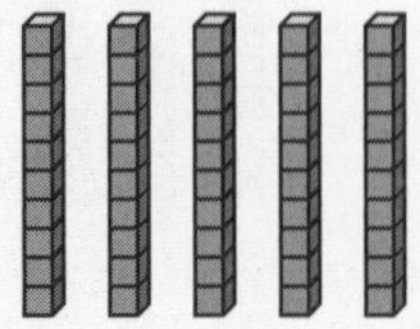

5 tens − ____ tens = 3 tens

50 − ____ = 30

Name ______________________

Subtracting Tens on a Hundred Chart

Reteaching
11-2

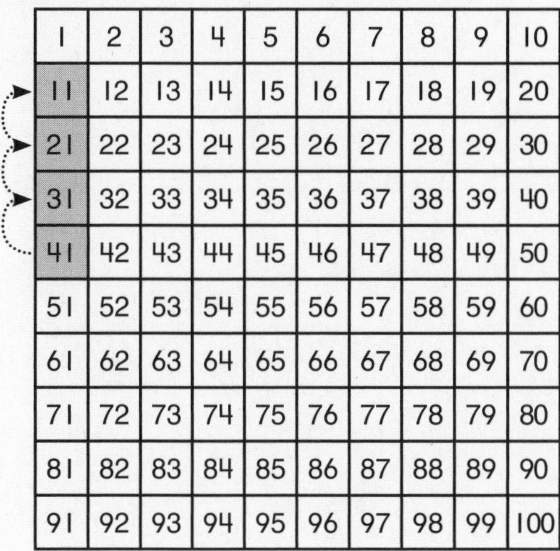

1	2	3	4	5	6	7	8	9	10
11	12	13	14	15	16	17	18	19	20
21	22	23	24	25	26	27	28	29	30
31	32	33	34	35	36	37	38	39	40
41	42	43	44	45	46	47	48	49	50
51	52	53	54	55	56	57	58	59	60
61	62	63	64	65	66	67	68	69	70
71	72	73	74	75	76	77	78	79	80
81	82	83	84	85	86	87	88	89	90
91	92	93	94	95	96	97	98	99	100

> To subtract by tens, you can count back by tens on a hundred chart. Move up a row for each ten you subtract. All of the numbers will end in the same number.

41 − 30 = ______

Count back by tens on the hundred chart to subtract.

1. 84 − 60 = 24

2. 59 − 10 = ☐

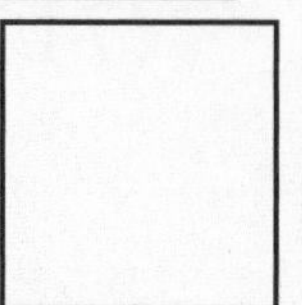

3. 45 − 30 = ☐

4. 78 − 40 = ☐

5. What numbers did you skip count on the hundred chart to find the answers? ______

Algebra

6. Fill in the missing digits to complete the pattern.

8______, 72, ______2, ______2

Name ______________________

Practice
11-2

Subtracting Tens on a Hundred Chart

1	2	3	4	5	6	7	8	9	10
11	12	13	14	15	16	17	18	19	20
21	22	23	24	25	26	27	28	29	30
31	32	33	34	35	36	37	38	39	40
41	42	43	44	45	46	47	48	49	50
51	52	53	54	55	56	57	58	59	60
61	62	63	64	65	66	67	68	69	70
71	72	73	74	75	76	77	78	79	80
81	82	83	84	85	86	87	88	89	90
91	92	93	94	95	96	97	98	99	100

Use the hundred chart to subtract tens.

1. 87 − 40 = ______ 53 − 30 = ______ 71 − 60 = ______

2. 98 − 10 = ______ 32 − 20 = ______ 83 − 50 = ______

3. 43 − 20 = ______ 71 − 50 = ______ 66 − 40 = ______

Algebra

4. Which number completes the subtraction sentence?

75 − ______ = 35

Ⓐ 20

Ⓑ 30

Ⓒ 40

Ⓓ 50

Name ______________________

Reteaching
11-3

Subtracting Tens from Two-Digit Numbers

You can count back by tens to subtract.

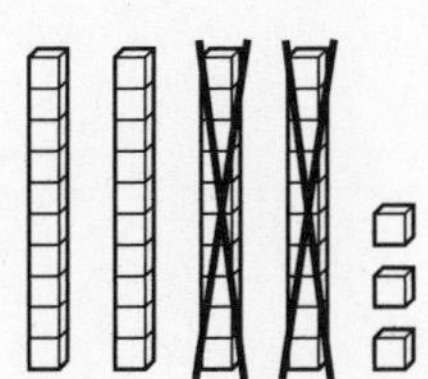

2 tens

10 10

43, 33, 23

43 − 20 is 43 − 2 tens

43 − 20 = 23

Solve each number sentence.

1. 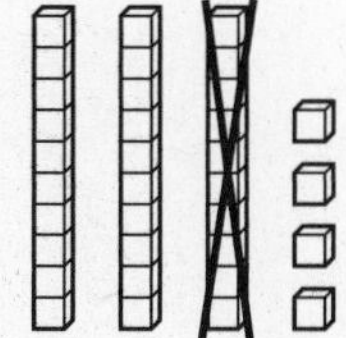

10

34, 24

34 − 10 is 34 − 1 ten

34 − 10 = 24

2. 

10

52, ______, ______, ______

52 − 30 is 52 − ______ tens

52 − 30 = ______

3. 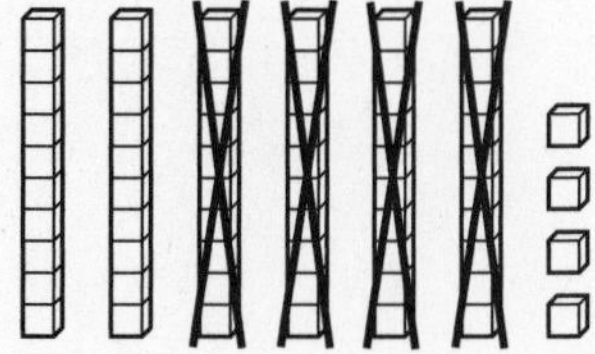

64, ______, ______, ______, ______

64 − 40 is 64 − ______ tens

64 − 40 = ______

Name ______________________

Practice
11-3

Subtracting Tens from Two-Digit Numbers

Cross out the tens. Write the difference.

1.

64 − 20 = ______

2.

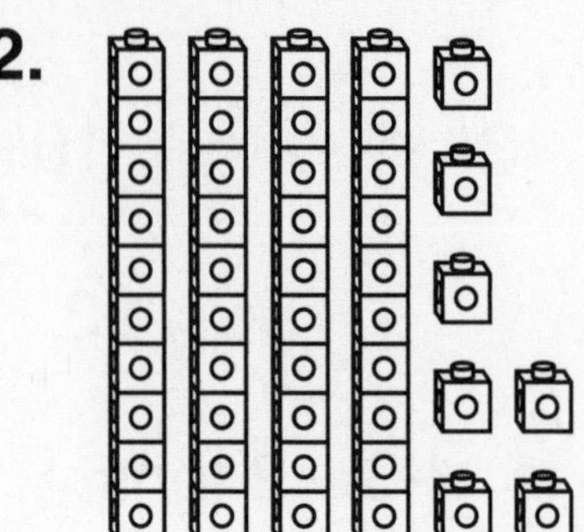

47 − 30 = ______

3.

55 − 40 = ______

4.

33 − 10 = ______

Journal

5. Roberto says that 75 − 30 = 35.
Is Roberto correct?
Explain.

____

____

Name ______________________

Using Mental Math to Subtract Tens

Here are two ways you can find 86 − 20.

1. Count back 2 tens, or 20.

When you subtract tens, only the tens digit changes.

86, 76, 66

2. Use cubes to subtract the tens.

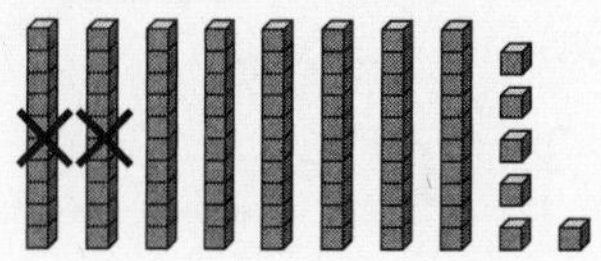

80 − 20 = 60

Then subtract the ones.

6 − 0 = 6

So, 86 − 20 = 66.

Count back to subtract tens. Use cubes if needed.

1. 34 − 30 =

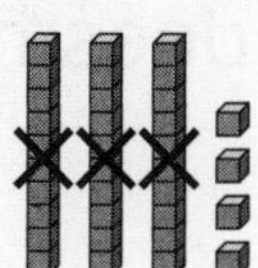

34, 24, 14, 4

34 − 30 = 4

2. 85 − 30 = ____

3. 26 − 10 = ____

4. 63 − 50 = ____

5. 84 − 70 = ____

6. 71 − 40 = ____

7. 48 − 20 = ____

Name ______________________

Using Mental Math to Subtract Tens

Subtract. Use mental math or ten-frame cards.

1. 66 − 50 = ____

2. 88 − 40 = ____

3. 48 − 20 = ____

4. 39 − 20 = ____

5. 23 − 10 = ____

6. 56 − 30 = ____

7. 87 − 70 = ____

Ⓐ 77
Ⓑ 57
Ⓒ 37
Ⓓ 17

8. 67 − 40 = ____

Ⓐ 20
Ⓑ 27
Ⓒ 36
Ⓓ 41

9. Use mental math to solve.

A jar holds 59 marbles. Laine is playing with 10 of them.

How many marbles are left in the jar?

Ⓐ 19
Ⓑ 29
Ⓒ 49
Ⓓ 59

10. **Number Sense** Marco had 82 cards. He gave 40 of them to Susan.

How many cards does he have left?

Ⓐ 82
Ⓑ 62
Ⓒ 52
Ⓓ 42

Name ______________________________

Reteaching
11-5

Subracting from a Two-Digit Number

Find the difference for the problem 32 – 6.

Show 32. Regroup 1 ten as 10 ones. Subtract.

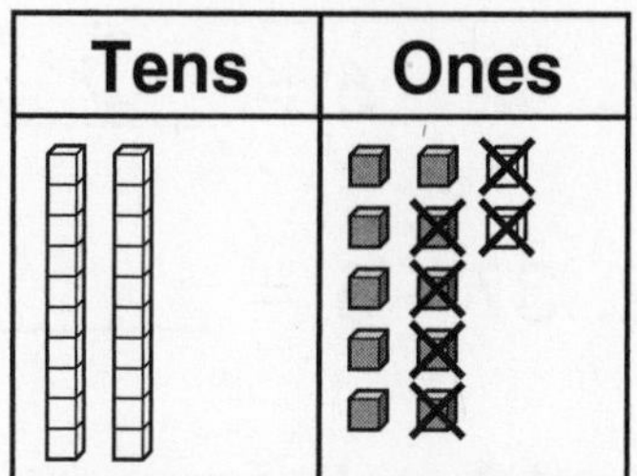

Subtract 6.

32 – 6 = 26

1. Find the difference for the problem 46 – 8.

Show 46. Regroup. Subtract.

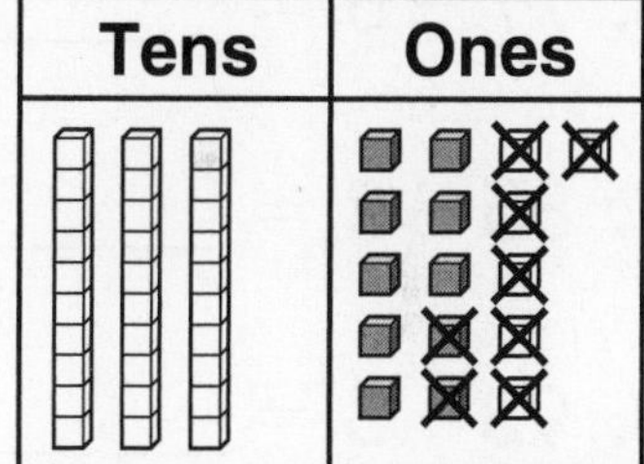

Subtract 8.

46 – 8 = 38

2. Find the difference for the problem 23 – 7.

Show 23. Regroup. Subtract.

Subtract 7.

23 – 7 = ______

Name ______________________

Subtracting from a Two-Digit Number

Write the difference.

Find the difference.	Do you need to regroup?	
1. 42 − 6 = 36	yes	no
2. 37 − 5 = ______	yes	no
3. 62 − 4 = ______	yes	no
4. 58 − 9 = ______	yes	no
5. 24 − 7 = ______	yes	no
6. 77 − 6 = ______	yes	no
7. 85 − 8 = ______	yes	no
8. 93 − 3 = ______	yes	no

Spatial Thinking

9. Draw cubes to show the same number in both place value mats.

Tens	Ones

Tens	Ones

Name ______________________________

Reteaching **11-6**

Problem Solving: Draw a Picture and Write a Number Sentence

Read and Understand

Mr. Yee has 40 pencils.
He gives away 30 pencils.
How many pencils does he have left?

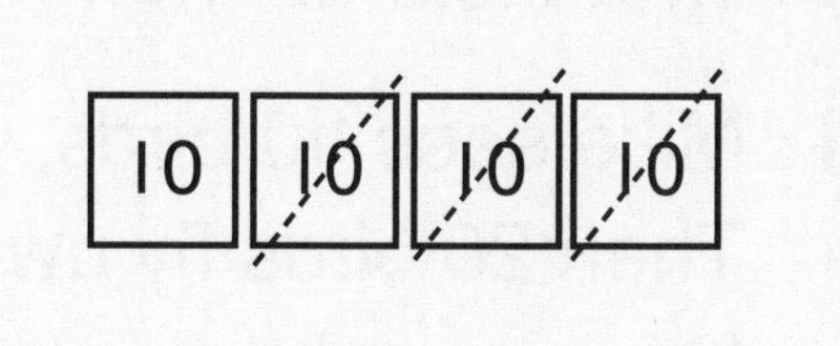

Plan

You can draw a picture and write a number sentence to solve.

Solve

Draw 4 squares for 40 pencils. Cross out 3 squares for 30 pencils.
Count the leftover squares. Then write a number sentence.

40 − __30__ = __10__, so Mr. Yee has __10__ pencils left.

Look Back and Check

You can check if your number sentence matches your picture.

Draw a picture. Then write a number sentence.

1. Alice gathered 60 flowers.
She gives 40 flowers to her friend.
How many flowers does
Alice have left?

_____ − _____ = _____

2. Jake counts 30 ants.
He counts 10 bees.
How many more ants
than bees does he count?

_____ − _____ = _____

Name ______________________

Practice
11-6

Problem Solving: Draw a Picture and Write a Number Sentence

Draw a picture. Then write a number sentence.

1. Mike sees 40 birds.
Then 20 birds fly away.
How many birds are left?

_____ − _____ = _____

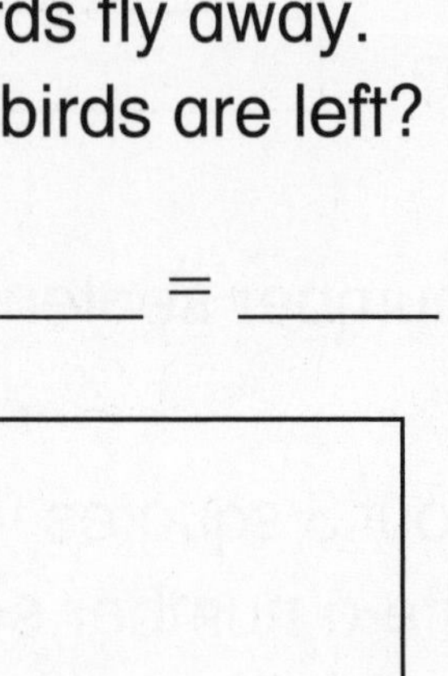

2. Sam has 60 stickers.
She gives away 50 stickers.
How many stickers does Sam have left?

_____ − _____ = _____

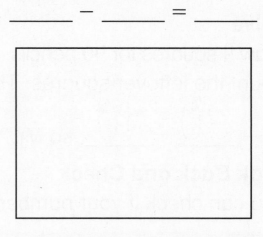

3. Tom drew 70 circles.
Then he drew 40 triangles.
How many more circles than triangles did he draw?

_____ − _____ = _____

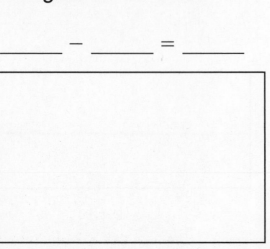

4. A farm has 30 cows and 20 pigs. How many more cows than pigs does the farm have?

_____ − _____ = _____

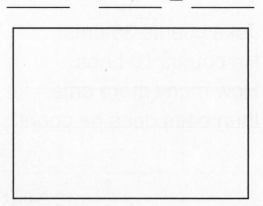

Name ______________________________

Reteaching
12-1

Comparing and Ordering by Length

You can compare and order objects by how long they are.

Line up the objects.

Look to see which object is longest and which is shortest.

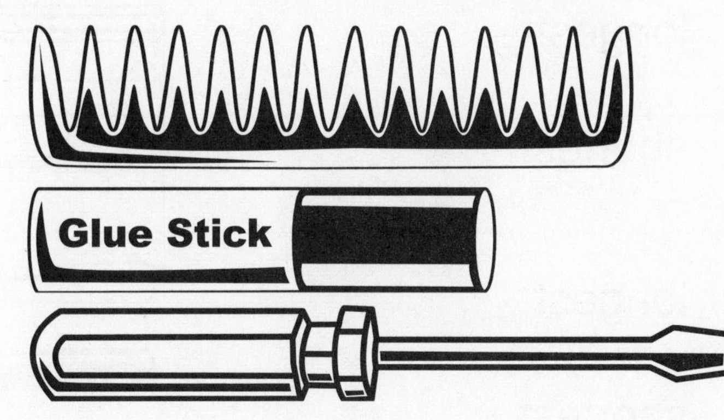

Then put the objects in order from longest to shortest.

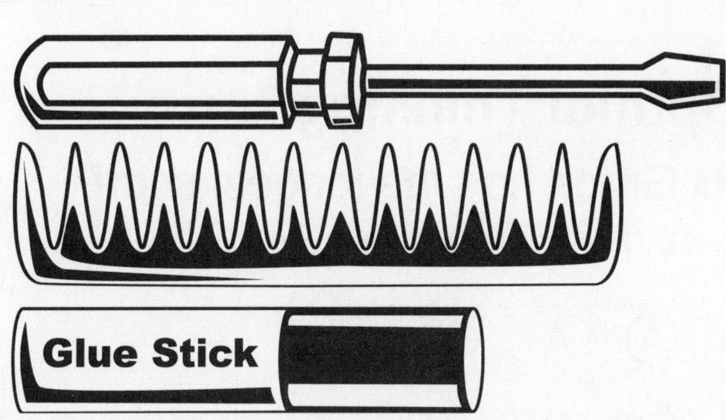

1. Complete the sentences.

Line A ______________________________

Line B ____________________________

Line C __________________________________

Line ______ is the longest. Line ______ is the shortest.

Reasoning

2. Use the clues to color the scarves.
The shortest scarf is red.
The green scarf is longer than the blue scarf.

Name ______________________________

Practice
12-1

Comparing and Ordering by Length

Draw lines to match the object with the word that describes it.

1. longest

shortest

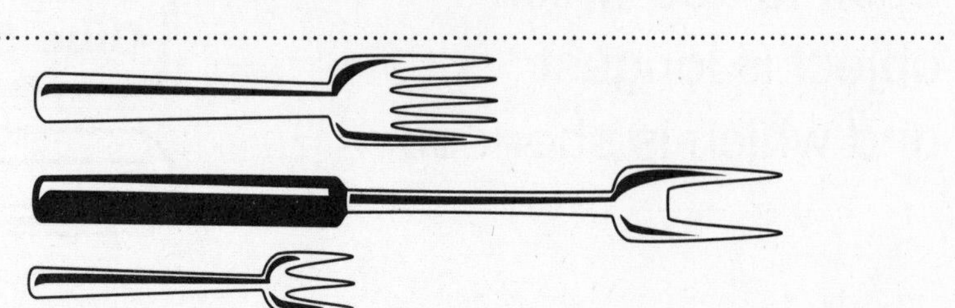

2. longest

shortest

Spatial Thinking

3. Grace has the longest scarf. Which child is Grace?

Ⓐ A

Ⓑ B

Ⓒ C

Ⓓ D

Reasoning

4. Use the clues to color the cars.

The shortest car is green.
The yellow car is longer than the red car.

Name ______________________

Indirect Measurement

You can compare two objects that are not together by using a third object.

The gray triangle is taller than the dotted triangle.
The white triangle is shorter than the dotted triangle.
So, the gray triangle is taller than the white triangle.

1. Circle the striped or gray object that is longer.

Use the white object to help.

2. Circle the dotted or black object that is shorter.

Use the white object to help.

3. Fill in the blanks.

The striped ribbon is ______________ than the gray ribbon.

The ___________ ribbon is shorter than the black ribbon.

Name ______________________

Practice
12-2

Indirect Measurement

Circle the black or white object that is shorter.
Use the gray object to help.

1.

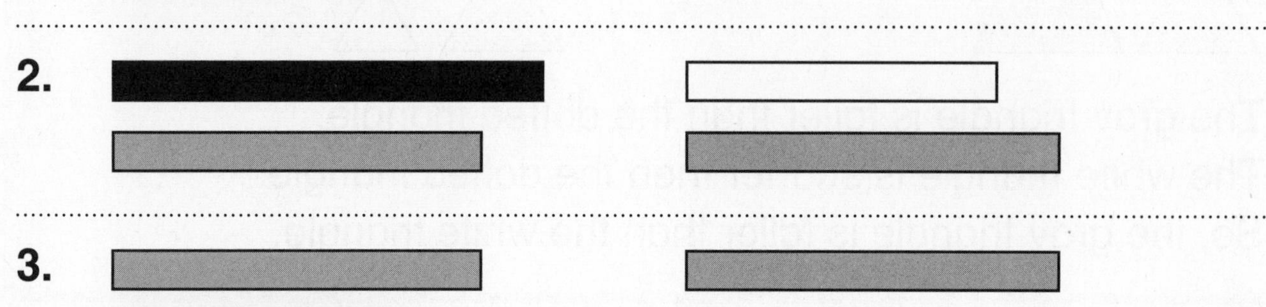

2.

3.

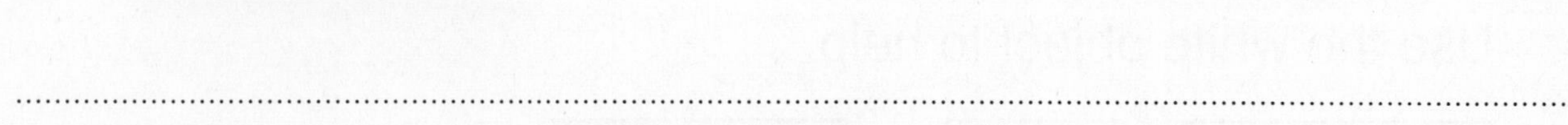

4. Which ribbon answers the riddle?

I am longer than the spotted ribbon.
I am shorter than the gray ribbon.

Ⓐ Ⓑ Ⓒ Ⓓ

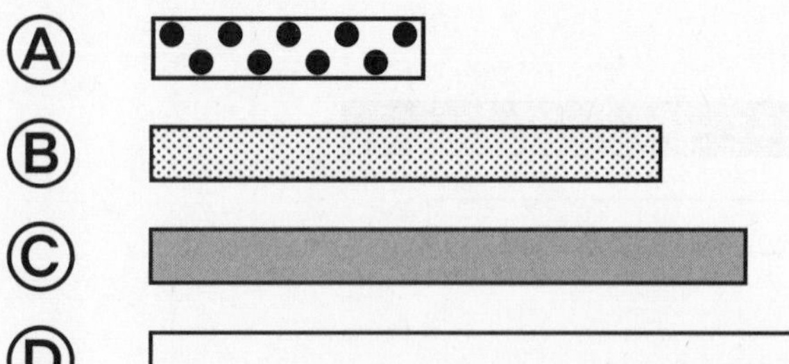

Name ____________________

Reteaching
12-3

Using Units to Estimate and Measure Length

Look at the paper clip.

Look at the string.

Estimate: How many paper clips long is the string?

About __5__ paper clips long.

Now measure.

Line up the first paper clip with the edge.

Be sure paper clips are all the same size.

Be sure you put the paper clips right next to each other.

Measure: About __3__ paper clips long.

That is close to the estimate.

Estimate. Then measure using paper clips.

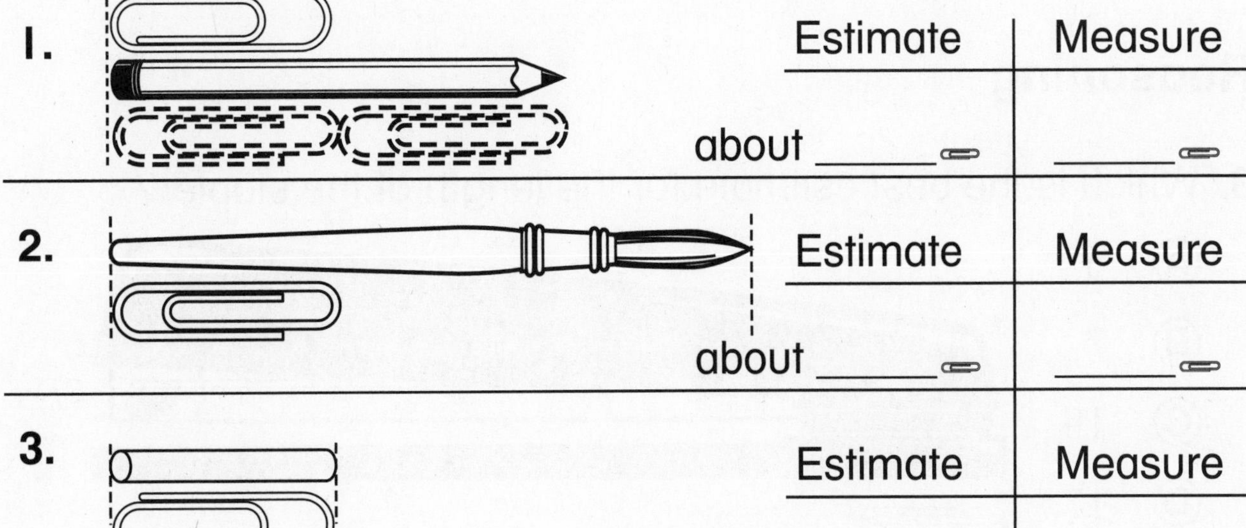

	Estimate	Measure
1.	about ______	______
2.	about ______	______
3.	about ______	______

Name ___________________

Practice
12-3

Using Units to Estimate and Measure Length

Estimate the length. Then use cubes to measure.

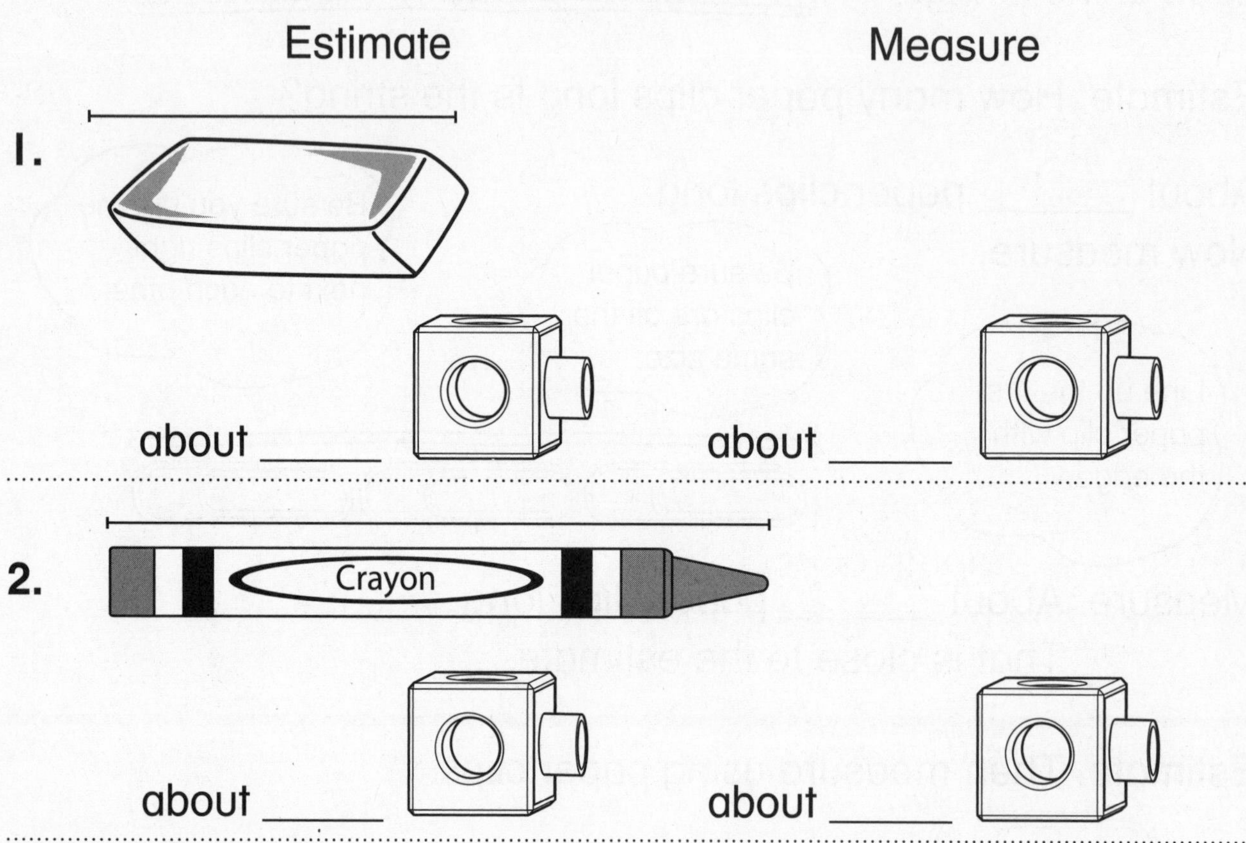

	Estimate	Measure
1.	about ____	about ____
2.	about ____	about ____

Reasoning

3. Which is the best estimate for the length of the stapler?

Ⓐ 6

Ⓑ 7

Ⓒ 14

Ⓓ 17

Name ______________________

More Measuring Length

You can compare and order the lengths of 3 objects.
First measure the length of each object. Use cubes to measure.

about 8 cubes   about 6 cubes   about 7 cubes

8 cubes is more than 6 cubes and more than 7 cubes.
The solid ribbon is the longest.

6 cubes is less than 8 cubes and less than 7 cubes.
The dotted ribbon is the shortest.

Measure the length of each ribbon.
Write which ribbon is the longest and which is the shortest.

Ribbon A   about 4 cubes

Ribbon B   about _____ cubes

Ribbon C   about _____ cubes

_____ cubes is more than _____ cubes and more than _____ cubes.

Ribbon _____ is the longest.

_____ cubes is less than _____ cubes and less than _____ cubes.

Ribbon _____ is the shortest.

Name ____________________

More Measuring Length

Find each object in your classroom.
Measure how long or how tall with cubes.

Measure

1. 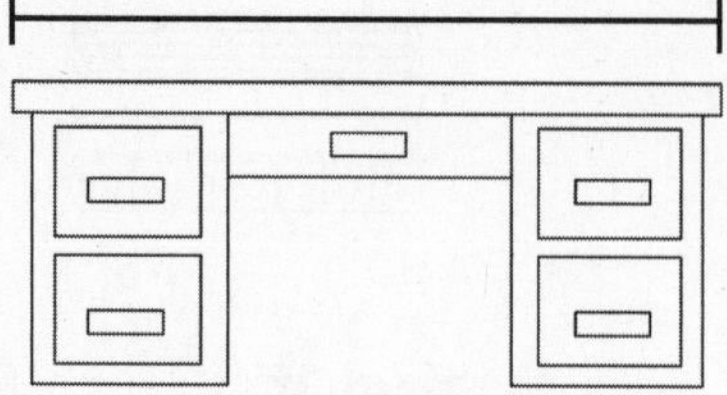

how long: about _____ cubes

2. 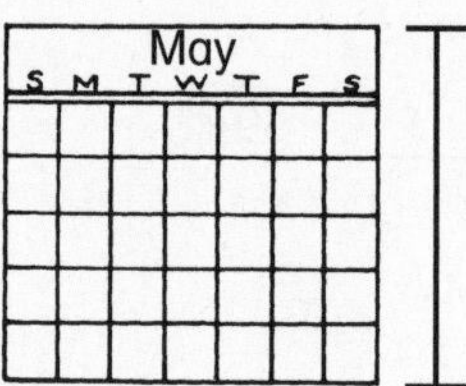

how long: about _____ cubes

3. 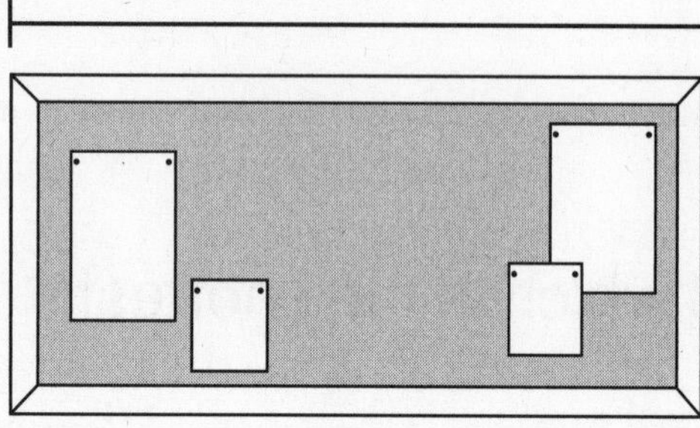

how long: about _____ cubes

4. Look at the desk and the bulletin board above.
Circle the longer object.
Draw an X on the shorter object.

5. Which shows these objects in order from shortest to tallest?

tall chair: about 30 cubes
tall book: about 10 cubes
tall basket: about 20 cubes

Ⓐ chair, book, basket
Ⓑ basket, chair, book
Ⓒ chair, basket, book
Ⓓ book, basket, chair

Name ______________________

Problem Solving: Use Reasoning

Predict: Will you need more chalk or more paper clips to measure the marker?

more 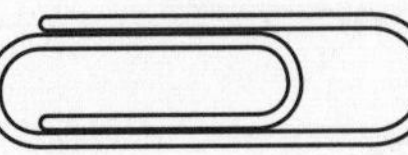 or more

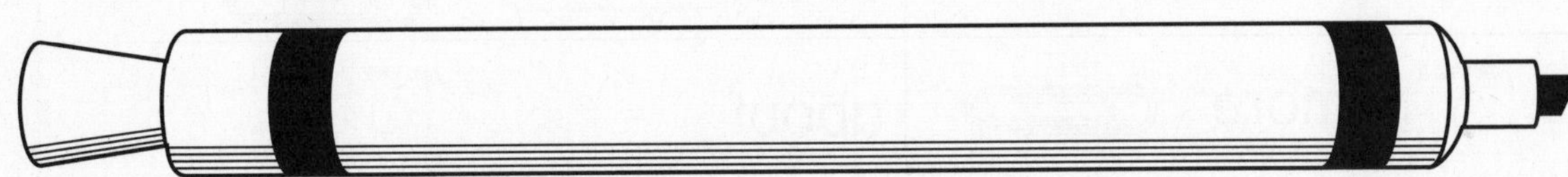

You must find out if you need more chalk or more paper clips.

Use reasoning to help you.
The paper clip is shorter.
You will probably need more paper clips.

more  more

Measure to check.

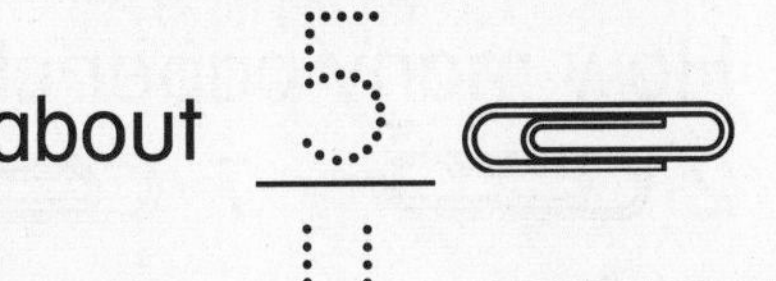

about 5 (paper clips)

about 4 (chalk)

Measure to check your prediction.
Was your prediction correct?

1. Will it take fewer pieces of chalk or fewer paper clips to measure the stapler? Circle your prediction. Then measure.

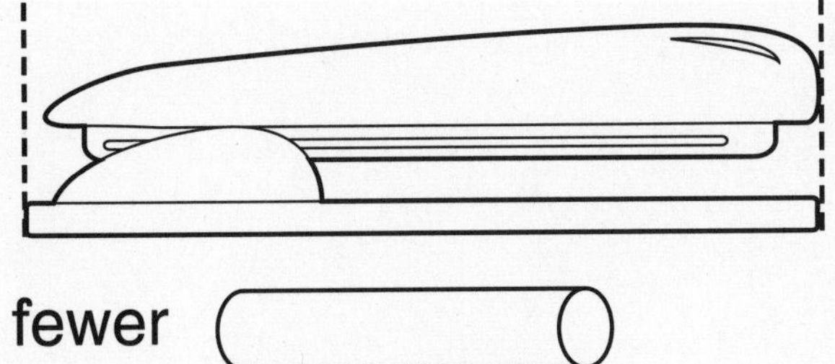

fewer (chalk)

fewer (paper clips)

Measure to check.

about ____ (paper clips)

about ____ (chalk)

Name ____________________

Problem Solving: Use Reasoning

Circle your estimate. Measure to check.

Estimate	Measure
1. fewer (cube) fewer (paper clip) (pencil)	about ______ (cube) about ______ (paper clip)
2. more (cube) more (paper clip) (crayon)	about ______ (cube) about ______ (paper clip)

Reasonableness

Circle your answer.

3. Eric has a paintbrush that is about 12 cubes long. How many paper clips long could it be?

2 (paper clip) 7 (paper clip) 12 (paper clip)

Spatial Thinking

4. Which object would you need the fewest of to measure how long the eraser is?

Ⓐ 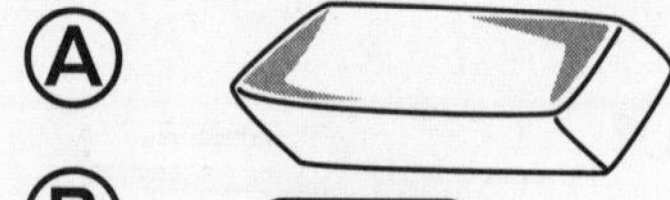

Ⓑ (small paper clip)

Ⓒ 

Ⓓ 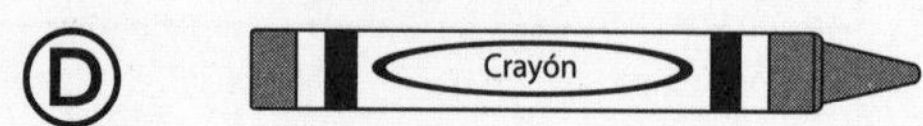

Name ________________________

Measuring using Different Units

This is 1 cube.

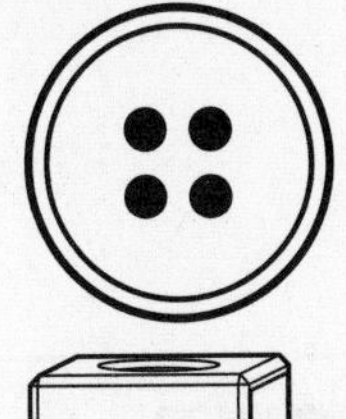

Cubes can be helpful for measuring shorter objects.

It's easier to say
"A ribbon is 3 cubes long"
than "A ribbon is not as long as a straw."
It's also easier to understand.

This is 1 straw.

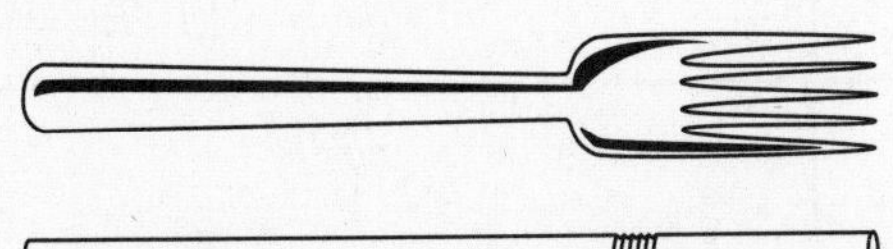

Straws can be helpful for measuring longer objects.

It's easier to say
"A rug is 6 straws long"
than "A rug is 32 cubes long."
It's also easier to understand.

Look at the items below. Decide if you would use cubes or straws to measure. Circle your answer.

1. 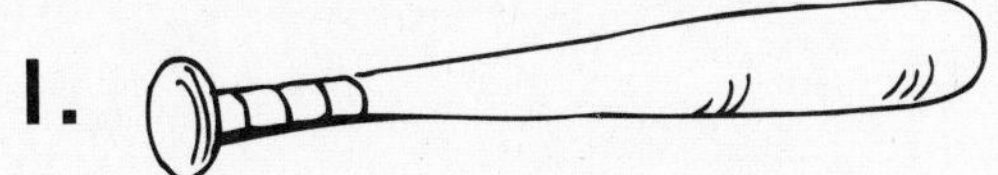 **cubes** **straws**

2.  **cubes** **straws**

3. 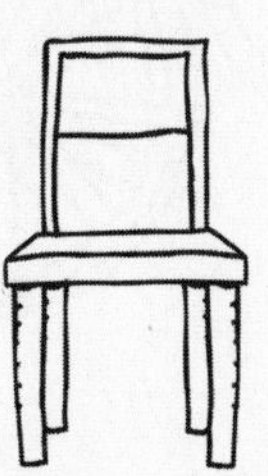 **cubes** **straws**

Name ___________________________

Practice
12-6

Measuring Using Different Units

Find each object in your classroom.
Estimate its length.
Then measure using straws.

	Estimate	Measure
1.	about ______ straws	about ______ straws
2.	about ______ straws	about ______ straws
3.	about ______ straws	about ______ straws

Reasonableness

4. Which is the best estimate for the length of the bicycle?

Ⓐ about 4 cubes

Ⓑ about 9 cubes

Ⓒ about 4 straws

Ⓓ about 9 straws

Name ______________________

Reteaching
13-1

Understanding the Hour and Minute Hands

The hour hand points to the 6. hour hand 6

The minute hand points to the 12. minute hand 12

When the minute hand points to 12, say o'clock. 6 o'clock

Write the time shown on each clock.

1. 

hour hand 3

minute hand 12

3 o'clock

2. 

hour hand ______

minute hand ______

______ o'clock

3. 

hour hand ______

minute hand ______

______ o'clock

4. 

hour hand ______

minute hand ______

______ o'clock

Reasoning

Write the times that come next.

5. 4 o'clock 5 o'clock ______ o'clock

6. 9 o'clock 10 o'clock ______ o'clock

Name ________________________________

Understanding the Hour and Minute Hands

Draw an hour hand and a minute hand to show each time.

1.

7 o'clock

2.

10 o'clock

3.

2 o'clock

4.

1 o'clock

5.

8 o'clock

6.

11 o'clock

Algebra

7. Mark the missing time.
2 o'clock, ______, 4 o'clock

Ⓐ 1 o'clock
Ⓑ 3 o'clock
Ⓒ 5 o'clock
Ⓓ 9 o'clock

8. Mark the missing time.
4 o'clock, ______, 6 o'clock

Ⓐ 10 o'clock
Ⓑ 5 o'clock
Ⓒ 3 o'clock
Ⓓ 2 o'clock

Name

Telling and Writing Time to the Hour

Both clocks show 4 o'clock.

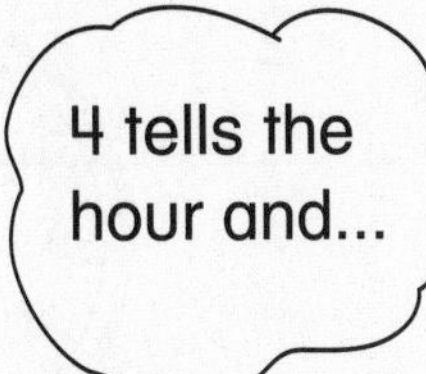

...00 tells the minutes.

The clocks show the same time.

Draw lines to match the clocks that show the same time.

1.

2.

3.

4.

Name ___________________________

Practice
13-2

Telling and Writing Time to the Hour

Draw the hands on each clock face.
Then write the time on the other clock.

1.

12 o'clock

2.

3 o'clock

3.

7 o'clock

4.

10 o'clock

Reasoning

5. Mark the clock that shows the same time as this clock.

Ⓑ 

Ⓒ 

Ⓓ 

Name ______________________

Telling and Writing Time to the Half Hour

When it is 7:30, the hour hand will be halfway between 7 and 8.
The minute hand will be on 6.

The hour hand is shorter than the minute hand.

Complete the sentences.
Then draw the hands on the clock face.

1. 

The hour hand will be halfway between 3 and 4.

The minute hand will be on 6.

2. 

The hour hand will be halfway between ______ and ______.

The minute hand will be on ______.

3. 

The hour hand will be halfway between ______ and ______.

The minute hand will be on ______.

Name ______________________________

Telling and Writing Time to the Half Hour

Write the time shown on each clock.

1.

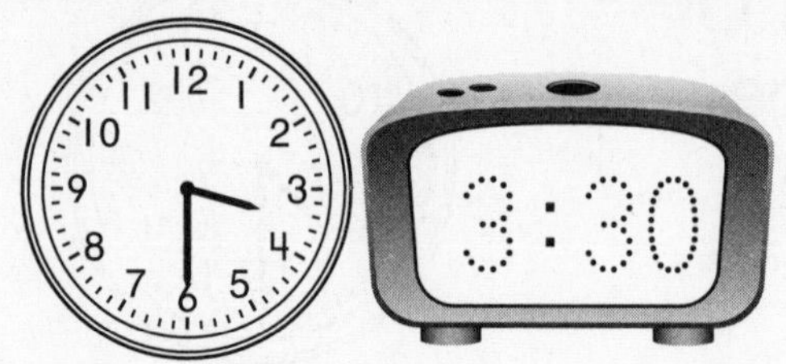

2.

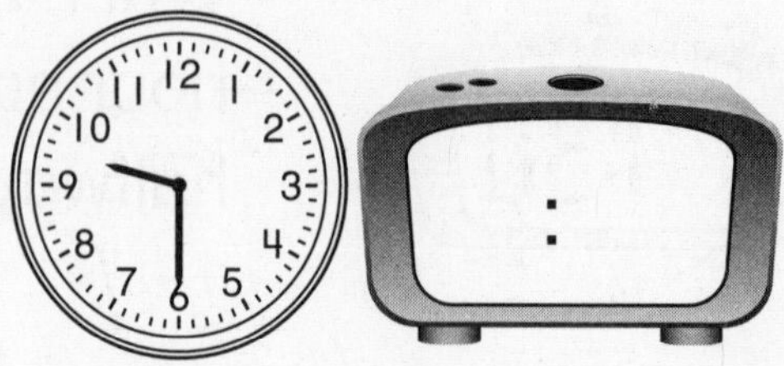

3.

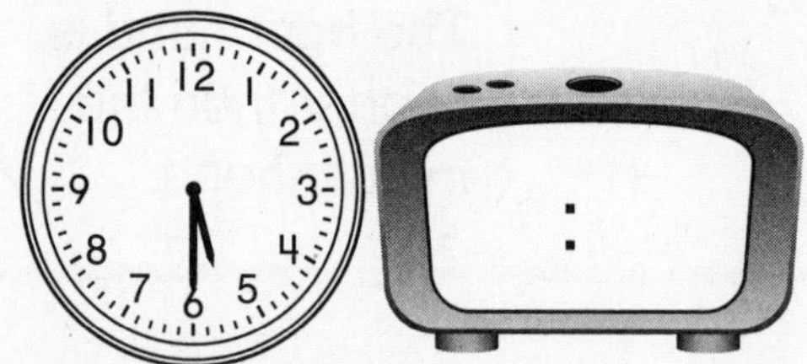

4.

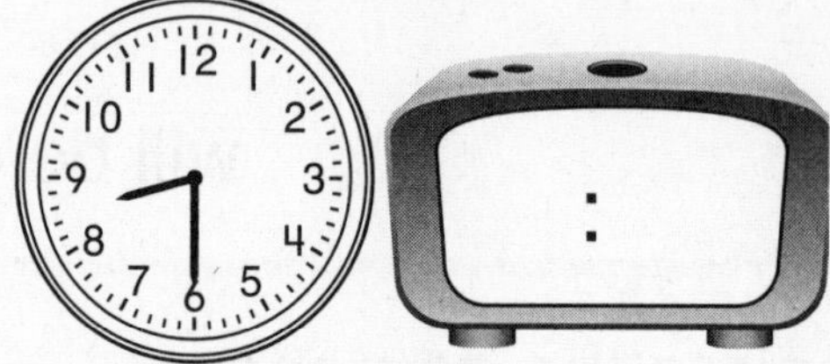

Journal

5. Show 3:00 on the first clock.
On the second clock, show the time 30 minutes later.
Is the hour hand still on 3?
Explain.

____

____

____

Name ______________________

Problem Solving: Use Data from a Table

Nature Center Schedule	
Activity	Time
Hike	9:00
Feed Turtles	10:00
Pick Flowers	11:00
Bird Watch	12:00

A schedule tells the time at which activities start.

Look for the activity.

The hike starts at 9:00.

Look at the time.

At 12:00 we bird watch.

Use the schedule to answer the questions. Circle your answer.

1. Which activity comes just before feeding the turtles?

Bird Watch   Hike   Pick Flowers

2. Which activity comes just after picking flowers?

Hike   Feed Turtles   Bird Watch

3. What time does the activity Pick Flowers begin?

9:00   10:00   11:00

4. Which activity starts at 10:00?

Hike   Feed Turtles   Bird Watch

Name ______________________

Practice
13-4

Problem Solving: Use Data from a Table

Use the schedule to answer the questions.

Time	Activity
9:00	Art
9:30	T-Ball
10:00	Music
10:30	Puppet Theater
11:00	Swimming

1. Which activity is at 9:00? ______________

2. Which activity is just before Music? ______________

3. Which activity is just after Puppet Theater? ______________

Reasoning

4. What time does Music begin?

9:00    9:30    10:00    10:30 Ⓓ

Name ______________________

Using Data from Real Graphs

You can use real objects to make a graph by arranging the objects in rows and columns.

This is a real-object graph because the counters are real objects.

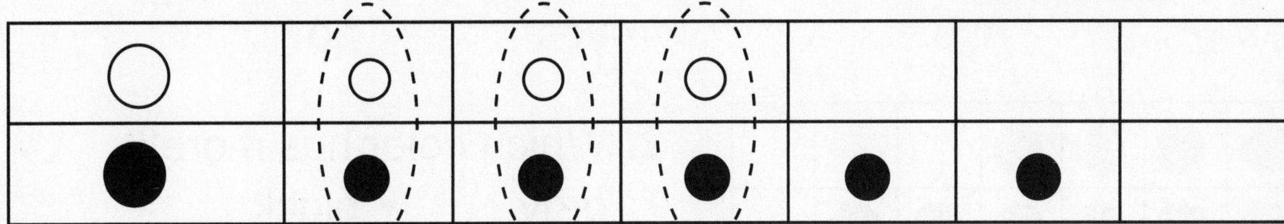

Circle each pair of counters in the graph. 

Is there the same number of colors? Yes  No

Which color has more?  Black White

How many counters do not have a partner? 2

1. Circle the correct answers. Write the number.

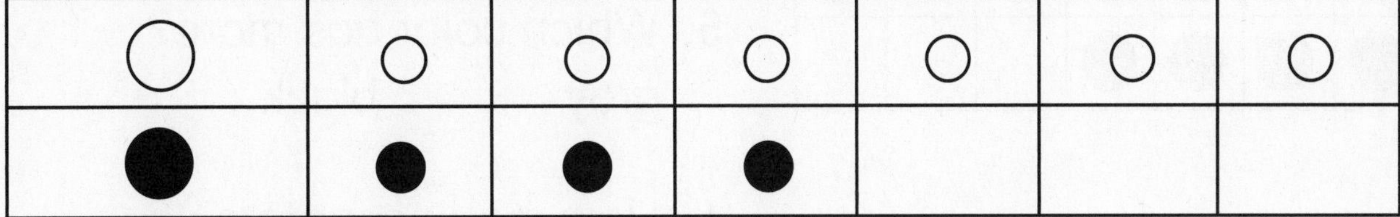

Is there the same number of colors? Yes No

Which color has more? Black White

How many counters do not have a partner? _______

Name ______________________

Practice
14-1

Using Data from Real Graphs

Look at the graph. Circle the correct answers.
Write the number.

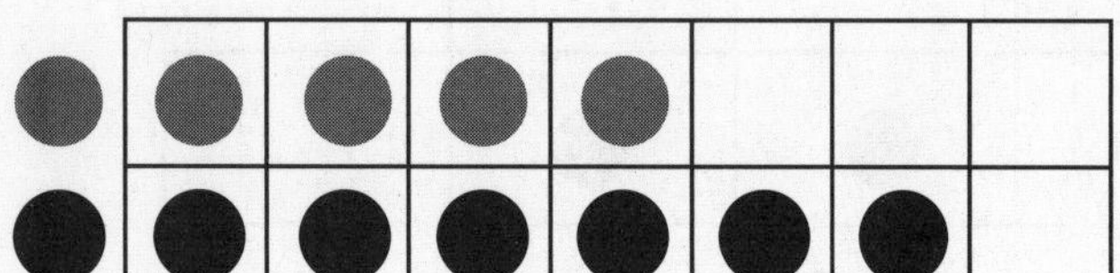

1. Is there the same number of colored counters?
   yes no

2. Which color has more?
   gray black

3. How many counters do not have a partner?
   ______

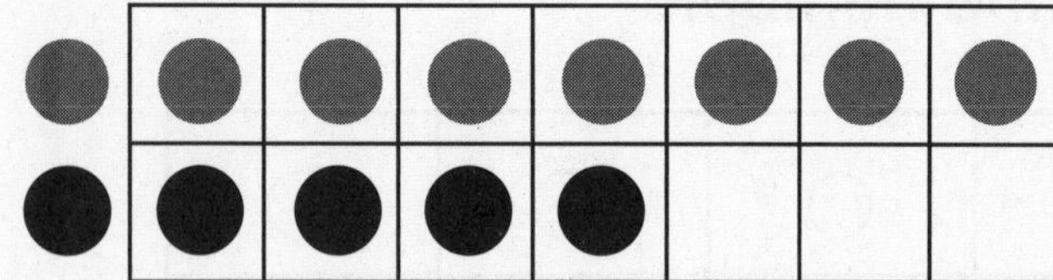

4. Is there the same number of colored counters?
   yes no

5. Which color has more?
   gray black

6. How many counters do not have a partner? ______

Journal

7. Draw black counters on the graph so there is 1 more black counter than gray.

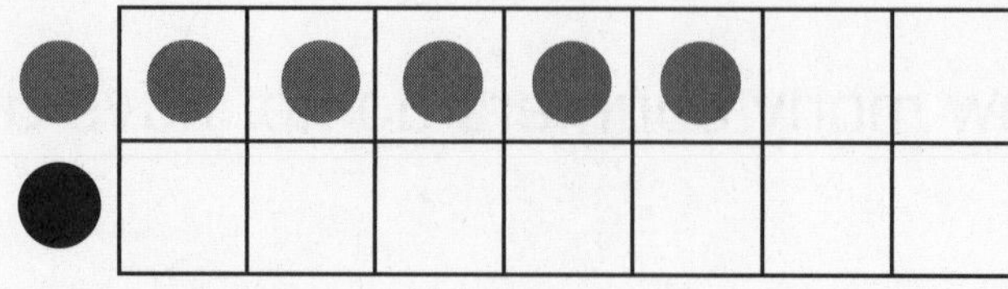

Name ______________________

Reteaching **14-2**

Using Data from Picture Graphs

You can use information in picture graphs to answer questions.

Each party hat stands for 1 vote.

10 children voted.

Favorite Party Hat						
Stripes	🎉	🎉	🎉	🎉		
Polka Dots	🎉	🎉	🎉	🎉	🎉	🎉

How many children voted for the hat with stripes? 4

How many children voted for the hat with polka dots? 6

How many more children voted for hats with dots than stripes?

2

Favorite Club						
Science	🔍	🔍	🔍	🔍	🔍	🔍
Art	🖌	🖌	🖌	🖌	🖌	

1. How many children in all voted for a favorite club? 11
2. How many children voted for Science Club? _______
3. How many fewer children voted for Art Club than the Science Club? _______
4. Which club got more votes? Science Art

Name ______________________

Practice
14-2

Using Data from Picture Graphs

Use the graph to answer the questions.

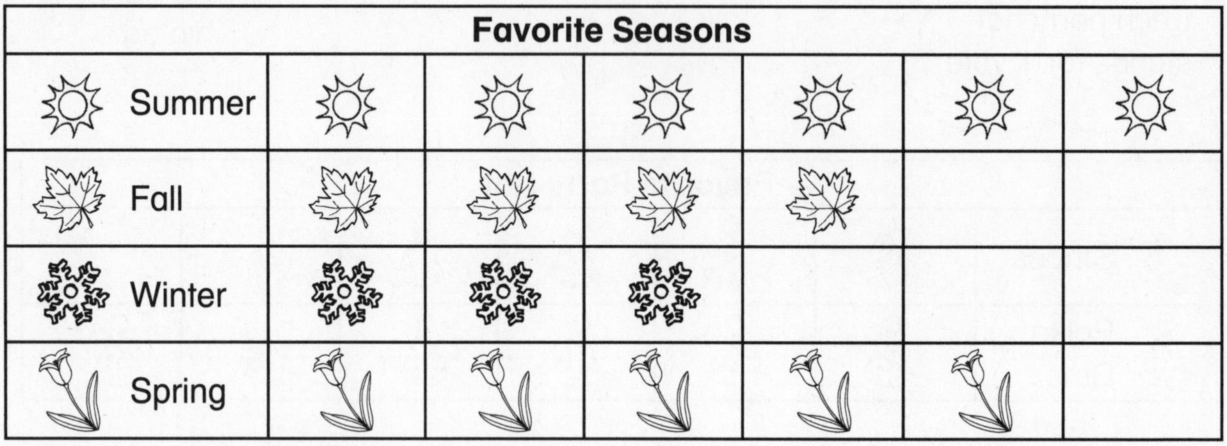

Favorite Seasons						
Summer	☼	☼	☼	☼	☼	☼
Fall	🍁	🍁	🍁	🍁		
Winter	❄	❄	❄			
Spring	🌷	🌷	🌷	🌷	🌷	

1. How many children chose winter? ________

2. How many fewer children chose Winter than Spring? ________

3. Which season did 4 children choose? ______________

Number Sense

4. How many more children chose summer than spring?

Ⓐ 11

Ⓑ 6

Ⓒ 5

Ⓓ 1

Reasoning

5. How many children voted in all?

Ⓐ 6

Ⓑ 14

Ⓒ 18

Ⓓ 20

Name ______________________

Using Data from Bar Graphs

You can use information in bar graphs to answer questions.

Each shaded square stands for 1 vote. The shaded squares in a row form a bar.

The least favorite day has the shortest bar.

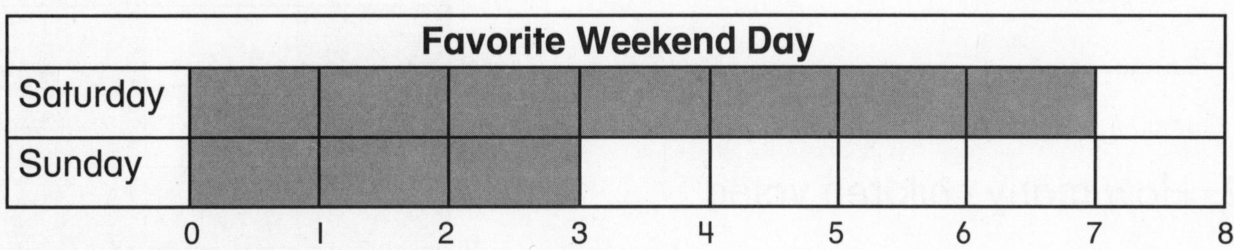

How many votes did each day get?

Saturday 7 Sunday 3

How many more children chose Saturday than Sunday? _____ more

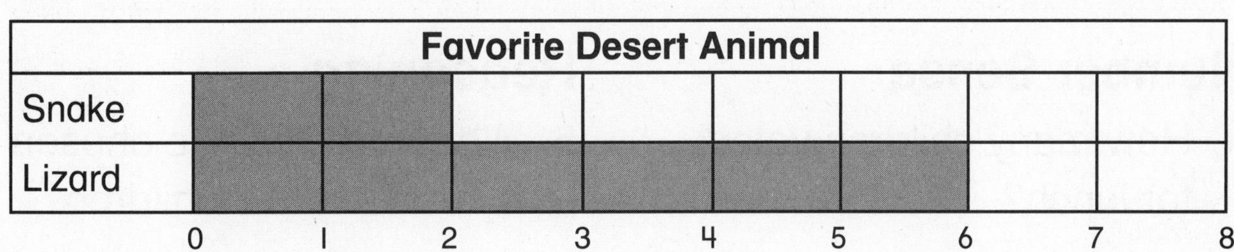

1. How many votes did each animal get?

Snake _____ Lizard _____

2. How many more children chose Lizard than Snake? _____ more

Name ______________________

Practice
14-3

Using Data from Bar Graphs

Use the graph to answer the questions.

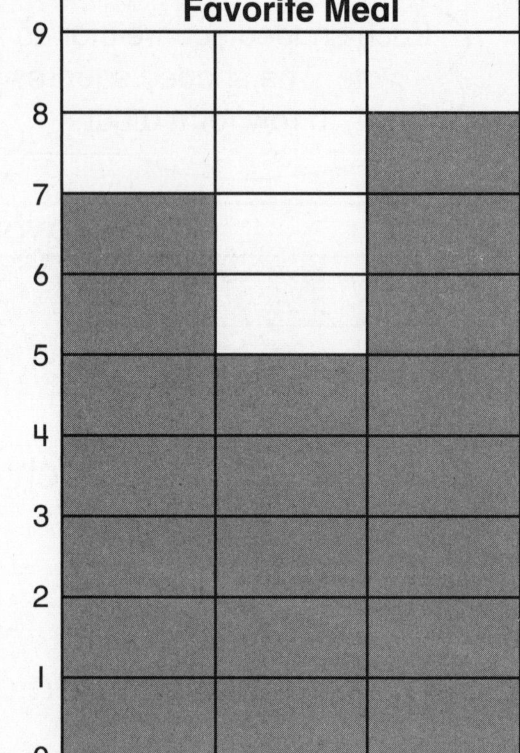

1. Mrs. Dunne's class made a graph of their favorite meals. Which meal is the least favorite?

____

2. How many children voted for breakfast? ________

3. How many more children voted for dinner than for lunch? ________

Number Sense

4. How many children voted for lunch?

- Ⓐ 5
- Ⓑ 7
- Ⓒ 8
- Ⓓ 9

Reasoning

5. Which meals were chosen by more than 6 children?

- Ⓐ breakfast and lunch
- Ⓑ breakfast and dinner
- Ⓒ breakfast, lunch, and dinner
- Ⓓ lunch and dinner

Name ___________________________

Reteaching
14-4

Collecting Data Using Tally Marks

The children made tally marks to show the ways children get to school.

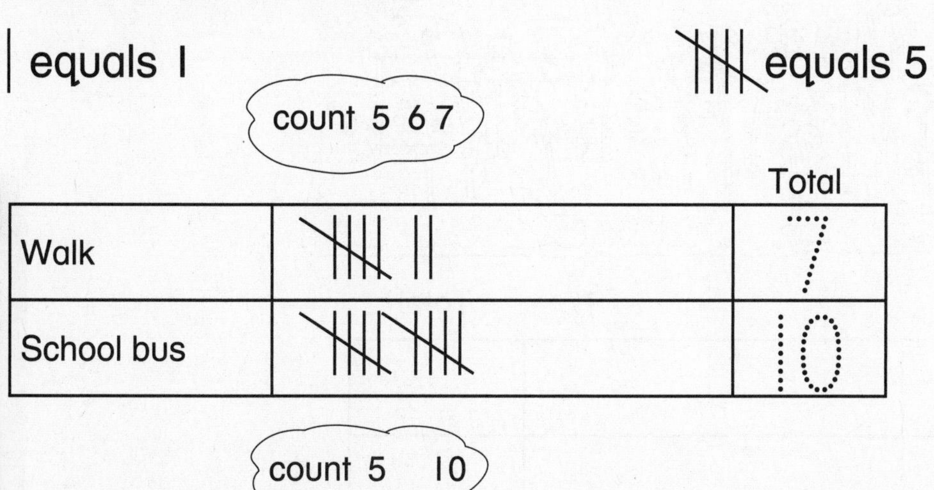

| equals 1
equals 5
count 5 6 7
Total
Walk
7
School bus
10
count 5 10

1. Color some balloons red. Color the rest blue. Use tally marks to show how many balloons there are in each color. Write the totals.

		Total
Red		
Blue		

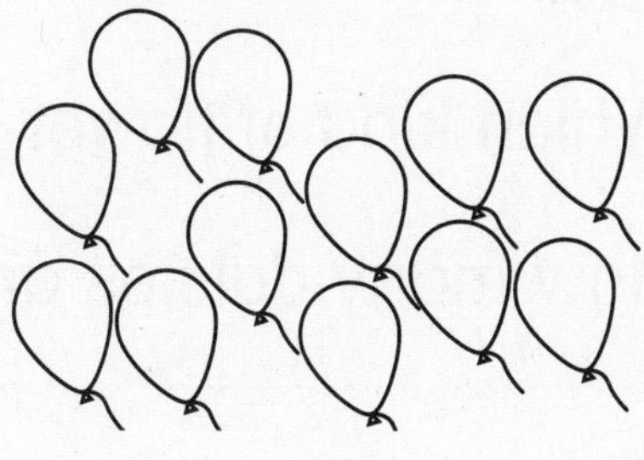

Use the tally chart to answer the questions.

2. Of which color are there more balloons? ____________

3. Of which color are there fewer balloons? ____________

4. How many balloons are there altogether? ________

Name ______________________

Practice
14-4

Collecting Data Using Tally Marks

Make tally marks to show how many flowers of each kind there are. Then write each total.

1.

		Total
Rose		
Tulip		
Daisy		

Use your tally to answer the questions.

2. Which kind of flower is there the most of? ______________

3. How many daisies and roses are there in all? ______

Algebra

4. How many more daisies than tulips are there?

Ⓐ 2
Ⓑ 3
Ⓒ 5
Ⓓ 7

Reasoning

5. How many roses and tulips are there in all?

Ⓐ 15
Ⓑ 13
Ⓒ 12
Ⓓ 3

Name ______________________________

Making Real Graphs

You can use a tally chart to make a real graph.

The chart shows Kim has 5 gray cubes and 3 white cubes.

Kim's Cubes – Tally Chart		
gray	𝍸	5
white	𝍷𝍷𝍷	3

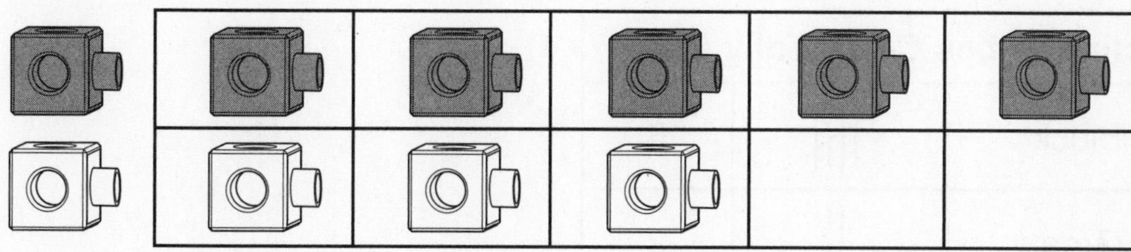

How many gray cubes will you put in the graph? 5

How many white cubes will you put in the graph? 3

1. Use the tally chart to make a graph with cubes.

Reba's Cubes – Tally Chart		
gray	𝍷𝍷𝍷𝍷	4
white	𝍸 𝍷	6

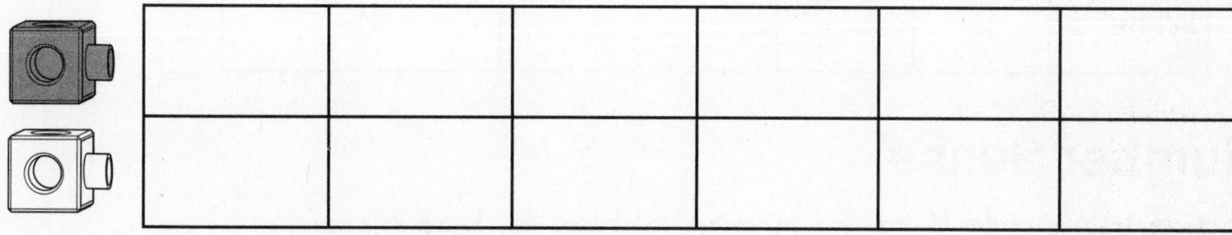

2. If you add 1 gray cube to the graph, how many gray cubes will there be? _____ gray cubes

Name ____________________

Practice
14-5

Making Real Graphs

Sarina used cubes to make a picture of a cow.
She used a tally chart to show how many cubes of each color she used in her picture.

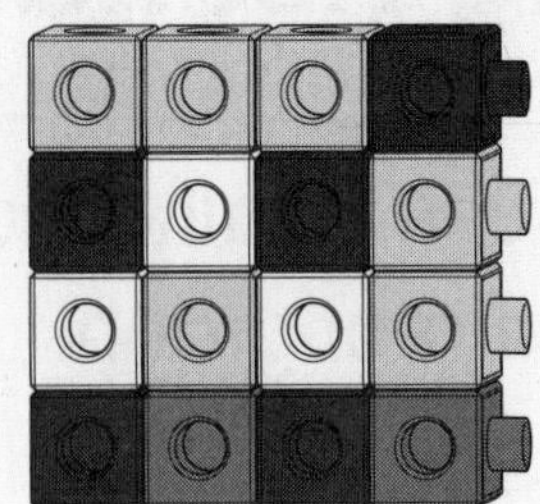

1. Use the tally chart to make a graph.

Connecting Cubes Cow – Tally Chart			
	Black	卌	5
	Green	‖	2
	Blue	卌 |	6
	White	|||	3

Connecting Cubes Cow – Real Graph						
Black						
Green						
Blue						
White						

Number Sense

2. Sarina adds 4 more green cubes to her picture.
How many green cubes are there now?

10 Ⓐ   9 Ⓑ   7 Ⓒ   6 Ⓓ

Name ______________________

Making Picture Graphs

You can use a tally chart to make a picture graph.

Draw a flower for each tally mark.

Favorite Flower	
Daisy	|||| (5)
Tulip	|||

Favorite Flower					
Daisy	✿	✿	✿	✿	✿
Tulip	✿	✿	✿		

In how many boxes did you draw a daisy? 5

In how many boxes did you draw a tulip? 3

How many more daisies did you draw than tulips? 2

1. Ask your friends to vote for apple juice or milk as their favorite drink. Make a tally chart and a picture graph.

Favorite Drink	
Juice	
Milk	

Apple Juice					
Milk					

2. How many of your friends voted for apple juice? ______

3. How many more friends voted for Apple Juice than Milk? ______

Name ____________________

Practice 14-6

Making Picture Graphs

Favorite Items to Collect	Tally Marks	Totals
Shells	|||	3
Stamps	~~||||~~ |	6
Coins	||||	4

1. Use the information in the tally chart. Draw pictures to make a picture graph.

Favorite Items to Collect						
Shells						
Stamps						
Coins						

2. Which item is the least favorite to collect? ____________

3. Write the items in order from most favored to least favored.

____________ ____________ ____________

most favored — least favored

Number Sense

4. How many more people chose stamps than coins?

Ⓐ 10 Ⓑ 6 Ⓒ 4 Ⓓ 2

Name ______________________

Problem Solving: Make a Graph

Each square that is colored gray equals 1 child's selection.

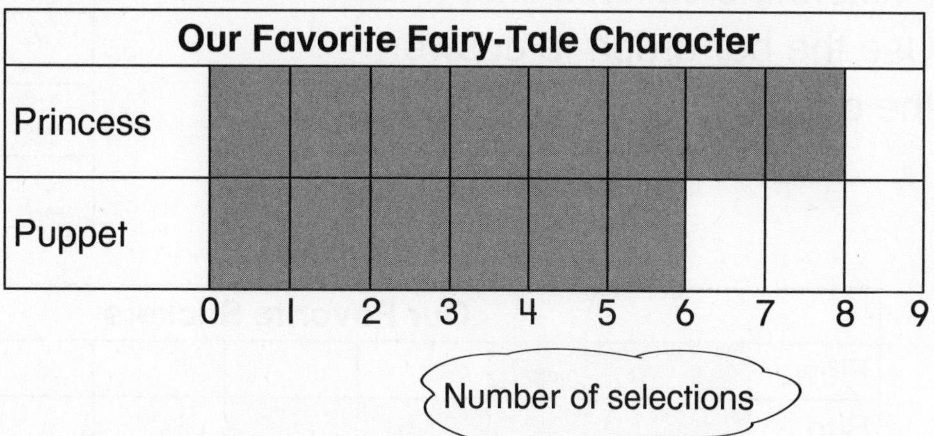

Look at the number of squares colored for the princess.

How many squares are colored? 8

Look at the number of squares colored for the puppet.

How many squares are colored? 6

How many more children chose the Princess than the Puppet?

______ more

1. Ask your classmates to select their favorite snack. Color to make a bar graph. Then answer the questions.

Yogurt									
Fruit									
	0	1	2	3	4	5	6	7	8 9

2. Which snack is the favorite? ______________________

3. How many children selected fruit? ______________________

Name ______________________________

Practice
14-7

Problem Solving: Make a Graph

The chart shows what kinds of stickers the children like. Use the bar graph to answer the questions.

Favorite Stickers	
Flower	2
Bird	4
Boat	7
Dog	3

Our Favorite Stickers

Flower	■	■						
Bird	■	■	■	■				
Boat	■	■	■	■	■	■	■	
Dog	■	■	■					

0 1 2 3 4 5 6 7 8

1. Which sticker do children like the most? ________

2. How many fewer children chose Flower stickers than Bird stickers? ______ fewer

3. Number Sense
Which of the following shows the stickers in order from most favorite to least favorite?

Ⓐ dog, boat, bird, flower

Ⓑ flower, dog, bird, boat

Ⓒ flower, bird, boat, dog

Ⓓ boat, bird, dog, flower

Name ______________________

Identifying Plane Shapes

Reteaching
15-1

Plane Shapes

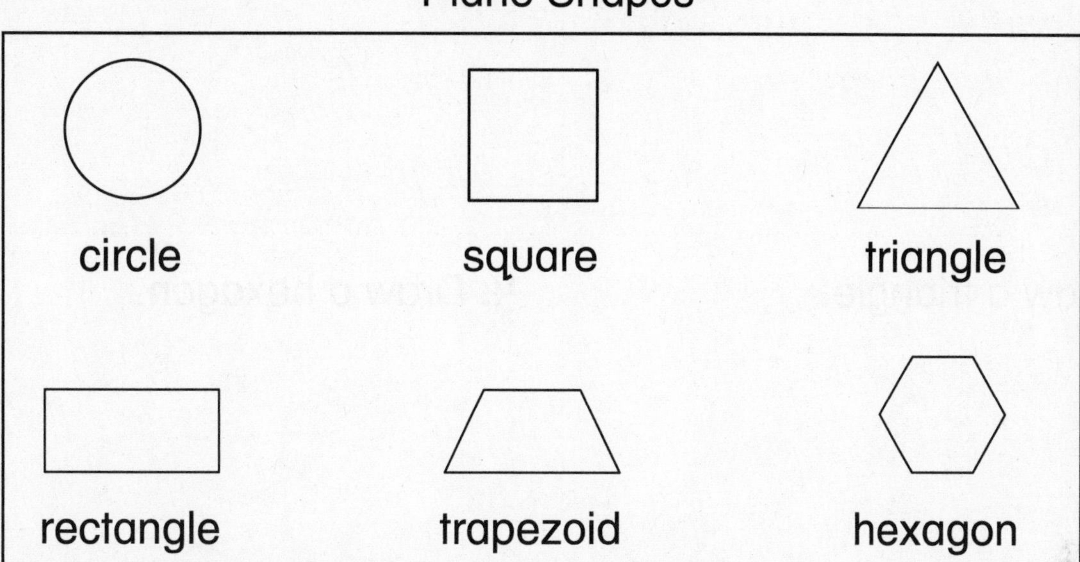

Color the shapes that are the same.
Circle the name of the shapes you colored.

1. 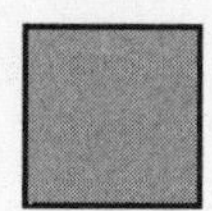 

square

triangle

2. 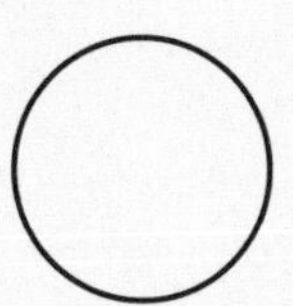 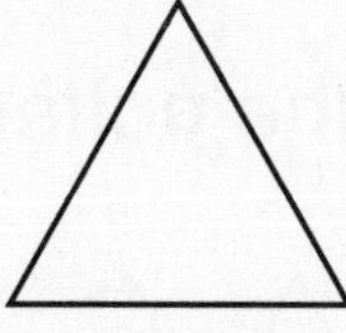 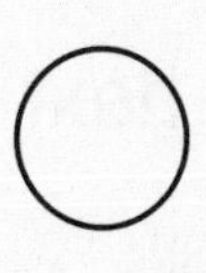

square

circle

3. 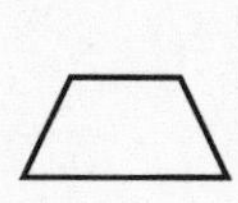 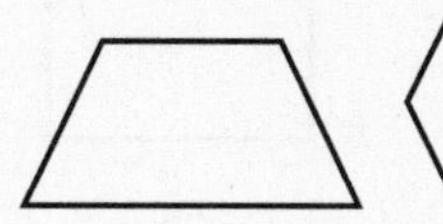

hexagon

trapezoid

Name ____________________

Identifying Plane Shapes

1. Draw a rectangle.

2. Draw a square.

3. Draw a triangle.

4. Draw a hexagon.

Geometry

5. I am not a rectangle.
I am not a triangle.
What shape am I?

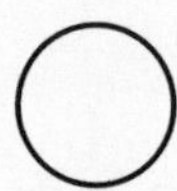
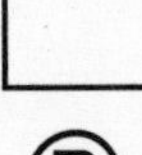

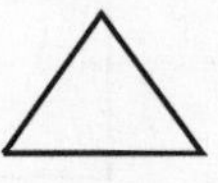

Ⓐ Ⓑ Ⓒ Ⓓ

Algebra

6. Which shape comes next in the pattern?

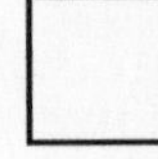
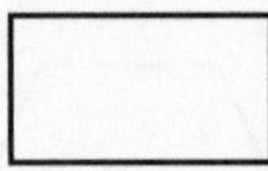
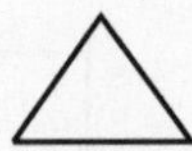

Ⓓ

Name ______________________________

Problem Solving: Make an Organized List

You can use pattern blocks to make another shape.

How many 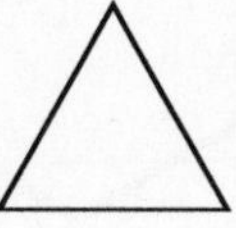 can fit in  ? 2  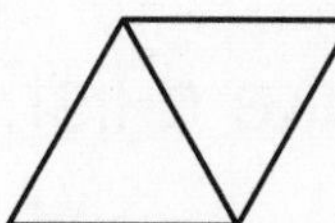

How many 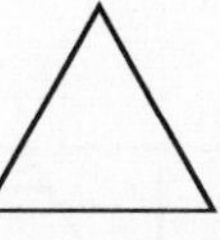 can fit in 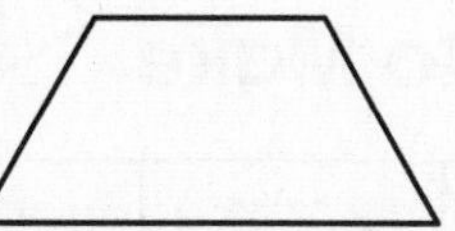 ? 3 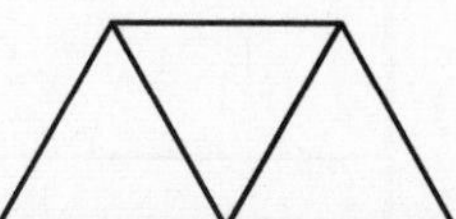

There are 3 ways you can make this shape using pattern blocks.

Complete the organized list.

Ways to Make			
	triangle	rhombus	trapezoid
Way 1	4	0	0
Way 2			
Way 3			

Name ______________________

Problem Solving: Make an Organized List

How many ways can you make this shape using pattern blocks?

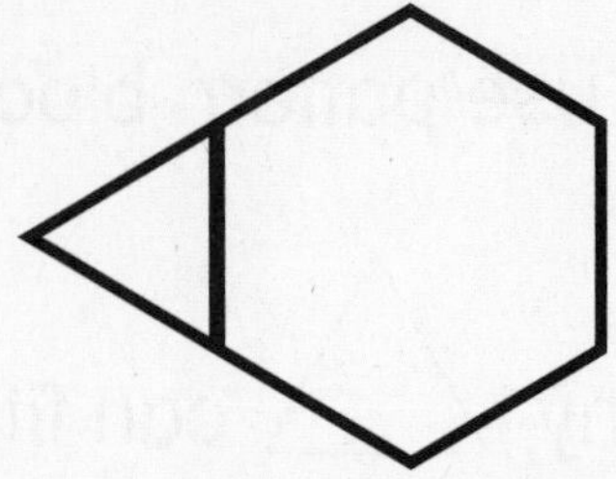

1. Make a list.

Ways to Make				
Shapes I Used	trapezoid	hexagon	triangle	rhombus
Way 1				
Way 2				
Way 3				
Way 4				
Way 5				
Way 6				

Journal

2. How many ways can you use pattern blocks to make a ▱? Explain.

Name ____________________

Properties of Plane Shapes

Count the straight sides.

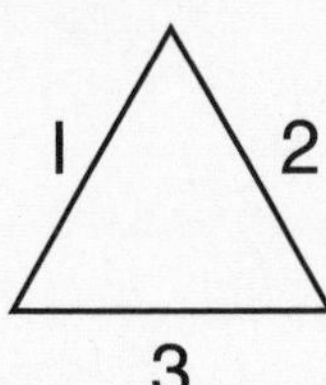

A triangle has

___ straight sides.

Count the corners.

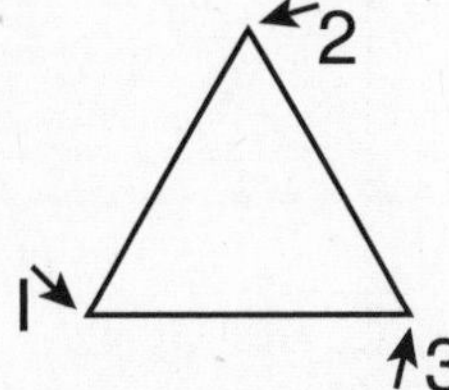

A triangle has

___ corners.

A circle has __0__ sides.

A circle has __0__ corners.

Count the straight sides. Count the corners.

1. 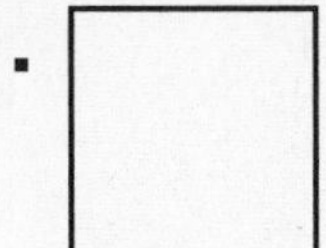

A square has __4__ straight sides.

A square has __4__ corners.

2. 

A rectangle has ______ straight sides.

A rectangle has ______ corners.

3. Draw a shape with more than 4 corners.

4. Draw a shape with more than 4 straight sides.

Name ______________________

Practice
15-3

Properties of Plane Shapes

1. Draw a shape with 4 corners.

2. Draw a shape with more than 4 straight sides.

3. Draw a shape with 3 sides and 3 corners.

4. I have 4 sides and 4 corners. Which shape am I?

Ⓐ circle
Ⓑ trapezoid
Ⓒ hexagon
Ⓓ triangle

Reasoning

5. Here is the way Brian sorted some plane shapes.

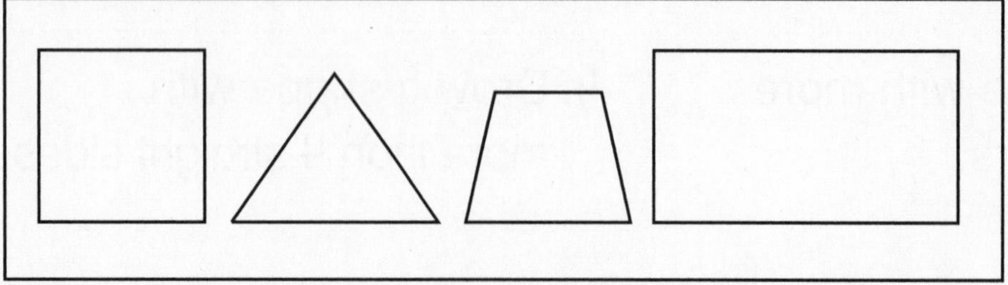

Circle the question Brian might have asked.

Does it have fewer than 5 corners?
Does it have more than 5 straight sides?

Name ___________________

Reteaching
15-4

Building with Shapes

You can use pattern blocks to make a picture.

Make a candle.

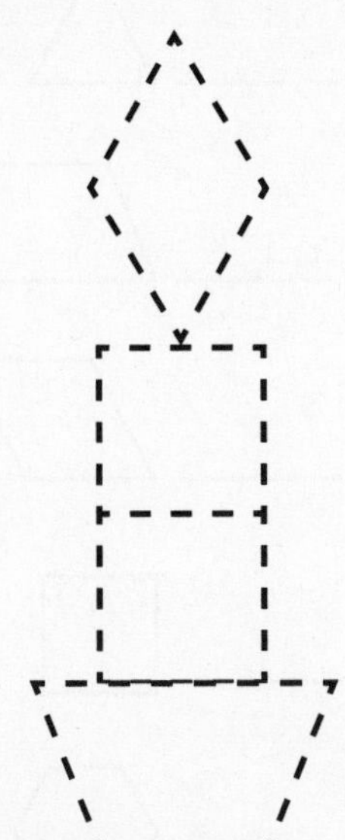

Then write how many of each shape you used.

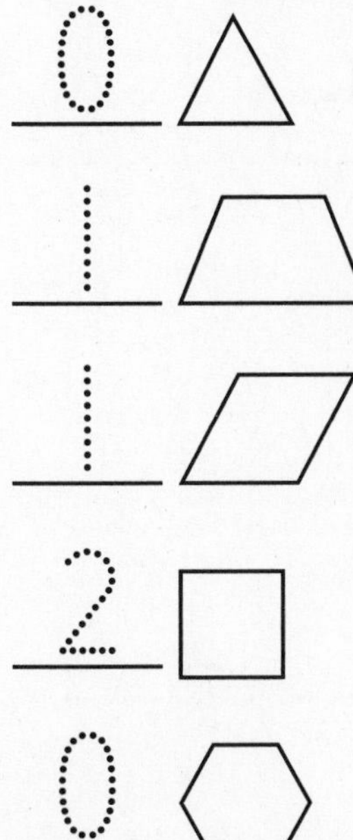

Use pattern blocks to make a picture.
Write how many of each shape you used.

1. The picture is a tree.

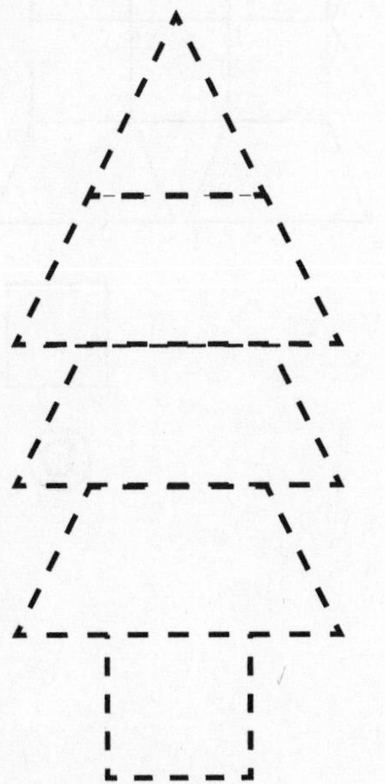

____ (triangle)

____ (trapezoid)

____ (rhombus)

____ (square)

____ (hexagon)

Name ____________________

Practice
15-4

Building with Shapes

Use pattern blocks to make a picture.
Write how many of each shape you used.

1.

____ triangle

____ trapezoid

____ rhombus

____ square

____ hexagon

Spatial Thinking

2. José is making a picture of a bunny.
He is missing one block.
Which block is missing?

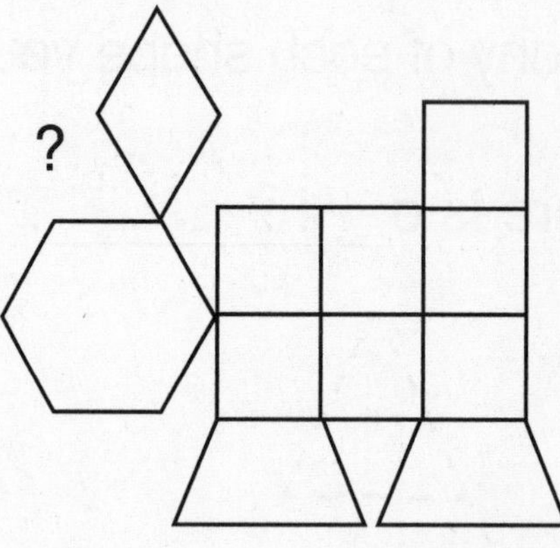

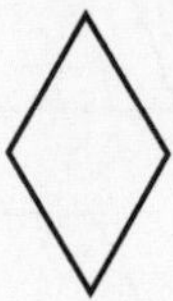

Ⓐ

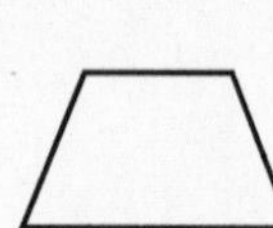

Ⓑ

Ⓒ

Ⓓ

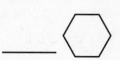

Name ______________________

Making New Shapes from Shapes

Give 3 ways you can make this shape using pattern blocks.

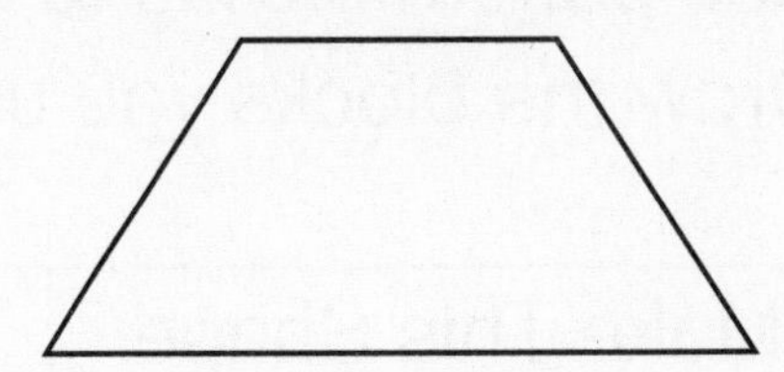

You need to find all the ways that pattern blocks can make the shape.

A list can help you keep track.

Ways to Make ⏢			
Shapes I Used	⏢	△	▱
Way 1	1	0	0
Way 2	0	3	0
Way 3	0	1	1

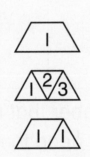

Did you find 3 ways? How do you know?

Give 3 ways you can make this shape using pattern blocks. Complete the list.

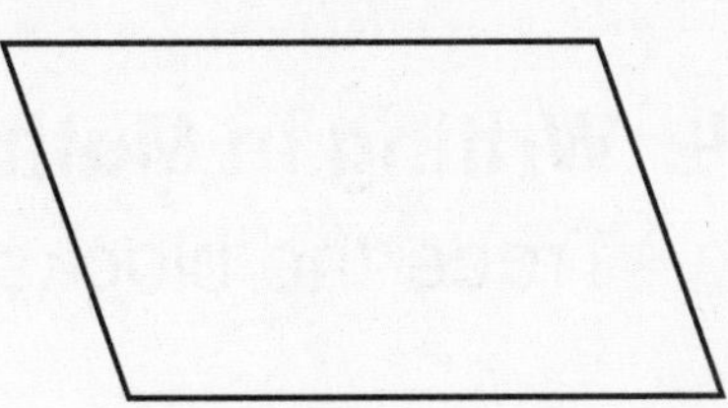

Ways to Make ▱			
Shapes I Used	⏢	▱	△
Way 1	1	0	1
Way 2			
Way 3			

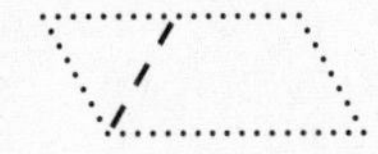

Name ______________________________

Making New Shapes from Shapes

Use pattern blocks to make each shape.
Draw the blocks you used.

Make This Shape	Use This Shape	Draw the Shapes
1. ⬡	⏢	
2. ⏢	△	

3. Mark the number that tells how many △ you need to make a ⬡.

4	5	6	7
Ⓐ	Ⓑ	Ⓒ	Ⓓ

4. **Writing in Math** Use pattern blocks to make a new shape. Trace the blocks you used below.

Name ______________________

Identifying Solid Figures

These shapes are solid figures.

sphere	cone	cylinder	cube	rectangular prism
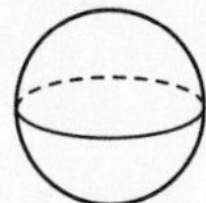				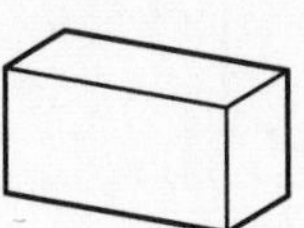

Color the spheres red. Color the cones blue.
Color the cylinders green. Color the cubes orange.
Color the rectangular prisms yellow.

1.

Name ______________________________

Practice
15-6

Identifying Solid Figures

1. Color each solid figure below.

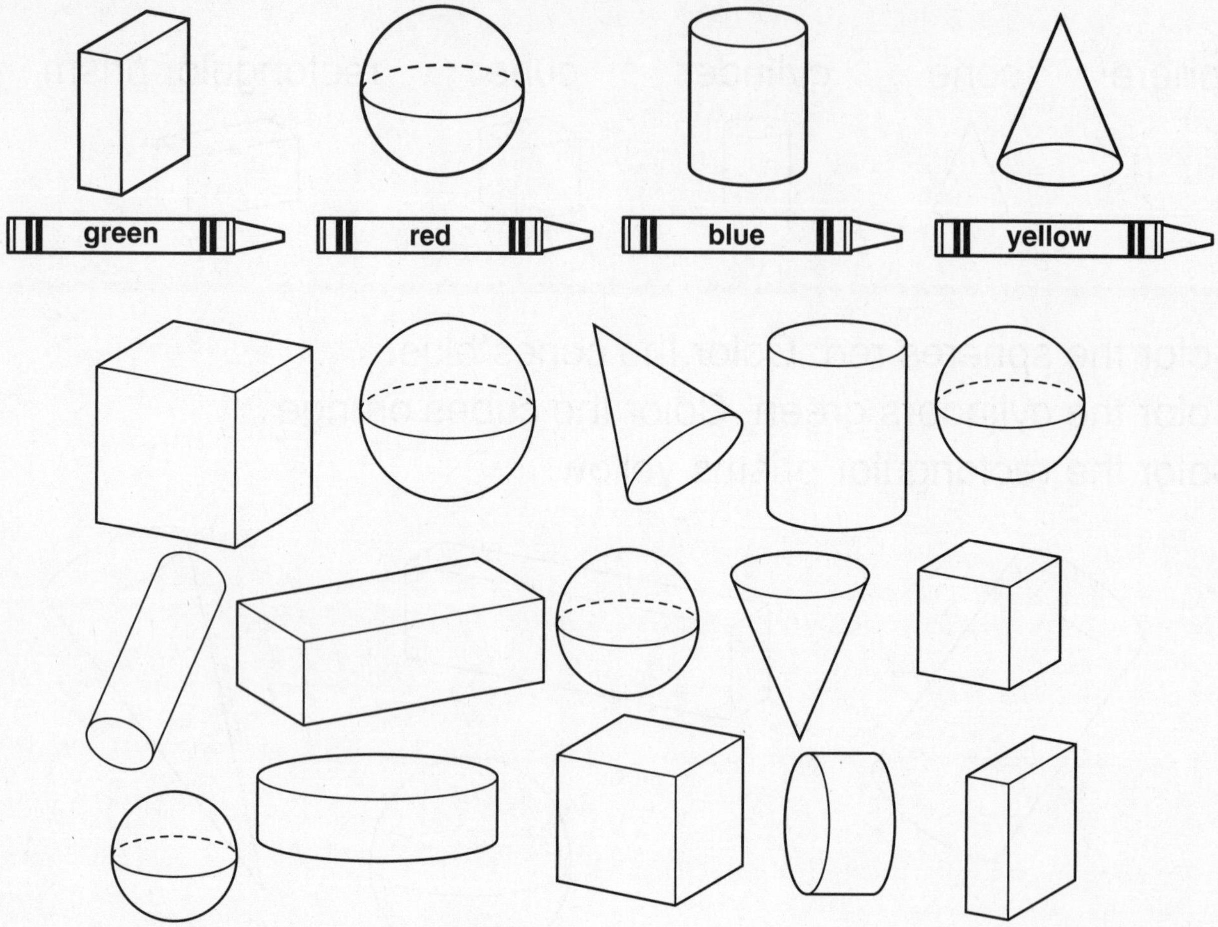

green
red
blue
yellow

2. Now put an X on each cube.

Algebra

3. Which solid figure comes next?

?

A
B
C
D

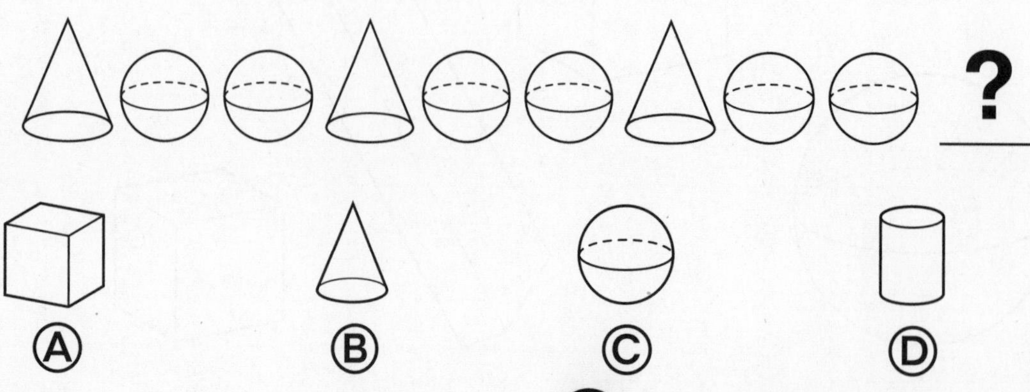

Name ______________________________

Reteaching
15-7

Flat Surfaces and Vertices

These solid figures have **flat surfaces.**

 cone

 cylinder

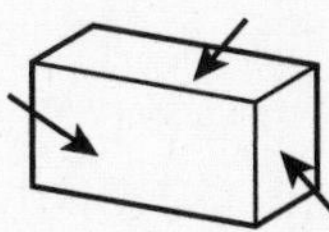 rectangular prism

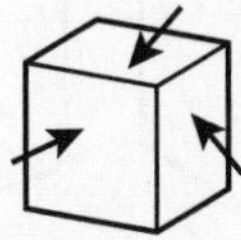 cube

These solid figures have **vertices** or corners.

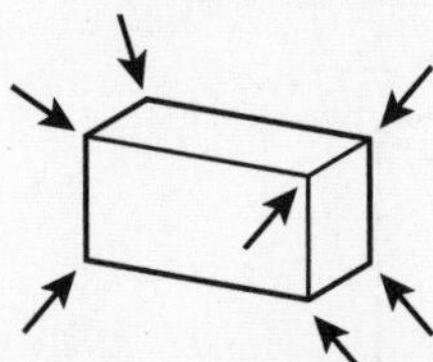

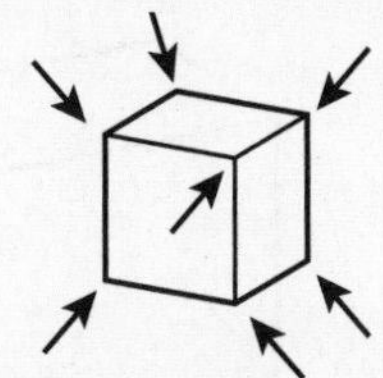

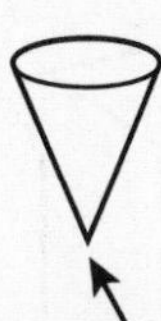

Use solid figures to complete the table.

Solid Figure	Number of Flat Surfaces	Number of Vertices (Corners)
1.  cube	6	8
2.  cone		
3. 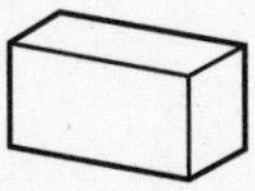 rectangular prism		
4. 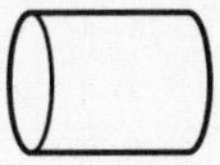 cylinder		

Name ______________________________

Flat Surfaces and Vertices

Circle the solid figure that answers each question.

1. Which solid figure has 2 flat surfaces and 0 vertices?

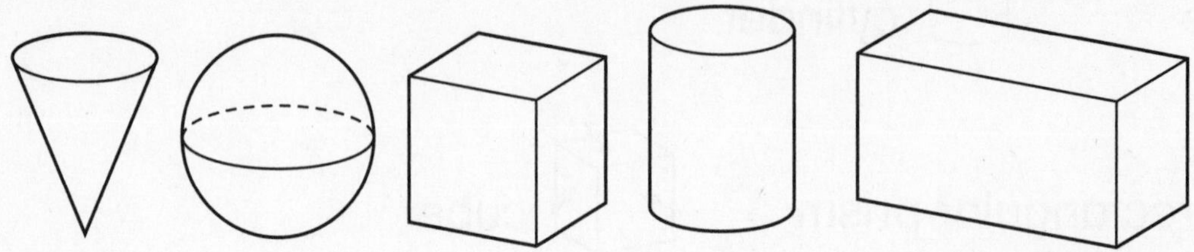

2. Which solid figure has 0 flat surfaces and 0 vertices?

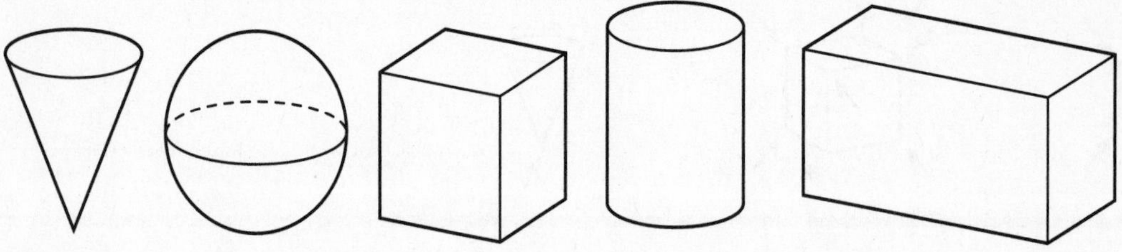

3. Which solid figures have 6 flat surfaces and 8 vertices?

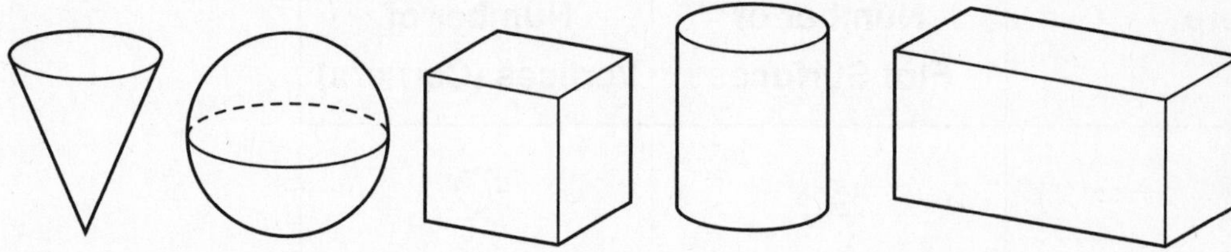

Reasoning

4. Mark the solid figure that answers the question.

I have 1 flat surface. I have 1 vertex.
Which solid figure am I?

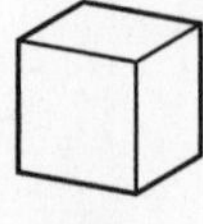

Name ________________________________

Reteaching
15-8

Sorting Solid Figures

You can sort solid figures in many different ways.

Some figures have flat surfaces and cannot roll. 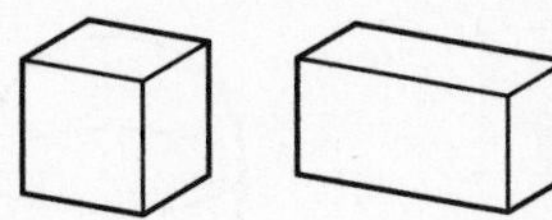

Some have flat surfaces and can roll. 

Some have vertices. 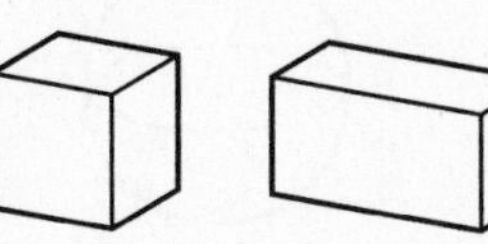 

Some have no vertices. 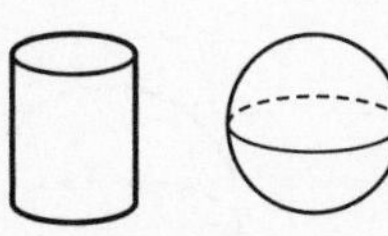

Circle the solid figure that follows the sorting rule.

1. It has all flat surfaces. 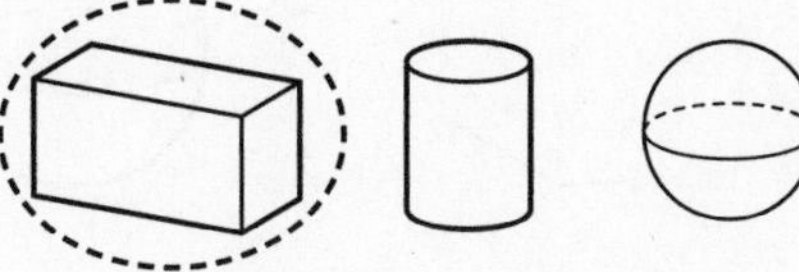

2. It has no flat surfaces. 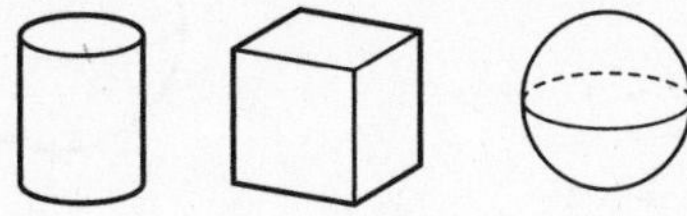

3. It can roll. 

4. Circle the 2 figures that have flat surfaces and curves. 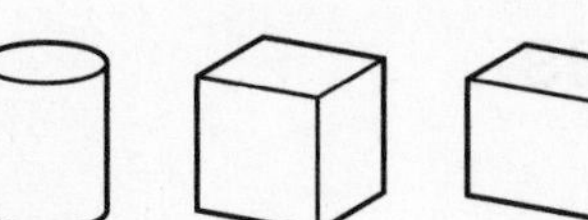  

Name ______________________

Sorting Solid Figures

Read the sorting rule.
Circle the solid figures that follow the rule.

1. 1 flat surface

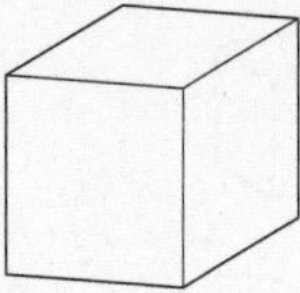 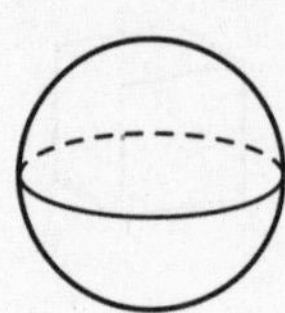 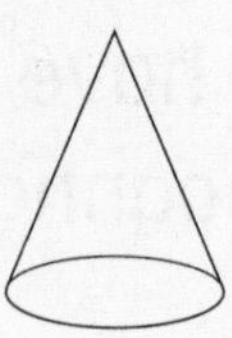 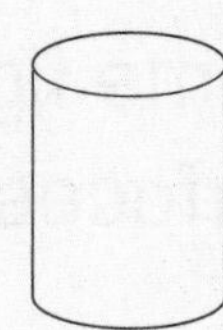

2. 8 vertices

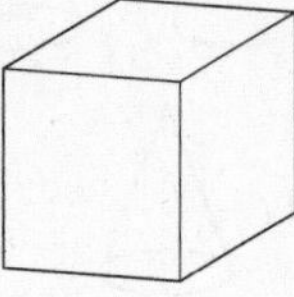 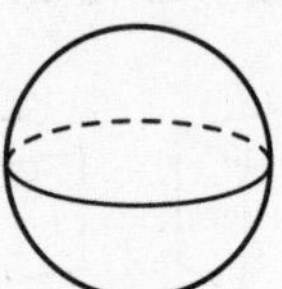 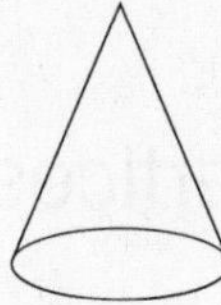 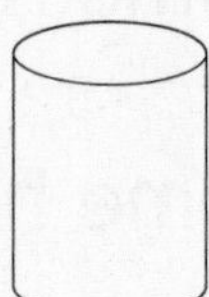

3. 2 flat surfaces

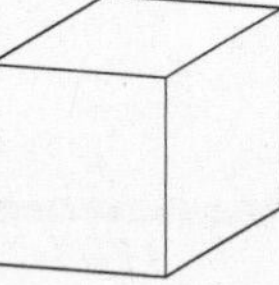 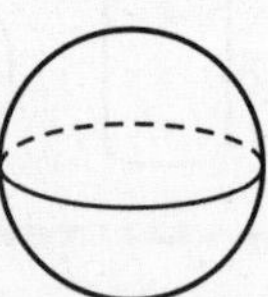 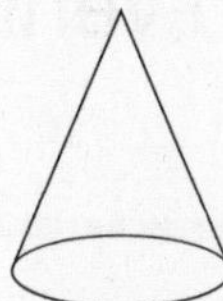 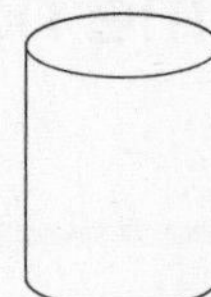

4. 6 flat surfaces

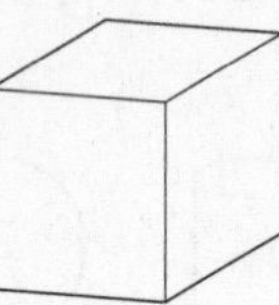 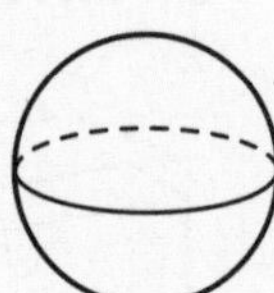 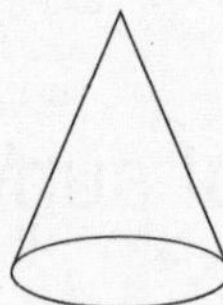 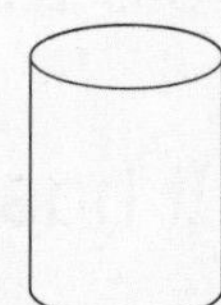

5. 0 vertices

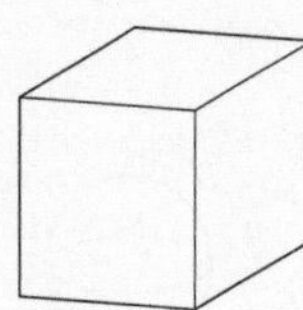 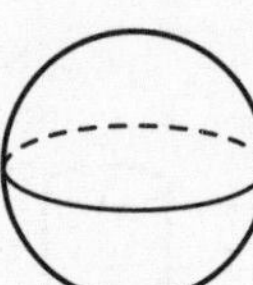 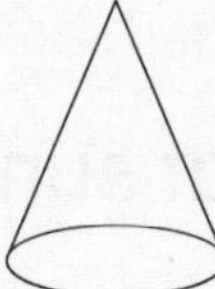 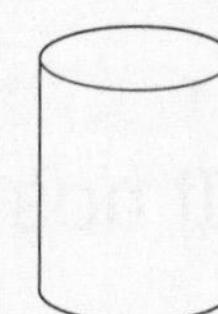

6. Which rule tells how these solid figures are alike?

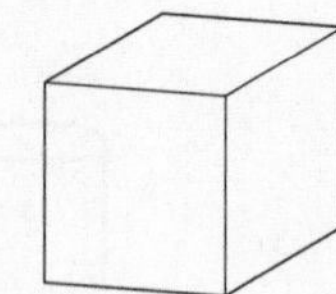 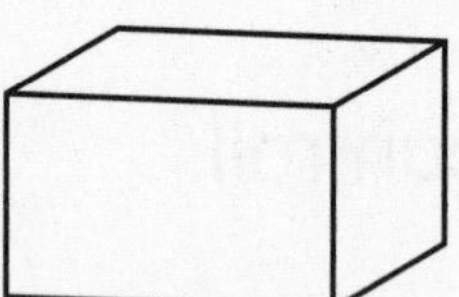

Ⓐ 3 vertices

Ⓑ 4 flat surfaces

Ⓒ 5 vertices

Ⓓ 6 flat surfaces

Name ______________________________

Building with Solid Figures

You can build an object by using solid figures.

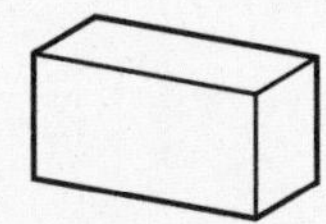
rectangular prism

cylinder

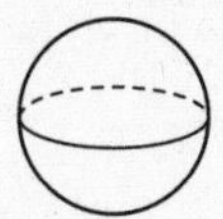
sphere

cone

cube

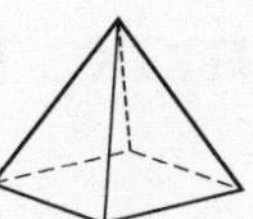
pyramid

Build a tower.

Step 1:
Start with a rectangular prism.

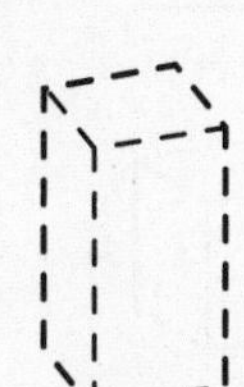

Step 2:
Put a cone on top.

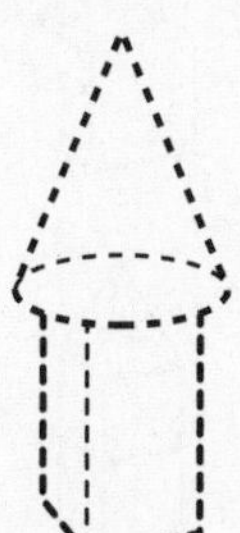

Build each object. Draw the solid figures.
Then write the solid figures you used to build the object.

1. Build a lamp post.

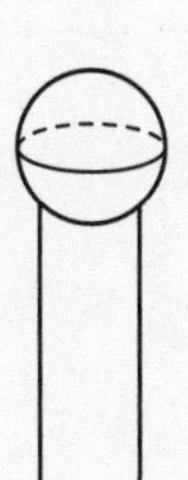

Step 1:
Start with a
__________.

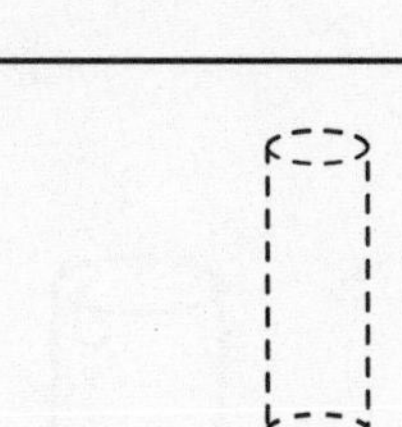

Step 2:
Put a __________
on top.

2. Build a tree.

Start with a
__________.

Put a __________
on top.

Name ______________________________

Building with Solid Figures

Look at the object.
Write how many of each solid figure is used to make the object.

1. ____ ____ ____ ____

2. ____ ____ ____ ____

3. ____ ____ ____ ____

Spatial Thinking

4. Kim used these 2 solid figures to make an object.
Which object did Kim make?

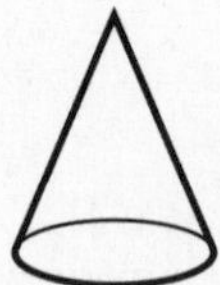

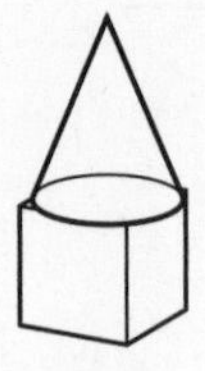
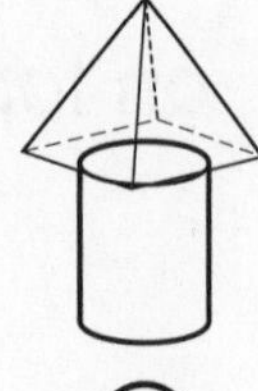
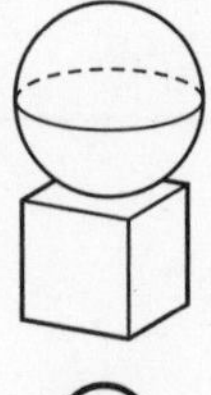

Ⓐ Ⓑ Ⓒ Ⓓ

Name ______________________

Problem Solving: Use Reasoning

All of these shapes are triangles.
Circle the words that are true of all triangles.

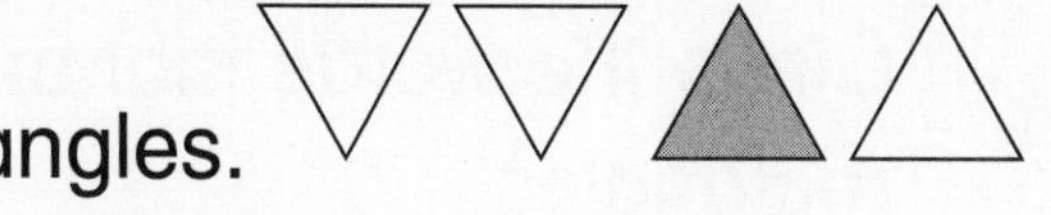

Look at each of the sentences below and then look at the triangles.

Circle the words that do match all the triangles.

For the first sentence, think: I can see a shape that is not gray but is still a triangle, so I do not circle this.

All triangles:

are gray

have 3 straight sides

have 3 corners

have a flat bottom

1. All of these shapes are cubes. Circle the words that are true of all cubes.

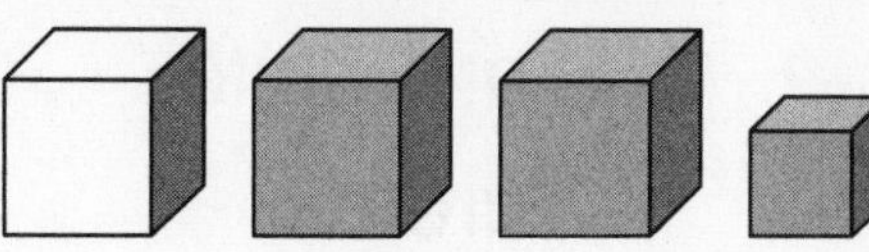

All cubes:

are gray

have 6 flat surfaces

are big

have 8 vertices

2. All of these shapes are circles. Circle the words that are true of all circles.

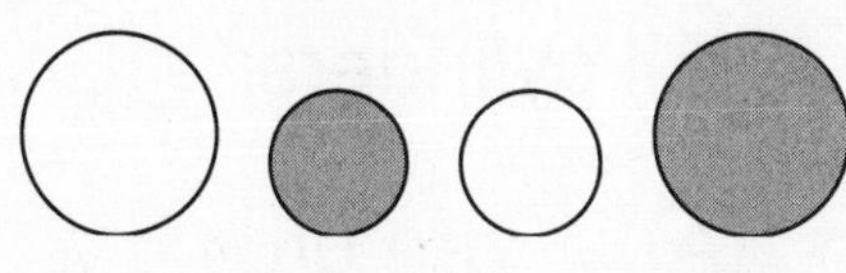

All circles:

have 0 straight sides

have 0 vertices

are big

are white

Name ______________________________

Practice
15-10

Problem Solving: Use Reasoning

1. All of these shapes are rectangles.
Circle the words that are true of all rectangles.
All rectangles:

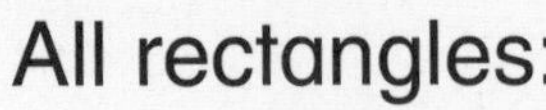

have 4 sides

have 4 corners

are white

have the longest side at the bottom

are big

2. All of these shapes are rectangular prisms.
Circle the words that are true of all rectangular prisms.
All rectangular prisms:

are white

are big

have 8 vertices

are gray

have 6 flat surfaces

3. Which shows something that is true of all cylinders?
All cylinders:

Ⓐ are gray

Ⓑ are small

Ⓒ have 2 flat surfaces

Ⓓ have a flat surface at the top

Name ______________________

Making Equal Parts

This apple pie is divided into equal parts.

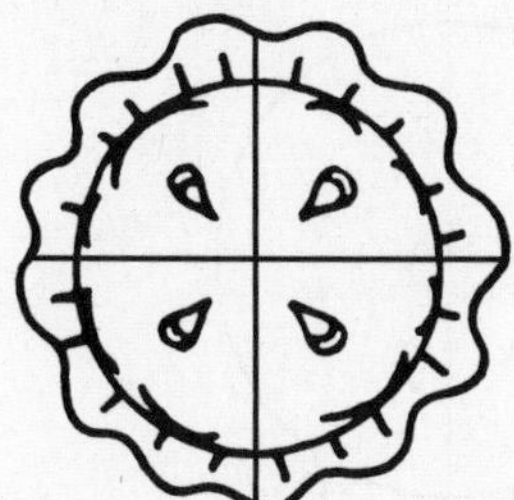

Each part is the same size.

There are 4 equal parts.

This apple pie is **not** divided into equal parts.

Each part is **not** the same size.

There are 0 equal parts.

Write the number of equal parts on each shape.

1. 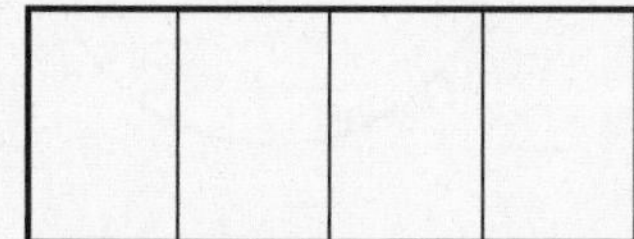

There are 4 equal parts.

2. 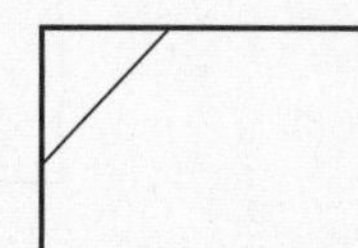

There are _____ equal parts.

3. 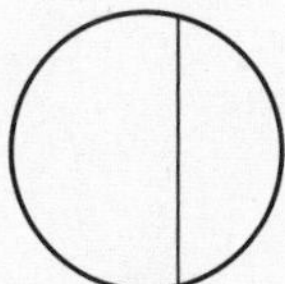

There are _____ equal parts.

4. 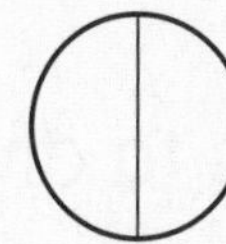

There are _____ equal parts.

5. 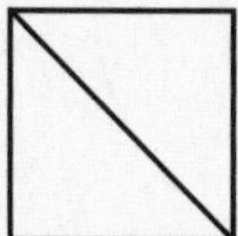

There are _____ equal parts.

6. 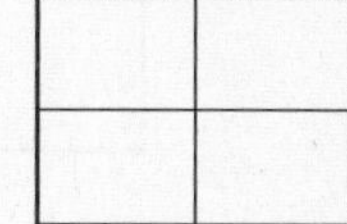

There are _____ equal parts.

Name ____________________

Making Equal Parts

Write how many equal parts the shape has.
If the parts are not equal, write 0.

1. 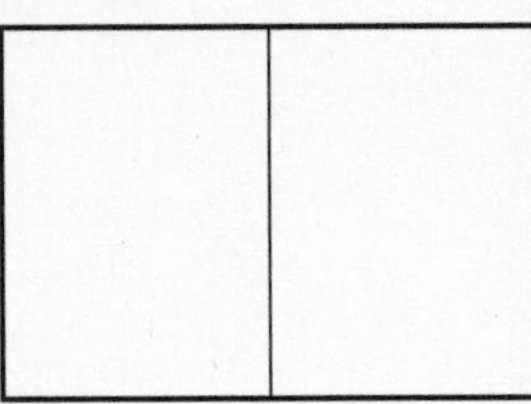

_____ equal parts

2. 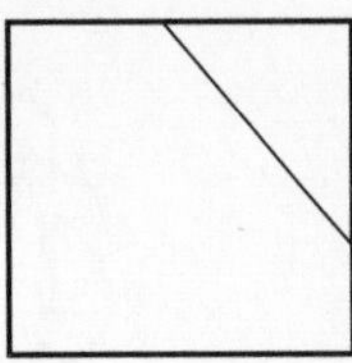

_____ equal parts

3. 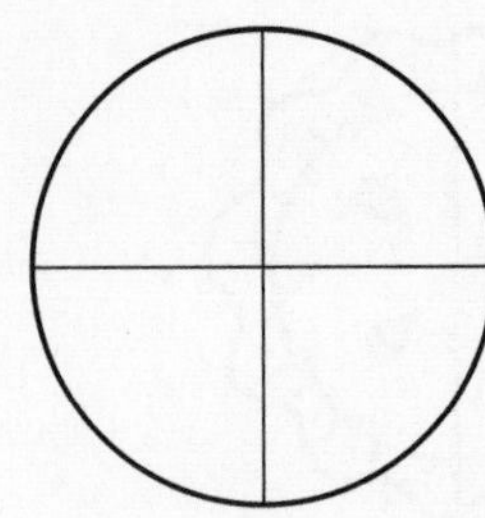

_____ equal parts

4. 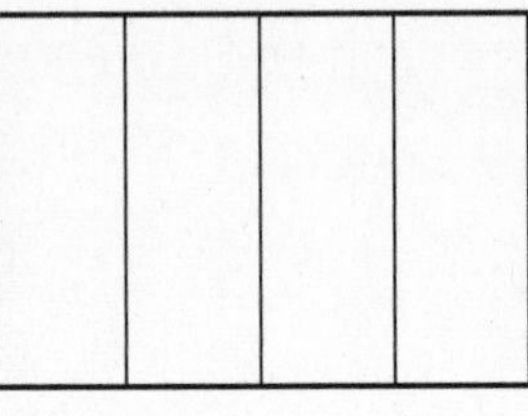

_____ equal parts

5. 

_____ equal parts

6. 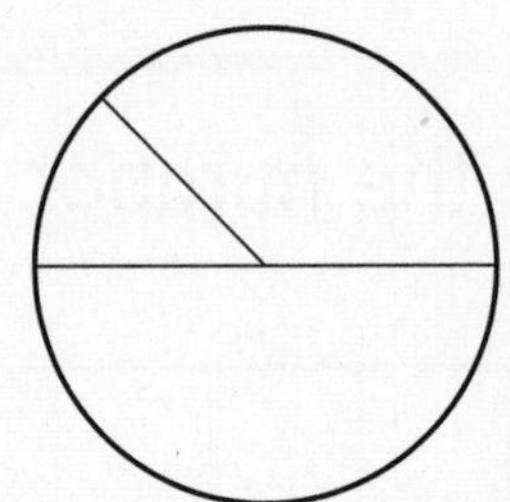

_____ equal parts

Journal

7. Draw straight lines to divide these shapes into the equal parts listed.

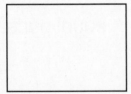

2 equal parts

4 equal parts

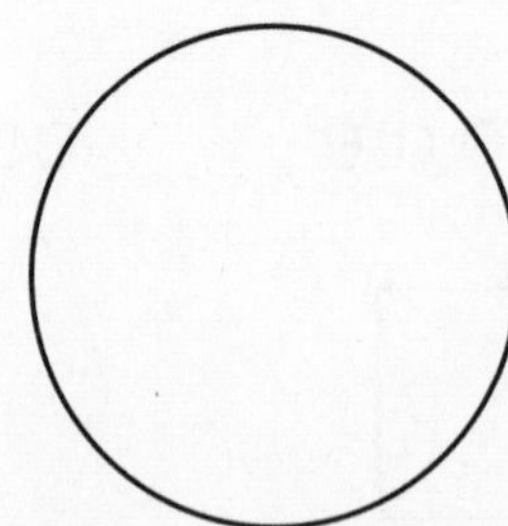

2 equal parts

Name ______________________________

Describing Equal Parts of Whole Objects

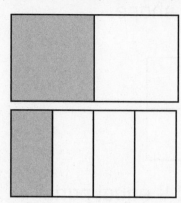

This rectangle has 2 equal parts.
1 out of 2 equal parts is shaded.

1 out of 4 equal parts is shaded.

1. Circle the shape that shows 1 out of 2 equal parts shaded.

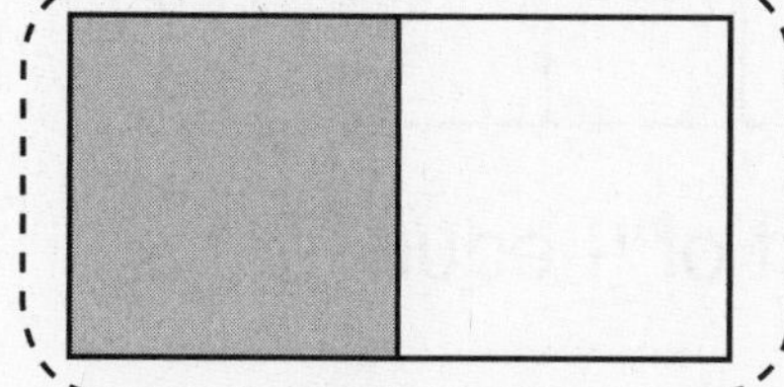

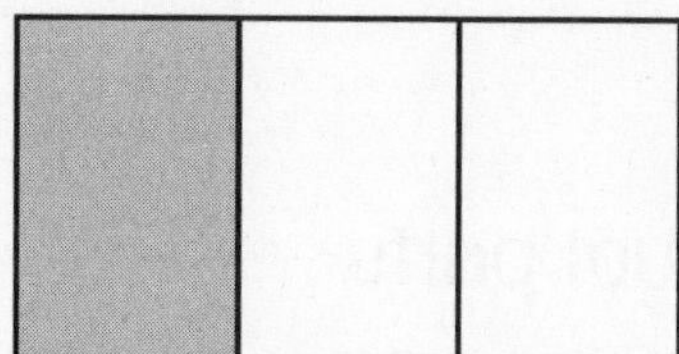

2. Circle the shape that shows 1 out of 4 equal parts shaded.

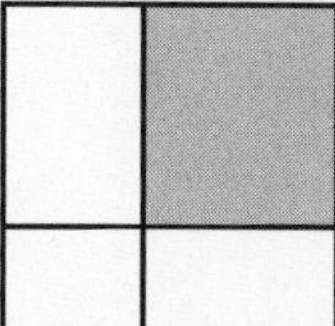

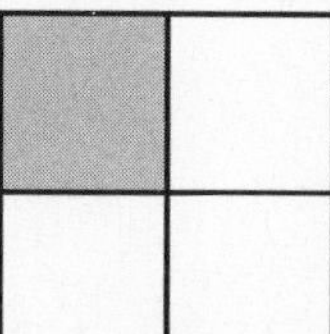

3. Circle the shape that shows 3 out of 4 equal parts shaded.

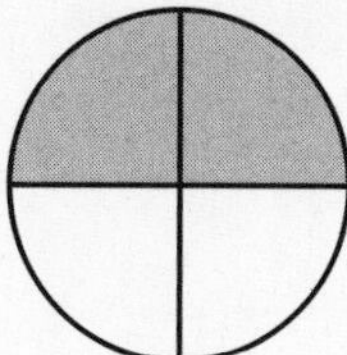

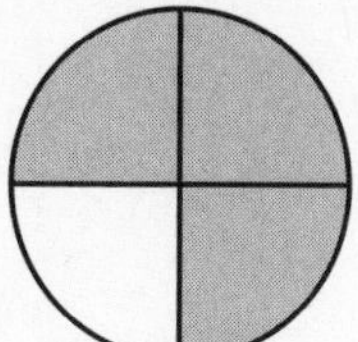

Name ______________________________

Practice
16-2

Describing Equal Parts of Whole Objects

Color the given number of equal parts in each shape.

1. 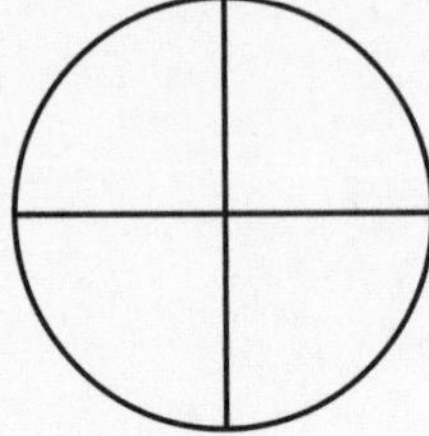

1 out of 4 equal parts

2. 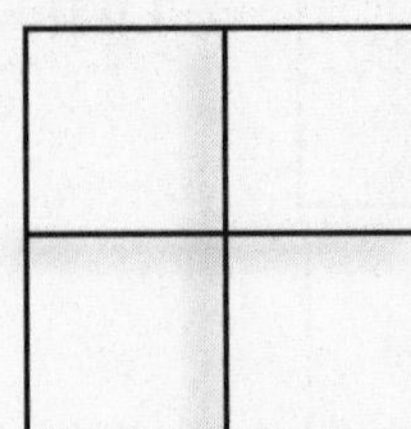

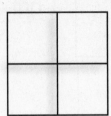

3 out of 4 equal parts

3. 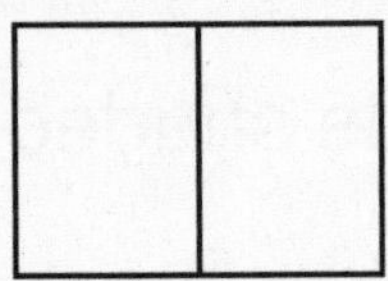

1 out of 2 equal parts

4. 

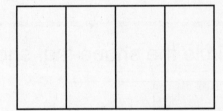

2 out of 4 equal parts

Spatial Thinking

5. Which picture shows 2 out of 4 equal parts shaded?

Ⓐ 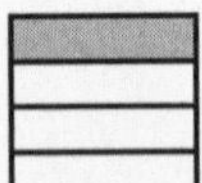

Ⓑ 

Ⓒ 

Ⓓ 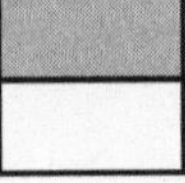

Number Sense

6. How many fourths equal one whole?

Ⓐ 4

Ⓑ 3

Ⓒ 2

Ⓓ 1

Name ______________________

Making Halves and Fourths of Rectangles and Circles

You can divide a figure into equal parts.

Two of the *halves* make the whole circle.

Each part is called a **half**.
A **half** of the circle is gray.

Four of the **quarters** make the whole rectangle.

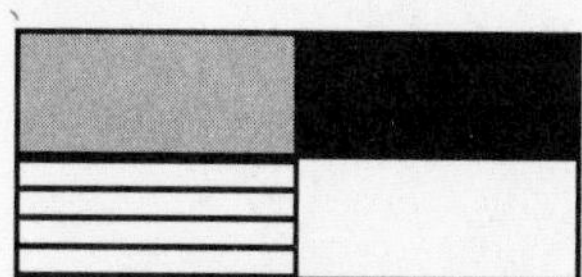

The rectangle is divided into **quarters.**
Each part is called a **quarter.**

Circle the shape that shows one half shaded gray.

1. 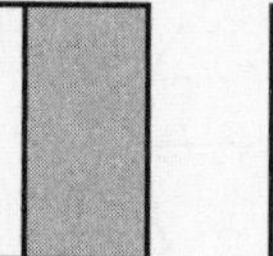 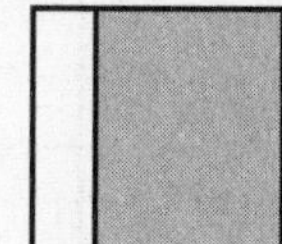

2. 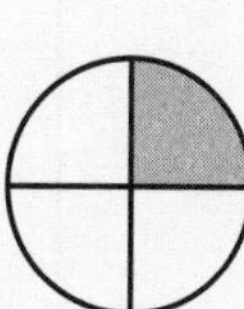 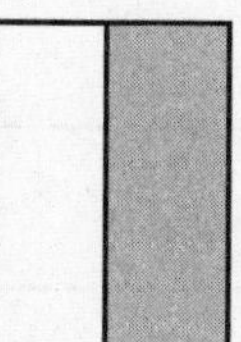

Circle the shape that shows one quarter striped.

3. 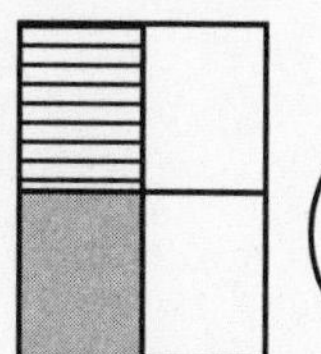 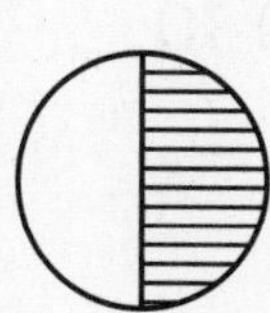

4. 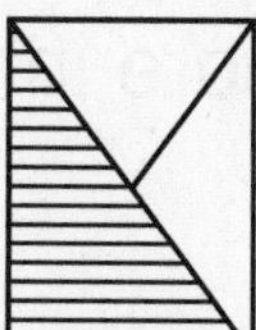 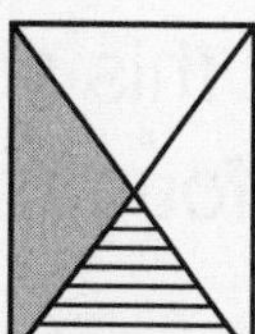

5. Julie colors half of the circle green. How many pieces does she need to color?
Color the parts.
Write the number.

______

Name ______________________________

Making Halves and Fourths of Rectangles and Circles

Color the shapes so that half of each shape is blue.

1. 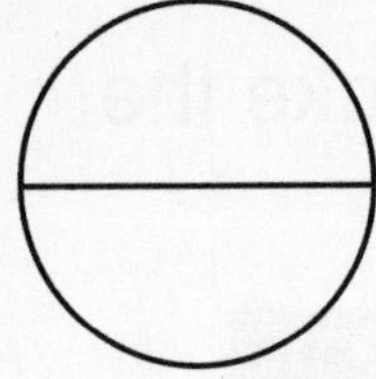

2. 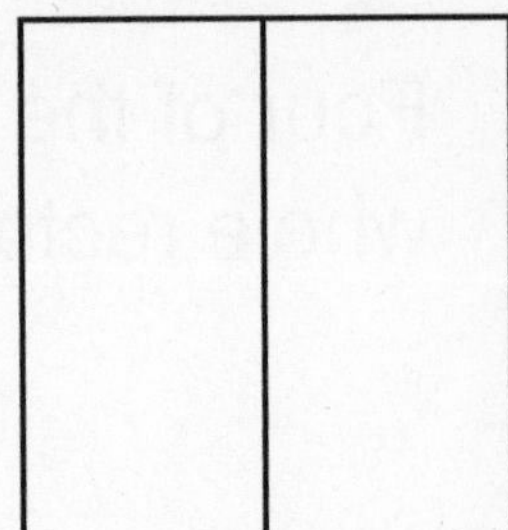

3. 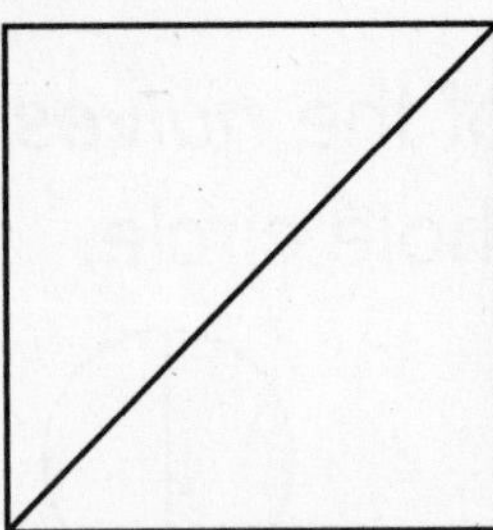

Color the shapes so that a quarter of each shape is orange.

4. 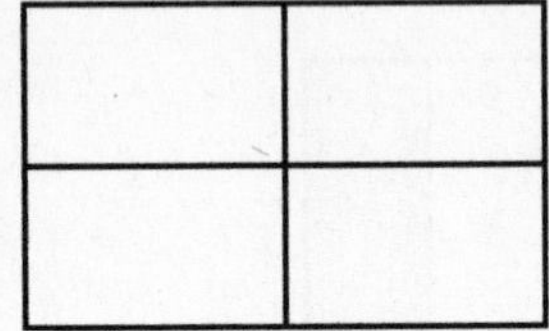

5. 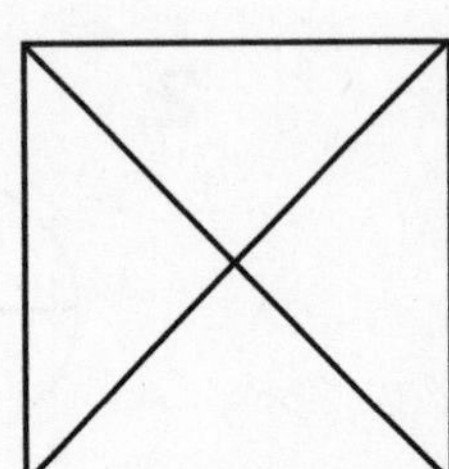

6. 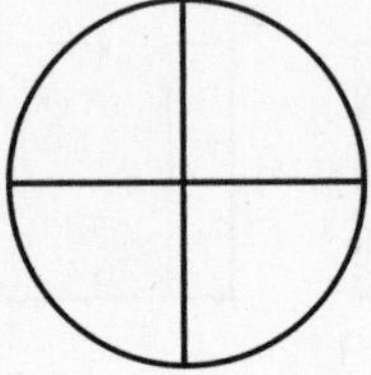

7. Marco cut this square into halves. Draw a line to cut it into fourths.

Name ______________________

Reteaching **16-4**

Problem Solving: Draw a Picture

You can draw a picture to solve a problem.

Mario's pizza has 4 equal parts.

2 of the parts have mushrooms on them.

What part of the pizza has mushrooms?

First, draw Mario's pizza.

Then draw mushrooms on 2 of the parts.

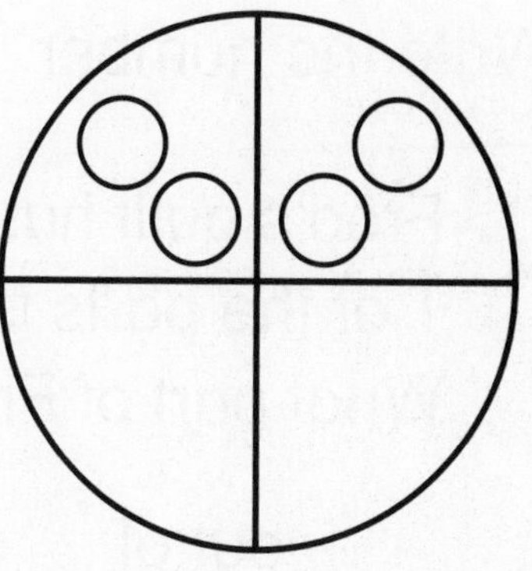

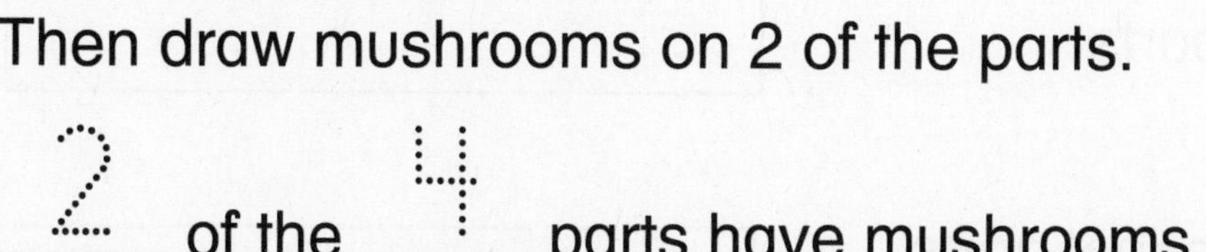

2 of the 4 parts have mushrooms.

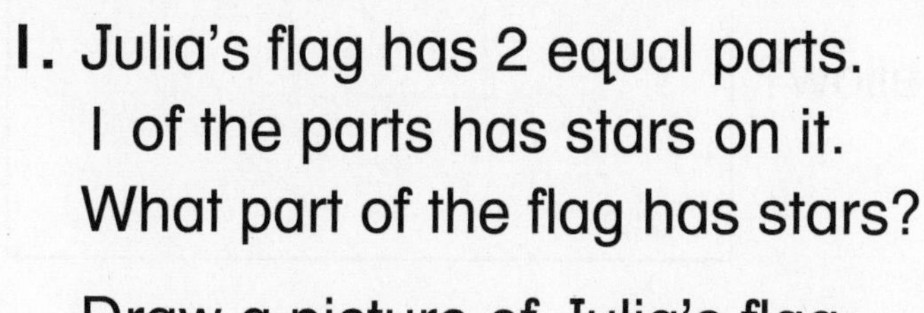

1. Julia's flag has 2 equal parts.
I of the parts has stars on it.
What part of the flag has stars?

Draw a picture of Julia's flag.

_____ out of _____ parts has stars.

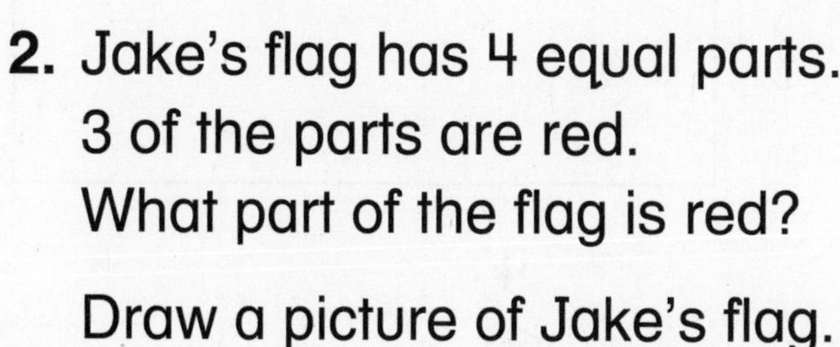

2. Jake's flag has 4 equal parts.
3 of the parts are red.
What part of the flag is red?

Draw a picture of Jake's flag.

_____ out of _____ parts are red.

Name ________________________________

Problem Solving: Draw a Picture

Read each story.
Draw a picture.
Write the number.

1. Fred's quilt has 2 equal parts.
I of the parts is blue.
What part of Fred's quilt is blue?

____ out of ____ parts

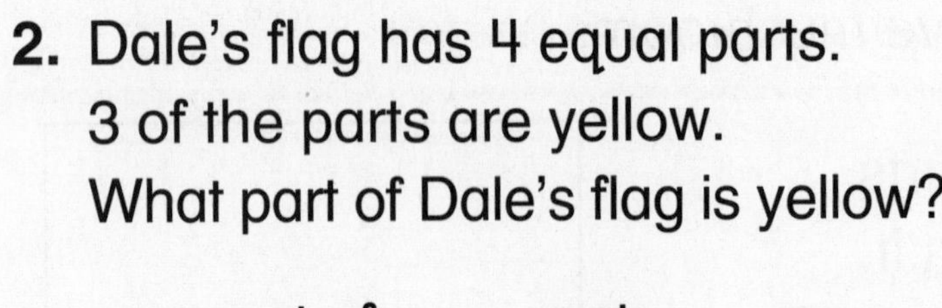

2. Dale's flag has 4 equal parts.
3 of the parts are yellow.
What part of Dale's flag is yellow?

____ out of ____ parts

3. **Reasoning** Tim's pizza has 4 equal parts.
He eats 2 of the parts.
How many parts are left for his friends?

Ⓐ I Ⓑ 2 Ⓒ 3 Ⓓ 4

Name ______________________

Building 1,000

Remember.

10 ones = __1__ ten

10 tens = __1__ hundred

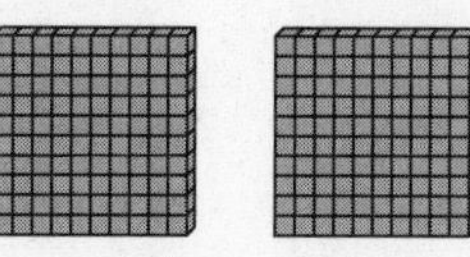

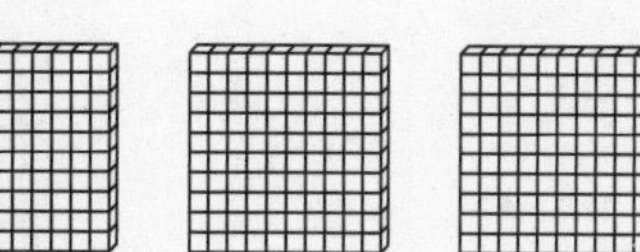

10 hundreds = __1__ thousand

Count by 100s to count hundreds.

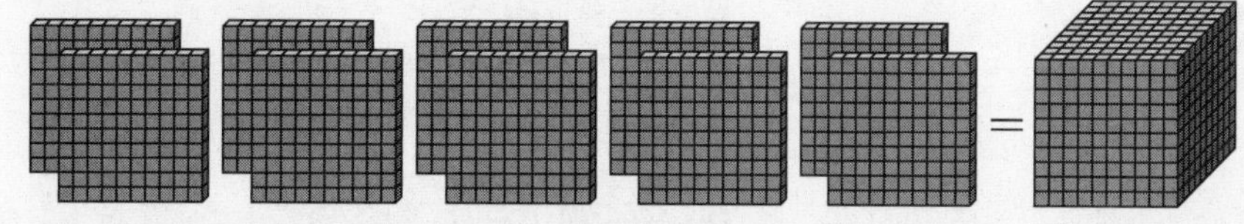

Color the models to show the hundreds.

1. 2 hundreds
200

2. 3 hundreds
300

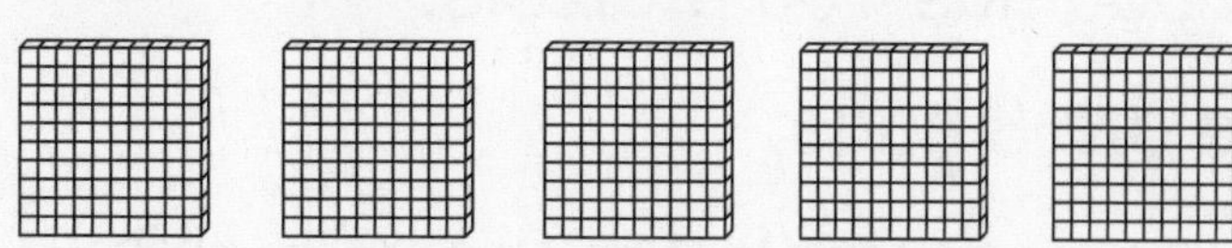

3. 1 hundred
100

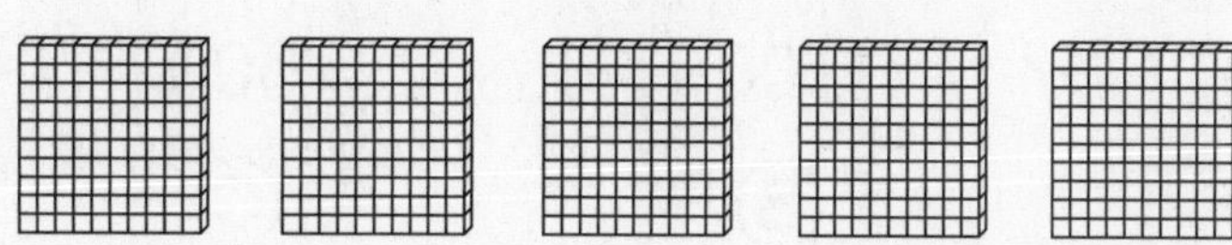

4. 5 hundreds
500

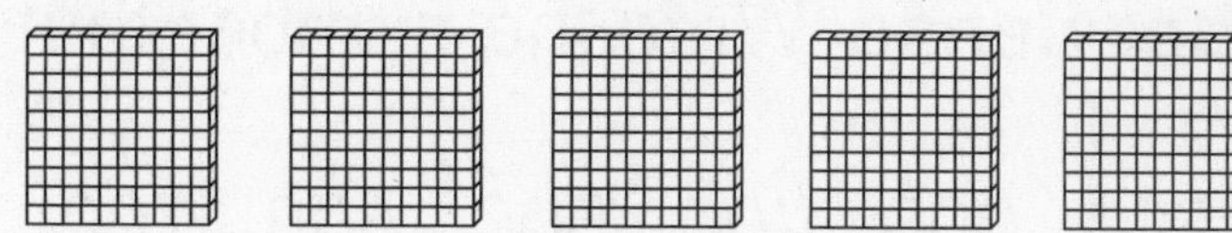

Name ______________________________

Step-Up 1
Practice

Building 1,000

Write how many. Use models if needed.

1.

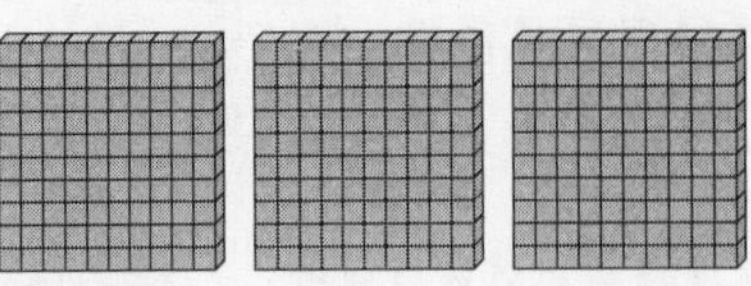

100 less is ________. ________ 100 more is ________.

2.

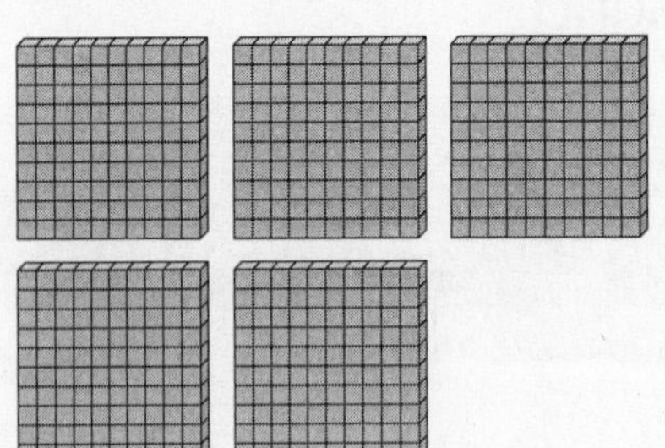

100 less is ________. ________ 100 more is ________.

3. Each bag has 100 pretzels.
There are 8 bags.
How many pretzels are there in all?

80	100	500	800
Ⓐ	Ⓑ	Ⓒ	Ⓓ

4. Number Sense Write the number that comes next:

100 200 300 400 500 600 700 800 900 ________

How many hundred flats would you need to show it?

_____ hundred flats

Name ____________________

Step-Up 2
Reteaching

Counting Hundreds, Tens, and Ones

Use models and your workmat to sort and count.

First, put the hundreds models on your mat.
Next, put the tens models on your mat.
Then, put the ones models on your mat.

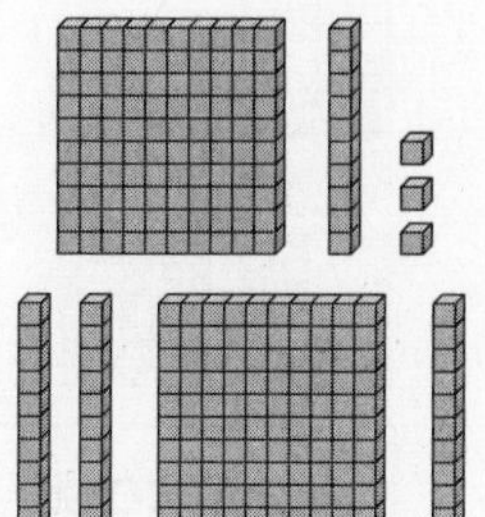

Write the number of hundreds, tens, and ones.

Hundreds	Tens	Ones
2	4	3

Write the numbers.
Use models and your workmat if needed.

1. 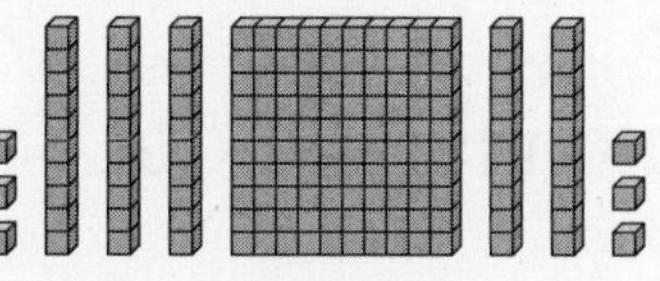

Hundreds	Tens	Ones
1	5	6

2. 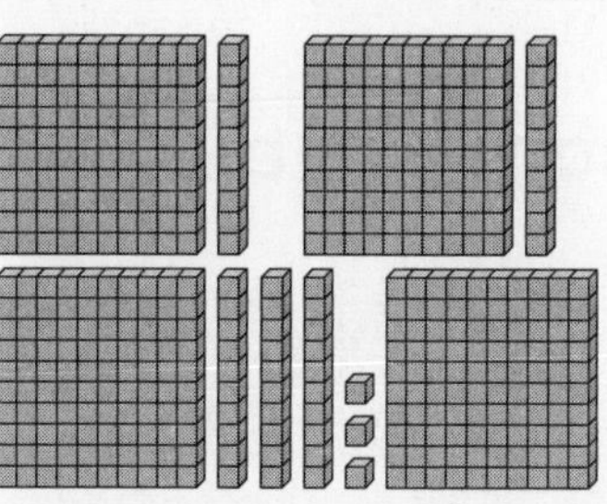

Hundreds	Tens	Ones

3. **Number Sense** How many hundreds are in 217? ____

Name ______________________________

Step-Up 2
Practice

Counting Hundreds, Tens, and Ones

Write the numbers. Use models and your workmat if needed.

1.

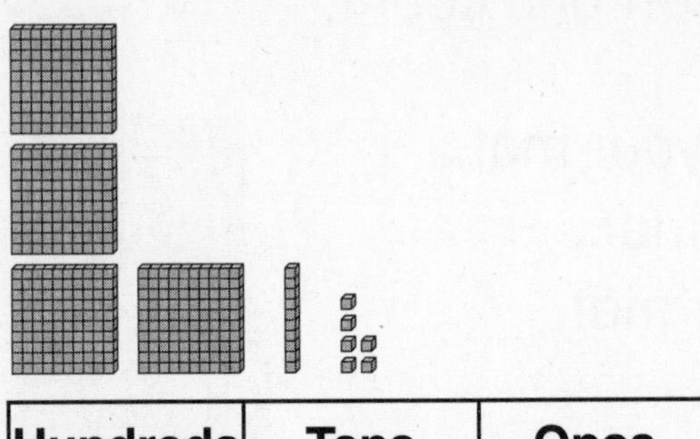

Hundreds	Tens	Ones

2.

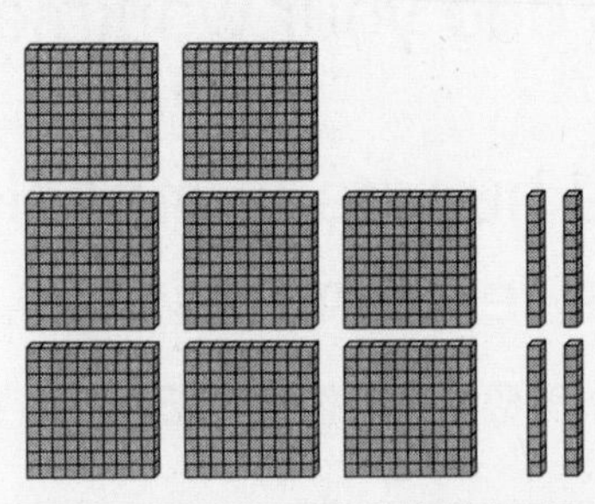

Hundreds	Tens	Ones

3.

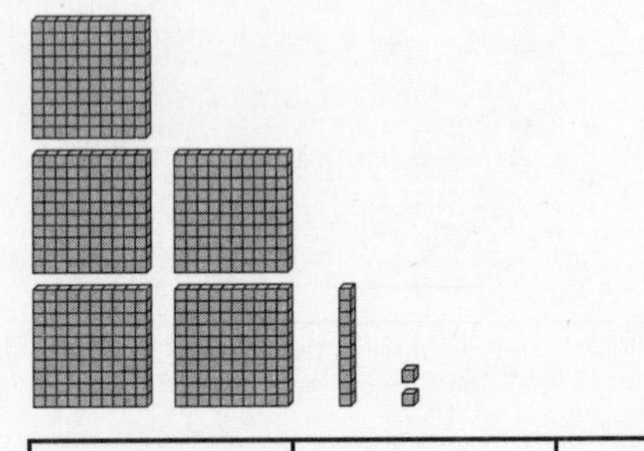

Hundreds	Tens	Ones

4.

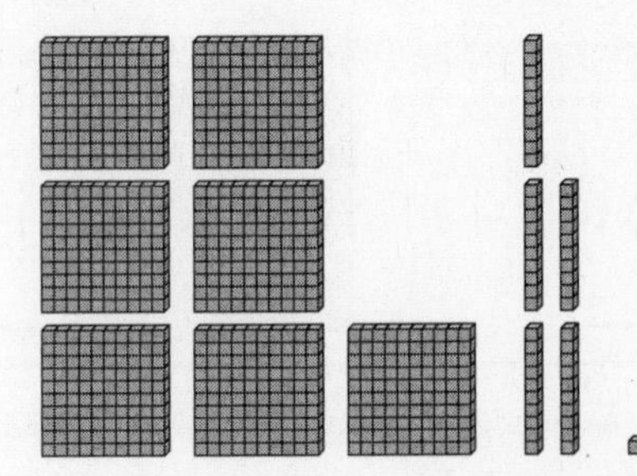

Hundreds	Tens	Ones

5. Reasonableness Kyra wrote **65** to match the model.

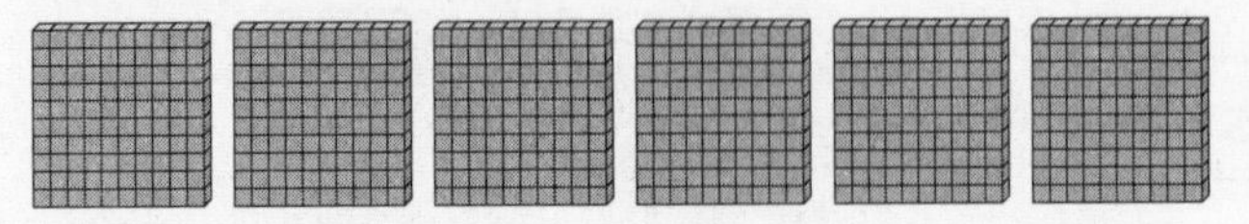

What mistake did she make?

____

What is the correct number to match the model?

650  605  506  56 Ⓓ

Name ______________________

Step-Up 3
Reteaching

Reading and Writing Numbers to 1,000

Expanded form uses plus signs to show hundreds, tens, and ones.

200 + 60 + 4

You can draw models to show expanded form.

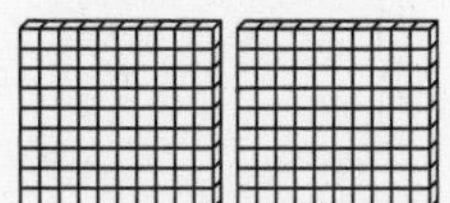 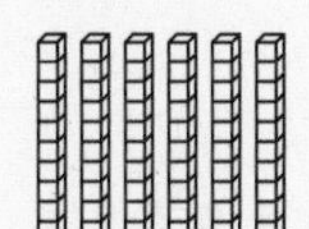

The **number word** is two hundred sixty-four.

The **standard form** is

 ______.

Draw models to show the expanded form.
Write the number in standard form.

1. 400 + 30 + 8 four hundred thirty-eight

______

2. 300 + 70 + 2 three hundred seventy-two

______

3. Write the number in expanded and standard form. five hundred fourteen

______ + ______ + ______ ______

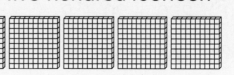

Name ______________________

Reading and Writing Numbers to 1,000

Circle the models to match the expanded form. Then write the standard form.

1. 200 + 70 + 5

two hundred seventy-five

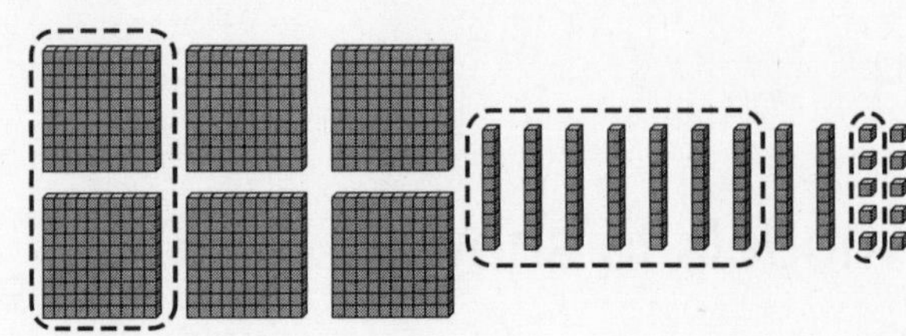

275

2. 100 + 40 + 0

one hundred forty

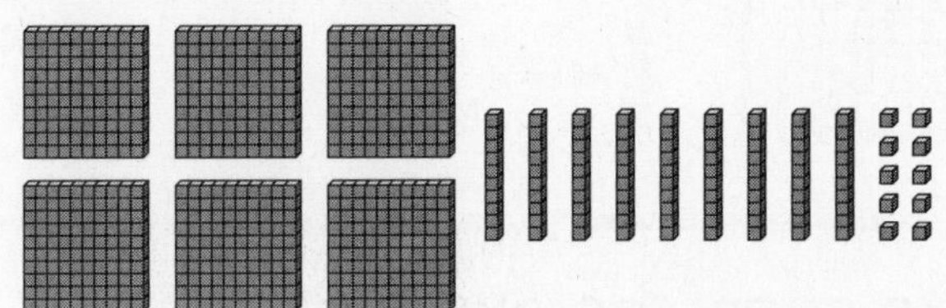

______

3. 300 + 60 + 2

three hundred sixty-two

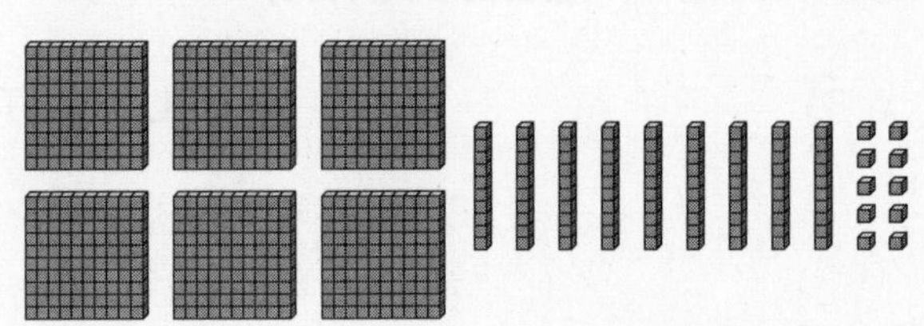

______

4. 329 cars are parked in a parking lot.

What is the expanded form of 329?

Ⓐ 200 + 90 + 3

Ⓑ 200 + 20 + 9

Ⓒ 300 + 20 + 9

Ⓓ 300 + 90 + 2

5. Reasoning What is the greatest number you can make using these digits?
5 7 2

Ⓐ 257

Ⓑ 572

Ⓒ 725

Ⓓ 752

Name ______________________

Step-Up 4
Reteaching

Comparing Numbers

Compare the digits with the greatest place value first.

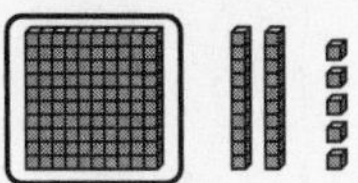

125 243

100 is less than 200. So, 125 < 243.

If the hundreds are equal, compare the tens.

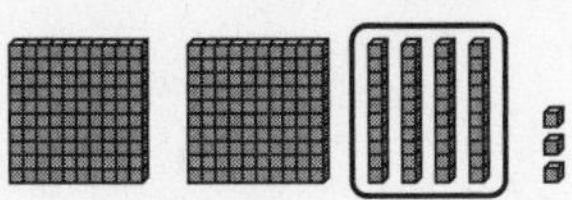

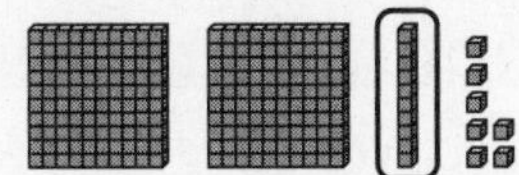

243 217

40 is greater than 10. So, 243 > 217.

If the tens are equal, compare the ones.

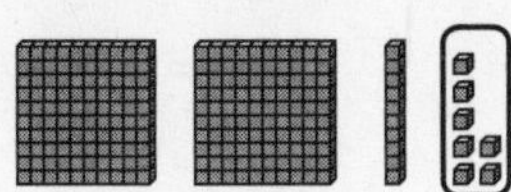

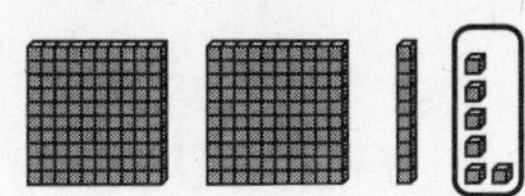

217 216

7 is greater than 6. So, 217 > 216.

Compare.
Write <, >, or =.

1. 341 ◯ 432

2. 890 ◯ 880

3. 621 ◯ 639

4. 546 ◯ 546

Name ______________________

Comparing Numbers

Compare. Write **greater than**, **less than**, or **equal to**. Then write >, <, or =.

1. 157 is less than 214. 157 (<) 214
2. 600 is ______________ 598. 600 ◯ 598
3. 771 is ______________ 771. 771 ◯ 771

4. This week, 261 fans watched a soccer game. Last week, 216 fans watched a soccer game. Which comparison is correct?

Ⓐ 216 = 261

Ⓑ 216 > 261

Ⓒ 261 < 216

Ⓓ 216 < 261

5. **Spatial Thinking** Circle hundreds, tens, and ones to show your answer.

This number is less than 200. The ones digit is 5 less than 10. The tens digit is 2 more than the ones digit. What is the number?

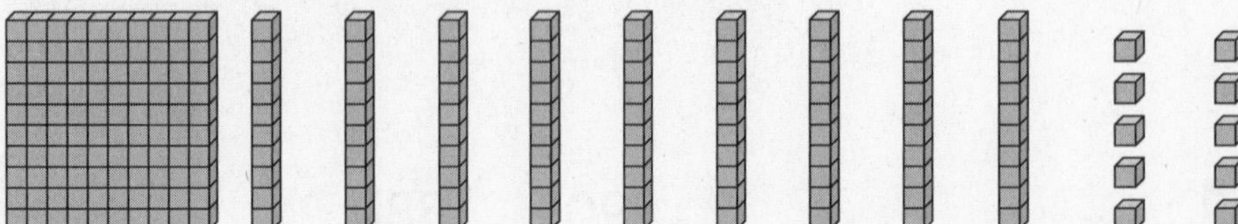

______

Name ____________________

Step-Up 5
Reteaching

Adding Two-Digit Numbers

Remember the steps for adding:

Step 1:	**Step 2:**	**Step 3:**
Add the ones.	Regroup if you need to.	Add the tens.

34 + 27 = ?
Regroup 11 ones as 1 ten and 1 one.

	Tens	Ones
	1	
	3	4
+	2	7
	6	1

12 + 36 = ?
You do not need to regroup 8 ones.

	Tens	Ones
	1	2
+	3	6
	4	8

Write the addition problem. Find the sum.

1. 15 + 26

	Tens	Ones
	1	
	1	5
+	2	6
	4	1

37 + 12

	Tens	Ones
	3	7
+	1	

28 + 15

	Tens	Ones
	2	8
+		

35 + 36

	Tens	Ones
+		

2. Algebra Begin with 24. Find the number that gives you a sum of 43. Use cubes to help you.

The number is _____.

	Tens	Ones
	2	4
+		
	4	3

Name ______________________________

Step-Up 5
Practice

Adding Two-Digit Numbers

Write the addition problem. Find the sum.

1. 36 + 21

	Tens	Ones
	☐	
	3	6
+	2	1

2. 31 + 19

	Tens	Ones
	☐	
+		

3. 63 + 19

	Tens	Ones
	☐	
+		

4. 56 + 34

	Tens	Ones
	☐	
+		

5. 63 + 26

	Tens	Ones
	☐	
+		

6. 54 + 28

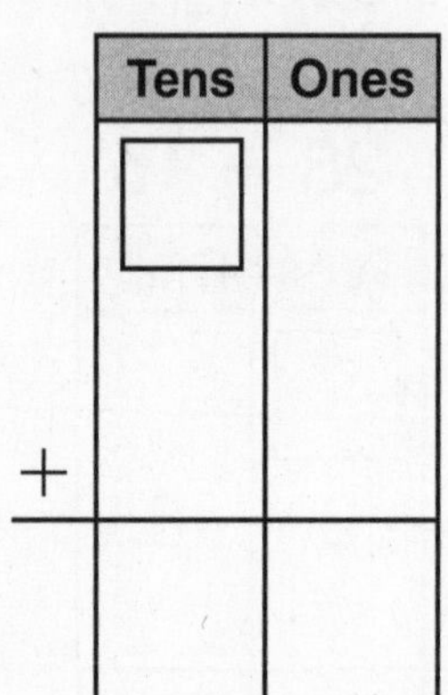

7. 68 + 29

	Tens	Ones
	☐	
+		

8. 33 + 47

	Tens	Ones
	☐	
+		

9. Ryan has a stack of 52 dimes and a stack of 29 dimes. How many dimes does he have in all?

Ⓐ 54
Ⓑ 59
Ⓒ 71
Ⓓ 81

10. Estimation One jar has 22 marbles. Another jar has 28 marbles. About how many marbles are in both jars?

Ⓐ about 40
Ⓑ about 50
Ⓒ about 60
Ⓓ about 70

Name ______________________

Subtracting Two-Digit Numbers

Step-Up 6
Reteaching

Remember the steps for subtracting.

Step 1
Think: Are there enough ones to subtract?

Step 2
Regroup the ones if you need to. Subtract.

Step 3
Subtract the tens.

Write the problems in the frames. Find the difference.

38 − 13

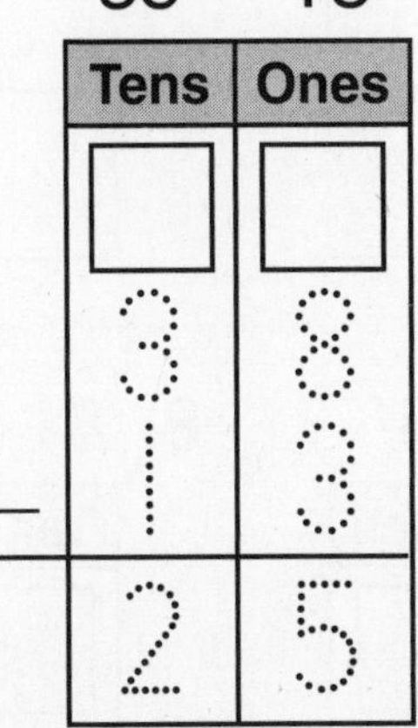

Tens	Ones
3	8
− 1	3
2	5

Regroup? Yes No

54 − 17

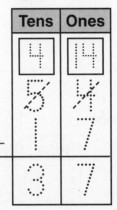

Tens	Ones
4	14
5	4
− 1	7
3	7

Regroup? Yes No

Write the problems in the frames. Find the difference.

1. 37 − 14

Tens	Ones
3	7
− 1	4
2	3

43 − 26

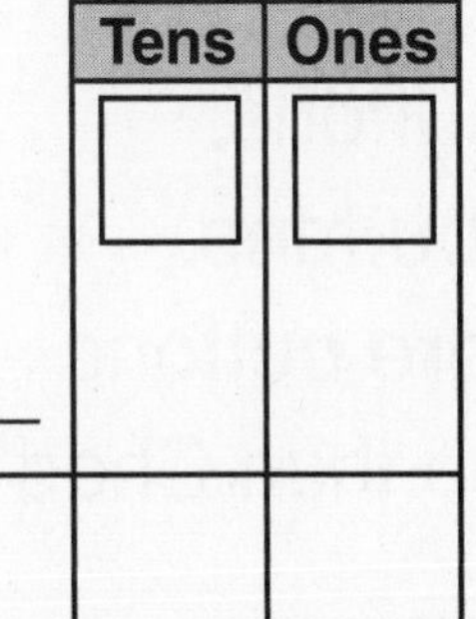

Tens	Ones
−	

66 − 37

Tens	Ones
−	

73 − 25

Tens	Ones
−	

2. Number Sense Write a number to make this a subtraction with regrouping problem.

Tens	Ones
− 2	8

Name ______________________

Step-Up 6
Practice

Subtracting Two-Digit Numbers

Write the subtraction problem. Find the difference.

1. 64 − 39

Tens	Ones
□	□
−	

2. 47 − 18

Tens	Ones
□	□
−	

3. 84 − 57

Tens	Ones
□	□
−	

4. 56 − 29

Tens	Ones
□	□
−	

5. 72 − 44

Tens	Ones
□	□
−	

6. 34 − 16

Tens	Ones
□	□
−	

7. 96 − 48

Tens	Ones
□	□
−	

8. 81 − 63

Tens	Ones
□	□
−	

9. Stan has 63 buttons. Chad has 47 buttons. How many more buttons does Stan have than Chad?

Ⓐ 26

Ⓑ 24

Ⓒ 23

Ⓓ 16

10. Number Sense Use each number only once. Write and solve the subtraction problem with the greatest difference.

2 3 5 6

Tens	Ones
□	□
− □	□

Name ______________________________

Step-Up 7
Reteaching

Using Addition to Check Subtraction

When you subtract, you start with the whole. Then you take part away. The other part is left.

37	Whole
− 12	Part
25	Part

Tens	Ones

To check your work, add to put the parts back together. Your answer should be the whole.

25	Part
+ 12	Part
37	Whole

Tens	Ones
and	and

Subtract. Check your answer by adding.

1.

	Tens	Ones
	3	3
−	2	1
	1	2

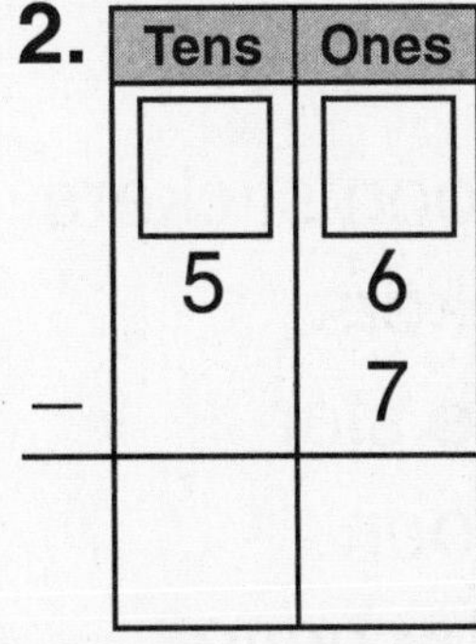

2.

	Tens	Ones
	5	6
−		7

3.

	Tens	Ones
	3	4
−	1	9

4.

	Tens	Ones
	6	3
−	3	7

Name ______________________

Step-Up 7
Practice

Using Addition to Check Subtraction

Subtract. Check your answer by adding. Write the missing part.

1.

$$\begin{array}{r} 62 \\ -\ 14 \\ \hline \end{array}$$

2.

$$\begin{array}{r} 83 \\ -\ 29 \\ \hline \end{array}$$

3.

$$\begin{array}{r} 73 \\ -\ 37 \\ \hline \end{array}$$

4.

$$\begin{array}{r} 48 \\ -\ 27 \\ \hline \end{array}$$

5.

$$\begin{array}{r} 94 \\ -\ 37 \\ \hline \end{array}$$

6.

$$\begin{array}{r} 75 \\ -\ 17 \\ \hline \end{array}$$

7. Betty has 48 moon stickers and 63 star stickers. How many more star stickers than moon stickers does she have?

Ⓐ 15

Ⓑ 19

Ⓒ 23

Ⓓ 27

8. Algebra Write the number that makes each number sentence true.

$60 - 20 = 20 +$ _____

$50 - 40 = 10 +$ _____

$70 - 30 = 10 +$ _____

$80 - 40 = 30 +$ _____

Name ______________________

Inches

Use a ruler to measure inches.

To measure to the nearest inch, look at the halfway mark between inches. If the object is longer, use the greater number. If the object is shorter, use the lesser number.

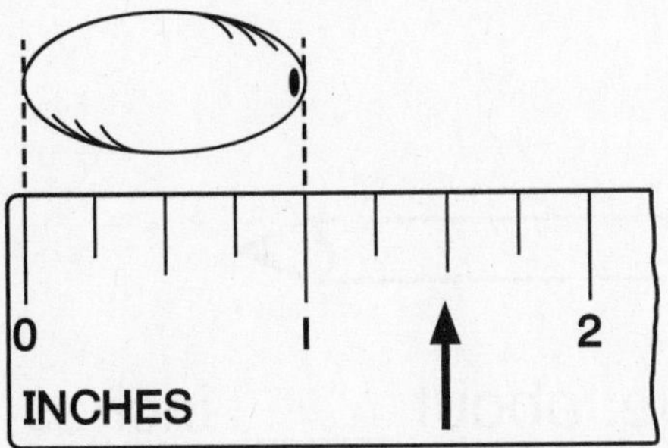

The bead is about

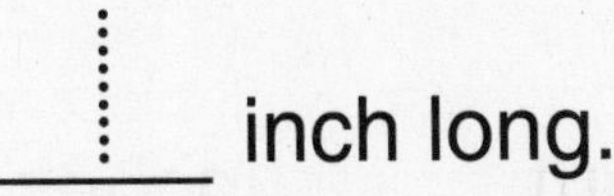

inch long.

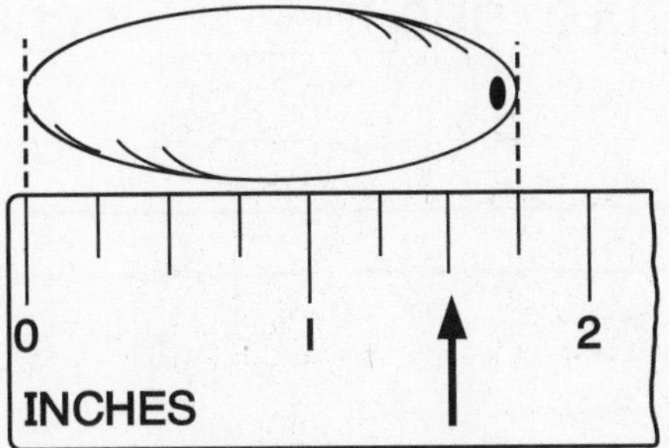

The bead is about

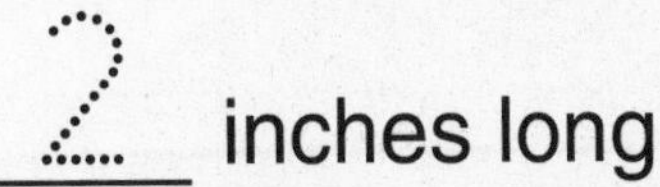

inches long.

1. Journal Find something in the classroom to measure in inches. Draw the object and write the measurement to the nearest inch.

Estimate the height or length. Then use a ruler to measure.

2. length of a pencil

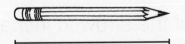

3. height of a book

	Estimate	Measure
2.	about _____ inches	about _____ inches
3.	about _____ inches	about _____ inches

Name ______________________________

Inches

Estimate the length of each object.
Then use a ruler to measure.

1\.

Estimate: about _____ inches

Measure: about _____ inches

2\.

Estimate: about _____ inches

Measure: about _____ inches

3\.

Estimate: about _____ inches

Measure: about _____ inches

4\.

Estimate: about _____ inches

Measure: about _____ inches

5\. **Reasonableness.** Measure the length of the straw in inches. About how long is the straw?

Ⓐ about 5 inches
Ⓑ about 6 inches
Ⓒ about 7 inches
Ⓓ about 8 inches

Name ______________________________

Centimeters

Use a ruler to measure centimeters.

To measure to the nearest centimeter, look at the halfway mark between centimeters. If the object is longer, use the greater number. If the object is shorter, use the smaller number.

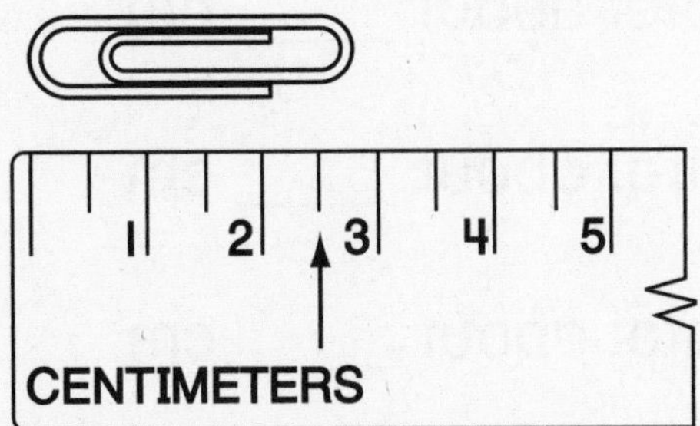

The paper clip is about

_____ centimeters.

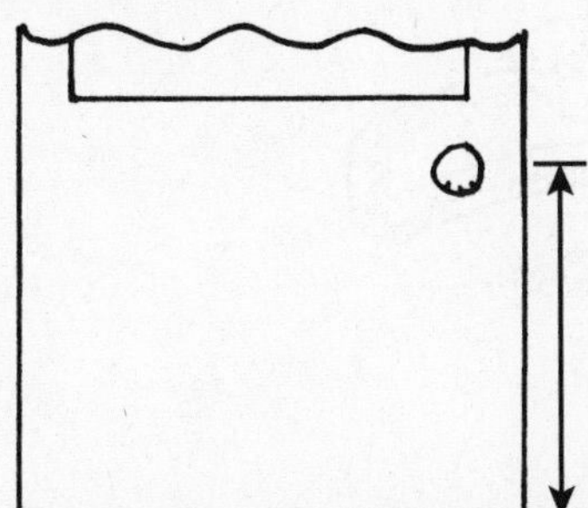

This part of the door is about

_____ centimeters.

1. Writing in Math Find something in the classroom to measure in centimeters. Draw the object and write the measurement to the nearest centimeter.

Estimate the height or length.
Then use a ruler to measure.

		Estimate	Measure
2. height of a book		about _____ centimeters	about _____ centimeters
3. length of a tape dispenser		about _____ centimeters	about _____ centimeters

Name ________________________

Centimeters

Estimate the length of each object.
Then use a ruler to measure.

1. Estimate: about _____ cm

Measure: about _____ cm

2. 

Estimate: about _____ cm

Measure: about _____ cm

3. 

Estimate: about _____ cm

Measure: about _____ cm

4. Look at the spoon. Measure the length of the spoon in centimeters. About how long is the spoon?

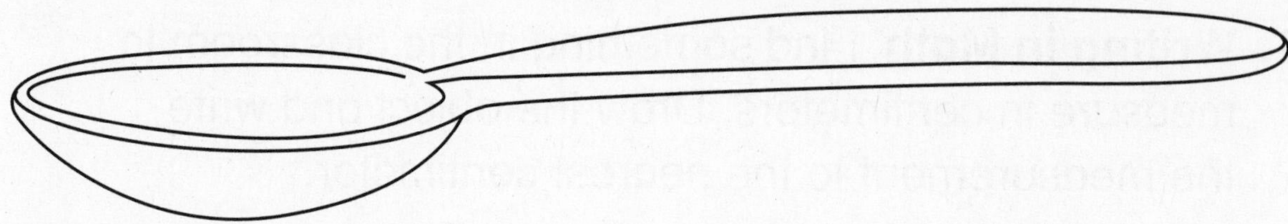

Ⓐ about 10 centimeters Ⓒ about 16 centimeters
Ⓑ about 13 centimeters Ⓓ about 18 centimeters

5. **Spatial Thinking** Choose the object that is about 4 centimeters long.

Ⓑ 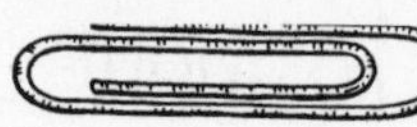

 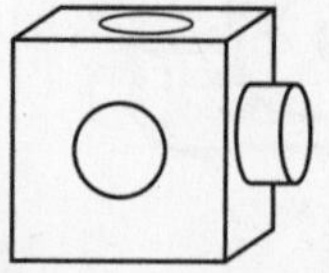

Name ______________________

Inches, Feet, and Yards

The stamp is about 1 inch long.

The book is about 1 foot long.

The table is about 1 yard long.

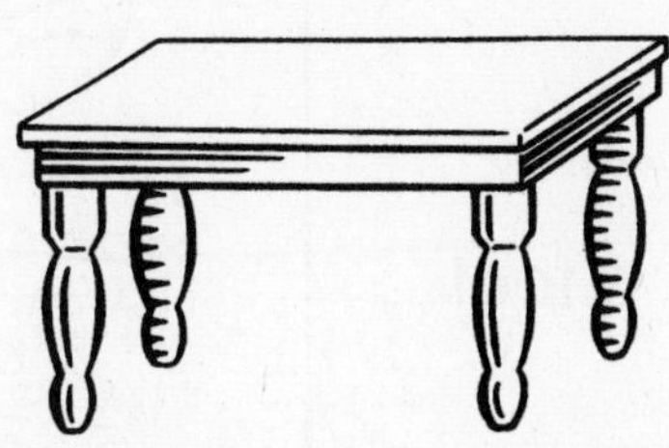

About how long or tall is each object? Circle the answer.

1. 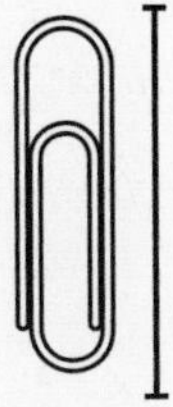

about 1 inch

about 1 foot

about 1 yard

2. 

about 1 inch

about 1 foot

about 1 yard

3. 

about 1 inch

about 1 foot

about 1 yard

4. 

about 1 inch

about 1 foot

about 1 yard

5. **Estimation** About how tall is the piece of paper?

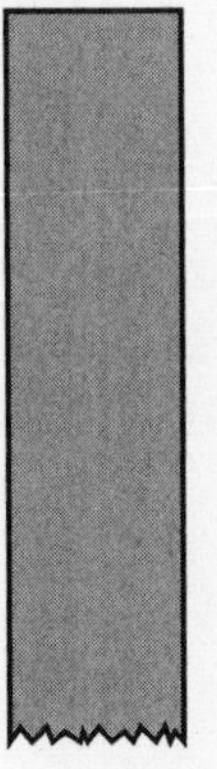

about 1 inch   about 2 inches   about 2 feet

Name ______________________________

Step-Up 10
Practice

Inches, Feet, and Yards

Circle the object that is about each length.

1. an inch

2. a foot

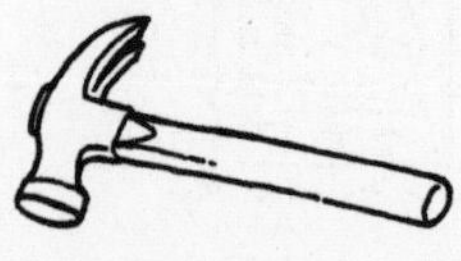

3. a yard

4. Measure from your fingertips to your elbow.

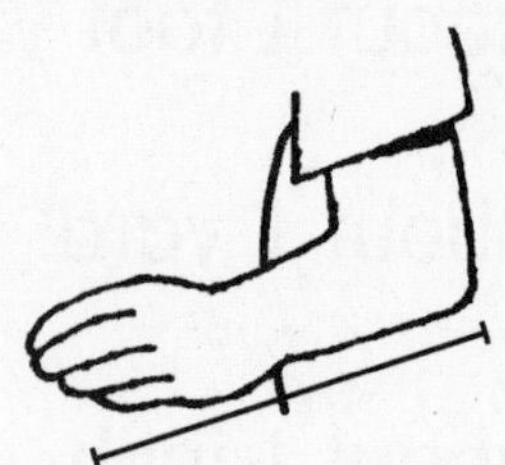

Estimate	Measure
about _____ inches	about _____ inches

5. Ingrid measures the length of a hockey stick. She says it is _____ long. Which measurement did she use?

Ⓐ 4 inches

Ⓑ 1 foot

Ⓒ 4 feet

Ⓓ 4 yards

6. **Reasonableness** Which is the best measurement for the height of the water bottle?

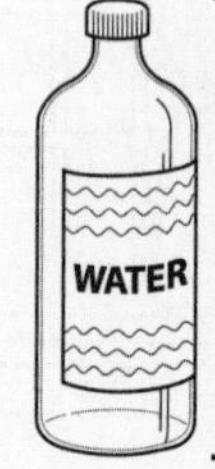

Ⓐ about 1 inch

Ⓑ about 9 inches

Ⓒ about 9 feet

Ⓓ about 9 yards